Immigration in Psychoar

Immigration in Psychoanalysis presents a unique approach to understanding the varied and multi-layered experience of immigration, exploring how social, cultural, political, and historical contexts shape the psychological experience of immigration, and with it the encounter between foreign-born patients and their psychotherapists.

Beltsiou brings together a diverse group of contributors including Ghislaine Boulanger, Eva Hoffman and Dori Laub, to discuss their own identity as immigrants and how it informs their work. They explore the complexity and the contradictions of the immigration process—the tension between loss and hope, future and past, the idealization and denigration of the other/stranger, and what it takes to tolerate the existential dialectic between separateness and belonging.

Through personal accounts full of wisdom and nuance, the stories of immigration come to life and become accessible to the reader. Intended for clinicians, students, and academics interested in contemporary psychoanalytic perspectives on the topic of immigration, this book serves as a resource for clinical practice and can be read in courses on psychoanalysis, cultural psychology, immigrant studies, race and ethnic relations, self and identity, culture and human development, and immigrants and mental health.

Julia Beltsiou is a psychologist in private practice in New York City, where she works with a diverse group of patients, and supervises clinicians. She is an advanced candidate at the NYU Postdoctoral Program in Psychoanalysis, and lectures nationally and internationally on the topic of the psychological experience of immigration.

Relational Perspectives Book Series

Lewis Aron & Adrienne Harris
Series Co-Editors

Steven Kuchuck & Eyal Rozmarin
Associate Editors

The Relational Perspectives Book Series (RPBS) publishes books that grow out of or contribute to the relational tradition in contemporary psychoanalysis. The term *relational psychoanalysis* was first used by Greenberg and Mitchell[1] to bridge the traditions of interpersonal relations, as developed within interpersonal psychoanalysis and object relations, as developed within contemporary British theory. But, under the seminal work of the late Stephen Mitchell, the term *relational psychoanalysis* grew and began to accrue to itself many other influences and developments. Various tributaries—interpersonal psychoanalysis, object relations theory, self psychology, empirical infancy research, and elements of contemporary Freudian and Kleinian thought—flow into this tradition, which understands relational configurations between self and others, both real and fantasied, as the primary subject of psychoanalytic investigation.

We refer to the relational tradition, rather than to a relational school, to highlight that we are identifying a trend, a tendency within contemporary psychoanalysis, not a more formally organized or coherent school or system of beliefs. Our use of the term *relational* signifies a dimension of theory and practice that has become salient across the wide spectrum of contemporary psychoanalysis. Now under the editorial supervision of Lewis Aron and Adrienne Harris with the assistance of Associate Editors Steven Kuchuck and Eyal Rozmarin, the Relational Perspectives Book Series originated in 1990 under the editorial eye of the late Stephen A. Mitchell. Mitchell was the most prolific and influential of the originators of the relational tradition. He was committed to dialogue among psychoanalysts and he abhorred the authoritarianism that dictated adherence to a rigid set of beliefs or technical restrictions. He championed open discussion, comparative and integrative approaches, and he promoted new voices across the generations.

Included in the Relational Perspectives Book Series are authors and works that come from within the relational tradition, extend and develop the tradition, as well as works that critique relational approaches or compare and contrast it with alternative points of view. The series includes our most distinguished senior psychoanalysts, along with younger contributors who bring fresh vision.

---

[1] Greenberg, J. & Mitchell, S. (1983). Object relations in psychoanalytic theory. Cambridge, MA: Harvard University Press.

Immigration in Psychoanalysis

Locating Ourselves

Edited by
Julia Beltsiou

Routledge
Taylor & Francis Group

LONDON AND NEW YORK

First published 2016
by Routledge
2 Park Square, Milton Park, Abingdon, Oxon, OX14 4RN

And by Routledge
711 Third Avenue, New York, NY 10017

Routledge is an imprint of the Taylor & Francis Group, an informa business

© 2016 Julia Beltsiou

British Library Cataloguing in Publication Data
A catalogue record for this book is available from the British Library

Library of Congress Cataloging in Publication Data
A catalog record for this book has been requested

ISBN: 978-0-415-74181-1 (hbk)
ISBN: 978-0-415-74182-8 (pbk)
ISBN: 978-1-315-66846-8 (ebk)

Typeset in Sabon
by codeMantra

Printed and bound in Great Britain by
TJ International Ltd, Padstow, Cornwall

For John and Yianna

Contents

Acknowledgements

This book has been a labor of love, the birth of which many people shared.

First and foremost, a big THANK YOU goes to the contributors of this book for their collaborative spirit in responding to my editorial communications, for their scholarship and wit and for sharing very personal aspects of themselves and their work with patients. I am fortunate to have come to know this diverse community of immigrant analysts and writers. They share my interest in this topic and have come up with exciting new angles on the experience of immigration, and I have learned much from them through this process.

I feel lucky to have had as my editors of the Routledge book series *Relational Perspectives*, Adrienne Harris and Eyal Rozmarin, both immigrants themselves. Their steady encouragement, interest, and enthusiasm for the project kept me going. Adrienne's close mentorship over the years in various roles—as clinical supervisor, writing group mentor, and as my editor for this book—has made me a better analyst and person and allowed my ideas on immigration and identity to flourish and evolve.

I am indebted to my writing group, which in addition to Adrienne Harris, includes Bob Bartlett and Lauren Levine. Their friendship, support, intelligence, and creative flow of ideas was the fertile soil that made it possible for me to think and write and gave me the confidence to develop the vision of this book. Special thanks to Donnel Stern to whom I am grateful for many things, including his careful reading and helpful remarks to my chapter. Warm thanks also to Tracy Simon for her friendship and for her thoughtful comments on my work. Donnel's and Tracy's fresh and wise eyes added important perspectives that improved what I have to say. Cleonie White offered supportive feedback on my work. Thanks to Jeanne Wolff Bernstein, contributor to this book, fellow international transplant and my dissertation adviser years ago, for her interest in and support of me and for her discussion of an earlier version of my chapter at the IARPP conference in Madrid in 2011.

I am indebted to my colleagues of the NYU Postdoctoral Program in Psychoanalysis, a vibrant and progressive community that has become my intellectual and professional home over the last decade. Thanks also to the Psychoanalytic Society for bestowing me with the 2013 Patrick Lane Award in support of this project.

I would like to express my appreciation for the excellent publishers, Kate Hawes and Susan Wickenden, and the staff at Taylor and Francis for bringing this book into fruition. Kristopher Spring deserves a special mention for his gracious assistance in obtaining copyright permissions.

This book is irrevocably linked to the immigration experiences of my grandparents, Ioulia and Nikos, Dimitris and Vassiliki, and my parents, Elisavet and Yiannis, whose migrations are part of my life's journey. I am indebted to my friends who are immigrants and international transplants or US born, who help me bridge worlds and give me an emotional home. Lastly, this book would have not been possible without my patients, many of whom are immigrants of one kind or another, who have taught me about loss and opportunity, hope and despair, otherness and belonging.

Permissions Acknowledgements

"Psalm" from *Poems New and Collected 1957–1997* by Wislawa Symborska, translated from the Polish by Stanislaw Baranczak and Clare Cavanagh. English translation copyright © 1998 by Houghton Mifflin Harcourt Publishing Company. Reprinted by permission of Houghton Mifflin Harcourt Publishing Company. All Rights Reserved.

Seeing Double, Being Double: Belonging, Recognition and Evasion in Psychodynamic Work with Immigrants by Ghislaine Boulanger, Ph.D. was originally published in shorter form in the *American Journal of Psychoanalysis*, 75(3), 2015 and is reused with their permission.

Out of Exile: Some Thoughts on Exile as a Dynamic Condition by Eva Hoffman, Ph.D. previously published in *European Judaism*, 46(2), 2013, pp. 55–60. Copyrighted by Author and reprinted with her permission.

The following five articles are reused in this book with permission of Taylor & Francis LLC:

Nell—A Bridge to the Amputated Self: The Impact of Immigration on Continuities and Discontinuities of Self by Hazel Ipp, Ph.D., *International Journal of Psychoanalytical Self Psychology*, 5(4), 2010, pp. 373–386. Also reprinted by permission of the International Association for Psychoanalytic Self Psychology.

The Immigrant's Neverland: Commuting from Amman to Brooklyn by Lama Zuhair Khouri, M.S., L.M.S.W., *Contemporary Psychoanalysis*, 48(2), 2012, pp. 213–237. Also reprinted by permission of the William Alanson White Institute of Psychiatry, Psychoanalysis & Psychology and the William Alanson White Psychoanalytic Society.

On Leaving Home and the Flight from Trauma by Dori Laub, MD, *Psychoanalytic Dialogues*, 23(5), 2013, pp. 568–580.

The Immigrant Analyst: A Journey from Double Consciousness towards Hybridity by Glenys Lobban, Ph.D., *Psychoanalytic Dialogues,* 23(5), 2013, pp. 554–567.

Strangers in Paradise: Trevor, Marley, And Me: Reggae Music and the Foreigner Other by Cleonie J. White, Ph.D., *Psychoanalytic Dialogues* (in press).

Contributors

Julia Beltsiou, PsyD grew up in Germany as the daughter of recent Greek immigrants and came to live in the US as a young adult. She is an advanced candidate at the New York University Postdoctoral Program in Psychoanalysis. She has presented nationally and internationally on the topic of immigration and identity. In 2013, she received the Patrick Lane Award of the Psychoanalytic Society of the Postdoctoral Program for her work on immigration in psychoanalysis. Julia Beltsiou is an adjunct supervisor at the Doctoral Program in Clinical Psychology, City University of New York. She maintains a private practice in New York City.

Jeanne Wolff Bernstein, PhD is the past president and supervising and personal analyst at PINC. She is on the faculty at PINC and at The Sigmund Freud PrivatUniversität, Vienna, Paris. Jeanne Wolff Bernstein is a contributing editor to *Psychoanalytic Dialogues* and on the Editorial Board of Studies in Gender and Psychoanalysis and Contemporary Psychoanalysis. She was the 2008 Fulbright Freud Visiting Scholar in Psychoanalysis at the Freud Museum, Vienna, Austria. Her most recent publications include, "Beyond the Bedrock" in Jill Salberg (Ed.), *Good Enough Endings*, (2010), Routledge Press and "The Space of Transition between Winnicott and Lacan" in Lewis Kirshner (Ed.), *Between Winnicott and Lacan,* (2011), Routledge Press. She currently lives and works in Vienna, Austria.

Ghislaine Boulanger, PhD is a psychologist and psychoanalyst in private practice in New York City and a member of the Relational faculty at New York University's Postdoctoral Program in Psychotherapy and Psychoanalysis. Dr. Boulanger has specialized in the treatment of immigrants and adults who have survived massive psychic trauma. She was the keynote speaker for the 2014 NIP Symposium "The Immigrant in the Consulting Room."

Irene Cairo, MD received her Medical Degree in her native Buenos Aires, Argentina. She resided in Europe during her teenage years and speaks fluently English, Spanish, and French. She completed her residency in Psychiatry in New York, where she is licensed and Board Certified in Psychiatry. She is a graduate, member, and faculty of the New York Psychoanalytic Institute, and Training and Supervising analyst as well as faculty of the Contemporary Freudian Society. She is currently North American Co-Chair of the Ethics Committee of the International Psychoanalytic Association. She maintains a private practice in Manhattan.

Francisco J. González, MD is personal and supervising analyst and faculty at the Psychoanalytic Institute of Northern California and has worked for over 17 years as a psychiatrist at Instituto Familiar de la Raza, a clinic focusing on the mental health needs of the Latino community in San Francisco. He has presented and published on a variety of topics including sociocultural processes, gender and sexualities, film, perversion, the Oedipal, and primitive states. Born in Havana, Cuba, he grew up in Chicano San Antonio, Texas, and lived in Germany before settling in the San Francisco Bay Area where he currently practices.

Eva Hoffman, PhD grew up in Cracow, Poland, where she studied music intensively before emigrating in her teens to Canada and then the United States. After receiving her BA from Rice University and her PhD in English and American literature from Harvard University, she worked as senior editor at the *New York Times*, serving for a while as the newspaper's regular literary critic. She is the author of four works of non-fiction: *Lost in Translation, Exit into History, Shtetl*, and *After Such Knowledge*, as well as two novels—*The Secret* and the forthcoming *Appassionata* (published in the UK as *Illuminations*). She has studied psychoanalysis and has written and lectured internationally on issues of exile, memory, Polish-Jewish relations, politics, and culture. She has taught literature and creative writing at various universities, including the University of East Anglia, MIT, and Columbia. She has written and presented radio programmes, and has received the prestigious Prix Italia for Radio. Her literary awards include the Guggenheim Fellowship, the Whiting Award, and an award from the American Academy of Arts and Letters. She holds an honorary doctorate from Warwick University and is a Fellow of the Royal Society of Literature. She currently lives in London and works as visiting professor at Hunter College, CUNY.

Hazel Ipp, PhD is a psychologist/psychoanalyst in private practice in Toronto, Canada. She is a founding board member, faculty and supervisor of the Toronto Institute for Contemporary Psychoanalysis. She is a founding board member and past president of the International Association for Relational Psychoanalysis and Psychotherapy. She also serves as faculty and supervisor for the Toronto Institute for Self Psychology, the Toronto Institute of Child Psychotherapy, and ISIPSé, Rome. She is co-editor of *Psychoanalytic Dialogues* and is on the editorial boards of *Contemporary*

Psychoanalysis and *The International Journal of Self Psychology*. She teaches and presents on a regular basis nationally and internationally.

Lama Zuhair Khouri (CAPC, LMSW, MS) is the Executive Director of the Circle Of Arab Students In Schools (Circle OASIS). She is an expert in issues of immigration and Arab adolescence. She has published scholarly articles; participated in national panels—such the American Psychological Association and the American Group Psychotherapy Association; and has been a speaker addressing professionals in symposiums and conferences on the topic of adolescent development and immigration. Lama Khouri has extensive experience in the area of international relations and peacekeeping. She worked for fourteen years as a Political Desk Officer at the United Nations Department of Peacekeeping Operations.

Dino Koutsolioutsos, MFCC grew up in Athens, Greece. He holds a diploma in Civil Engineering from ETH Zurich, Switzerland, and is a retired licensed marriage and family therapist in Los Angeles, California. In 1991, he created the first HIV/AIDS-focused clinical training program for mental health student interns at the AIDS Project Los Angeles. From 1996 through 2009, he taught at a graduate program in Marriage and Family Therapy (MFT) at Pacific Oaks College, Pasadena, CA, where he was the Clinical Training Coordinator and collaborated in the development of the first graduate program specializing in the mental health needs of the Latino/a community. He currently writes a column on politics and the economy of Greece and the Eurozone for a web-based financial newspaper of Greece. He has presented at conferences both nationally and internationally on a variety of issues, including Latino/latina mental health, and the Adverse impact of the culture of psychotherapy on american society.

Dori Laub, MD was born in Cernauti, Romania, on June 8, 1937. He is currently a practicing psychoanalyst in Connecticut who works primarily with victims of massive psychic trauma and their children. He is a clinical professor of Psychiatry at the Yale University School of Medicine and Co-Founder of the Fortunoff Video Archive for Holocaust Testimonies. He obtained his MD at the Hadassah Medical School at Hebrew University in Jerusalem, Israel and his MA in Clinical Psychology at the Bar Ilan University in Ramat Gan, Israel. He was acting director of the Yale Genocide Study Program (GSP) in 2000 and 2003. Since 2001, he has served as the Deputy Director for Trauma Studies for the GSP.

Glenys Lobban, PhD is a graduate of the New York University Postdoctoral Program in Psychoanalysis and Psychotherapy. She is in full-time private practice in New York City. She is a faculty member at the Stephen A. Mitchell Center for Relational Studies and an adjunct clinical supervisor at the City University of New York's Clinical Psychology Doctoral Program. She wrote three chapters in the book entitled *With Culture in Mind: Psychoanalytic Stories*, which was edited by Muriel Dimen and published in 2011. She also edited *Psychodynamic Psychotherapy in South Africa: Contexts, Theories and Applications* with Michael O'Loughlin and Cora Smith, which was published in 2013.

Pratyusha (Usha) Tummala-Narra, PhD is an Associate Professor in the Department of Counseling, Developmental and Educational Psychology at Boston College. She is also in independent practice in Cambridge, MA. Dr. Tummala-Narra received her doctoral degree from Michigan State University and completed her post-doctoral training in the Victims of Violence Program at the Cambridge Hospital in Cambridge, MA. She has published widely on the topics of immigration, race, ethnic minority issues, trauma, and psychoanalytic psychotherapy. Her research concerns experiences of acculturation, acculturative stress, and traumatic stress on mental health among immigrant communities, and culturally informed psychotherapy practice. Dr. Tummala-Narra has served as the chair of the Multicultural Concerns Committee and Member-at-Large in the Board of Directors for Division 39 (Psychoanalysis), as a member of the Committee on Ethnic Minority Affairs (CEMA) in the American Psychological Association, and as a member of the APA Presidential Task Force on Immigration.

Introduction

Julia Beltsiou, PsyD

Immigration is both a polarized and an idealized subject in current politics, and in the history of the USA. In recent years, political debates about immigration policy and reform have become increasingly divided and contentious, in particular on the question of how to address the issue of 11 million illegal immigrants currently living in the United States. As I write this, Europe is experiencing a refugee inflow of a scale not seen since World War II. Immigrants to the United States enter an established narrative in which their status is both iconic and marginalized. Americans and aspiring immigrants alike treasure the long-held ideal of the United States as a country of immigrants, with the metaphor of the melting pot signifying how different cultures blend into a new, plentiful, and vibrant community.

In her essay "Wanderers by Choice" (2000), Eva Hoffman notes that we have come to romanticize and idealize the traits that displacement demands: uncertainty, fragmented identity, and otherness. Being a stranger—a person on the edge who escapes definitions—has become fashionable and sexy, a preferred positioning in the world. The exciting narrative of the sexy foreigner always co-exists with the painful experiences of unbelonging, non-recognition, struggle, alienation, and trauma inherent in immigration. Having an interesting, varied background may have caché at a party in the West Village, but it does not feel exciting while waiting in the immigration line at JFK as a "non-resident alien," wondering whether we will be granted entry.

This volume presents a unique approach to understanding the varied and multilayered experience of immigration by inviting a diverse group of foreign-born psychoanalysts and writers to discuss aspects of their own identity as immigrants and their work with immigrant patients. While our voices are diverse, and our discourses wide-ranging, what we have in common is our interest in how the social, cultural, political, and historical contexts shape the psychological experience of immigration and with it the encounter between foreign-born patients and their psychotherapists. In our essays, we all maintain the tension and contradiction between critique and idealization of the possibilities and the hardships of immigration.

The chapters written by psychoanalysts trace—from a personal and theoretical perspective—clinical moments that illustrate how the experience of immigration in our own and our patients' lives is part of our analytic journey together. We examine aspects of the therapeutic relationship and process that serve as a conduit for sorting through our cultural, historical, and familial legacy in order to locate ourselves in the world. Examples of our work with patients speak to the varied dilemmas stirred up in the process of immigration, involving dependency and control, loss and opportunity, freedom and constraint, our difference from each other and simultaneous need to belong.

Immigration is part of the history of psychoanalysis. While psychoanalysis had its beginnings in central European cities, hundreds of analysts, most of them survivors of the Shoah, fled to countries such as England, the USA, Argentina, and Israel. According to Makari (2008), by 1943, 149 exiled psychoanalysts had been relocated to the United States with the help of an emergency commission. How this collective experience of analysts in exile affected and informed our theory and practice has only recently been explored in depth by psychoanalysts and historians (see Kuriloff, 2013; Laub, 2013, reprinted in this volume). One of the reasons it has taken this long for psychoanalysis to address the experience of forced migration lies in the traumatic impact of the Holocaust on psychoanalysis. This trauma of persecution, fascism, and authoritarianism was subsequently enacted in a general conservatism and dogmatism in psychoanalytic institutes (see Jacoby, 1983; Kuriloff, 2013; Makari, 2008). European émigré/survivor analysts rarely linked their trauma to how they understood and practiced psychoanalysis and instead privileged their theories as objective truths that transcend subjectivity. Many survivors coped with their massive trauma by using adaptive and defensive ways of dissociating. Minimizing or suppressing the relevance of their experiences was a way to focus energies on building a new life.

In her book, *Contemporary Psychoanalysis and the Legacy of the Third Reich* (2013), Kuriloff uses previously unpublished source material and interviews with émigré/survivor psychoanalysts to trace how exile, loss, trauma, and resilience affected the psychoanalytic community and our intellectual and therapeutic tradition. Through her interviews with Holocaust survivor analysts, Kuriloff brings to life many examples of how these analysts suppressed traumatic experiences and how they dismissed the relevance of adult trauma by exclusively focusing on early childhood trauma in their clinical theory and practice. Processing massive collective trauma takes several generations. It is the voices of the second and third generation post-Holocaust who are able to speak, feel, and think more freely about the effects of this historic legacy.

One example of psychoanalytic books on the topic of immigration and identity is Leon and Rebeca Grinberg's *Psychoanalytic Perspectives on Migration and Exile* (2004). The Grinberg couple, Argentinian psychoanalysts raised by Jewish immigrant parents, sought exile in Spain in 1976, in response to the Videla dictatorship. The couple studied normal and pathological reactions to migration and exile linking it to Kleinian developmental theory. In their book the Grinbergs look at the various ways that the changes brought about by immigration impose great threat to the identity of the recently migrated and how it triggers latent psychopathology. They focus on different anxieties that get stirred up through dislocation: persecutory, depressive, and confusional anxieties that interact with various defense mechanisms and then produce psychopathology.

Another well-known psychoanalytic book on immigration is *Immigration and Identity* (1999). In it, psychoanalyst Salman Akhtar, an Indian immigrant to the United States, examines from the lens of ego psychology, the traumatic impact that migration has on one's identity and adaption to a new country. He examines the psychological defenses mobilized by loss of home, such as nostalgia and fantasies of return.

To date, no books address the experience of immigration from a relational or interpersonal perspective, an approach that recognizes the significance of the analyst's personal life and values in clinical work with patients and focuses on the role of relationships in becoming a person and feeling and knowing ourselves. Over the last few years, there has been a surge of relational journal articles on the topic of immigration, some of which were written by contributors to this book, and a few recently published articles are reprinted here (Ipp, 2010; Khouri, 2013; Laub, 2013; Lobban, 2013).

The final impulse for this book was my experience at the conference of the Psychoanalytic Division 39 of the American Psychological Association, April 2013. At this conference—"Psychoanalysis in a Social World"—it was apparent that there is a thirst for understanding the immigrant's subjectivity: Four panels at the conference focused on the topic of immigration in our clinical work, all of them well attended. After presenting on the panel "Locating Ourselves—Immigration Stories and Psychoanalytic Process," my fellow panelists and I were approached not only by many members of the audience who were moved by our papers and wanted to read more on the subject, but also by a book agent of an academic press who encouraged us to submit a proposal on the topic of immigration and psychoanalysis, further highlighting the urgency and timeliness of this topic. A conference in May 2014 organized by the National Institute of the Psychotherapies in New York City followed, entitled: "The Immigrant in the Consulting Room." Several contributors of this book presented there: Ghislaine Boulanger gave the keynote address; Lama Khouri and Usha Tummala-Narra also gave talks on the topic. These conferences show that there is a strong interest and need for relational psychoanalytic accounts of clinical work with immigrants, and that the topic of immigration is emerging in contemporary psychoanalytic inquiry.

Unlike the psychoanalytic literature on immigration, there is a rich tradition of immigrant literature that gives voice to those experiences of uncertainty, possibility, loss, struggle, freedom, and constraint. These accounts have a both/and quality that transcends binaries of self/other, internal and external. Immigrant writers describe the social contexts in their homeland that prompted their leaving, their experience of the migration itself, and the psychological experience of adjusting to a foreign world. Cultural and language differences, class, and race are important vectors in the stories of immigration, as immigration experiences often alter one's class position (Ainslie, 2011). Immigrant writers explore their sense of rootlessness and the search for identity resulting from displacement and cultural diversity.

What exactly constitutes immigrant literature is not clearly defined, as writing by second-generation authors is considered to be immigrant literature, such as novels by Amy Tan and Jhumpa Lahiri. Many immigrant authors choose to write in the language of their host culture (e.g., Eva Hoffman and Edward Said are second-generation writers who grew up bilingual and thus are "polyphonic"). Taghi Modharessi, an Iranian novelist and psychiatrist wrote in his native tongue and translated his novels from Farsi into English: "I call it writing with an accent. (...) And I prefer that. Because that way of writing also gives a background, creates an atmosphere so that you immediately know these people are not born American. So that something that could have been a handicap has become for me a voice" (1997). Which language we choose to convey our experience shows how we position ourselves and to whom we explain ourselves: Do we choose to enter a dialogue with our new culture or to the ones we left behind in our native country? Practical reasons may also be part of this decision, as writing in English may increase the likelihood of getting published and allow for wider circulation and recognition.

One example of immigrant literature is the Pulitzer Prize winning novel *Brooklyn* by Colm Toibin (2009). It depicts the experience of a poor and uneducated young woman, Eillis, who is sent from rural Ireland to New York by her family for economic opportunities in the 1950s. She finds her way to a working-class existence in Brooklyn and gradually fits herself into the new world. When she visits Ireland a few years later, engaged to be married to a young Brooklyn man of Italian heritage, Eillis struggles to face the pain of choice: Stay in Ireland or return to Brooklyn? She is forced to grapple with questions about her desire and face her own agency in the choice of where and how to live her life. For a while she inhabits parallel lives, each equally viable. When she decides to leave Ireland, Eillis soothes herself by imagining a time in the future when she will fully inhabit her life abroad as an immigrant: "'She has gone back to Brooklyn,' her mother would say. And, as the train rolled past Macmire Bridge on its way towards Wexford, Eilis imagined the years already when these words would come to mean less and less to the man who heard them and would come to mean more and more to herself. She almost smiled at the thought of it, then closed her eyes and tried to imagine nothing more" (p. 262). This is a moment of maturation, in which Eillis actively grapples with the loss and opportunity of her choice to immigrate. It is easy to relate to the pain of leaving behind the continuity of a particular identity she had in her homeland, a story left unfinished for a new narrative elsewhere with unknown possibilities.

The Namesake by Jhumpa Lahiri (2003) depicts the history of an educated Indian family moving among Calcutta, Boston, and New York City. It considers the nuances in living between two cultures with vastly different religious, social, and ideological values and practices. As the immigrant parents and their American-born children live their lives in the US, India always hovers in the background. In their own ways, each family member struggles with what it means to live in the US, to belong and not belong: "Though no longer pregnant, she continues, at times, to mix Rice Krispies and peanuts and onions in a bowl. For being a foreigner, Ashima is beginning to realize, is a sort of lifelong pregnancy—a perpetual wait, a constant burden, a continuous feeling out of sorts. It is an ongoing responsibility, a parenthesis in what had once been ordinary life, only to discover that that previous life has vanished, replaced by something more complicated and demanding. Like pregnancy, being a foreigner, Ashima believes, is something that elicits the same curiosity from strangers, the same combination of pity and respect" (p. 49). Tasting the flavors of hybridity—Rice Krispies, peanuts, and onions—her own creation, is what comforts us immigrants as we hold the tension between the two worlds inside of us. As Ashima gives American foods the spiciness she needs, she adds her own accent.

Edward Said's memoir *Out of Place* (1999) describes his recurrent feeling of "not being quite right." As the child of a wealthy Palestinian family in Egypt, Palestine, and Lebanon; Christian in a Muslim world; Arab holding an American passport; he portrays a confusing and complicated experience of feeling different and not fitting in. Grappling with his multitude of allegiances, interests, and abilities turns Said into an international public intellectual, humanist, literary academic, and music aficionado as he learns to accept his "cluster of flowing currents." Claiming our diasporic identity is an important step in locating ourselves and offers a lens that we can put to use by continuously questioning local conventions. In his 1994 essay "Intellectual Exile: Expatriates and Marginals" Said speaks to the merits of deliberately positioning ourselves on the margins: "Even if one is not an actual immigrant or expatriate, it is still possible to think as one, to imagine and investigate in spite of barriers, and always to move away from the centralizing authorities towards the margins, where you see things that are usually lost on minds that have never travelled beyond the conventional and the comfortable" (quoted in Bayoumi and Rubin, 2000, p. xiv).

Immigrant accounts like these, each written in its own accent, mend the discontinuity we experience in our lives in different places. We find reverberations of the after in the before and of the past in the present and taste the pain and excitement of holding complexity.

The existing psychoanalytic literature on immigration has some catching up to do to reach the wisdom, nuance, and psychological sophistication of autobiographical and fictionalized accounts of immigration. My hope is that the following volume gives voice to the complexity and psychological shades of migration.

Part I, *Immigration as Psychological Opportunity* looks at the sense of possibility and creative edge that lies in immigration. Francisco J. González, a Cuban-born, Texas-raised psychiatrist and psychoanalyst currently practicing in San Francisco, examines the generative force of migration for the individual, in psychoanalysis and in the encounter between foreigner and native. He understands the idea of the foreigner as an existential register beyond a difference in nationality: "Our aching humanness, the inheritance of separation and division and loss, is soaked with foreignness." Francisco J. González considers how immigration aids us in elaborating abstract notions of transitional space by complementing it with the idea of material place. He points out that the immigrant signifies a crisis of identity for the native as well as for the stranger, and that in the place where irreconcilable difference meets, the new arises.

Part II is comprised of three chapters that examine *The Effects of Immigration on Self-Experience*, such as discontinuities of self pre- and post-migration, the segregation of painful parts from our old life, and what one author calls "the journey from double-consciousness to hybridity."

Hazel Ipp is a psychologist and psychoanalyst who grew up during apartheid in South Africa and practices in Toronto, Canada. She shares her analytic work with a woman who moved from the same politically complex and contradictory country yet with her own, very different, social and political history. Leaving our place of origin allows us to have a protective barrier from painful parts of our lived experience. Hazel Ipp carefully traces how, through struggling together over many years, she and her patient formed a bridge for each other that over time allowed them to re-link amputated parts of themselves and helped both of them to create a more alive and complex experience: "Nell has been my gift. Apart from providing me with the opportunity to dismantle many of my own prejudices and stereotypes, she has enabled me to reconnect with that part of me that I refer to as my amputated self, to grieve my losses and open new spheres of reflective space. ... Locating oneself within the other, with all the struggles and angst that that stimulates, is perhaps the essence of what we need to grapple with as contemporary psychoanalysts." She emphasizes as crucial in this work the shared effort to maintain an openness to inhabit and utilize the unavoidable moments where we are emotionally challenged, "rather than anxiously moving away from the stirrings of traumatic memories to places of 'certainty' and conviction."

Ghislaine Boulanger is a psychologist and psychoanalyst who grew up in a French and English family in England and lives and practices in New York

City. Her Chapter, "Seeing Double, Being Double: Longing, Belonging, Recognition, and Evasion in Psychodynamic Work with Immigrants," explores the complex task of immigrants to continuously hold several identities in dialectical tension. Ghislaine Boulanger points out: "Psychically, immigrants are always refocusing, automatically keeping both worlds in mind." She describes her work with a professional woman who was not only the child of immigrants in the country in which she was born, but also immigrated to America herself. Their analytic process traced the patient's subtle shifts of identity, often manifested in the form of dreams, as she struggled to feel accepted in America and to also find a sense of self. Ghislaine Boulanger carefully teases apart the various, incongruent self-states of this patient, shared by many immigrants: our loyalty to and wish for freedom from old ties and the tension between longing for recognition and the yearning to belong. She concludes that in this new framework, assimilation is no longer a goal.

Glenys Lobban is a psychologist and psychoanalyst born and raised in South Africa, who moved first to Britain and then immigrated to New York City. In Chapter Four, she examines how being an immigrant in North America shapes one's subjectivity. Lobban observes how mainstream North American cultural values are privileged in the dominant culture and foreign cultures are viewed as "other" and inferior. This puts a particular pressure on immigrants to assimilate and causes us to experience a double consciousness, viewing ourselves negatively by seeing our country of origin through the lens of the dominant culture. She describes her own experience as an immigrant analyst in training in North America and how it affected her work with two patients. She further analyzes the concept of double consciousness: how it develops, how is perpetuated, and how it becomes part of our subjectivity. She examines how immigrant analysts can contend with double consciousness in ourselves and our patients in a way that allows for resignification with the goal to view ourselves through multiple lenses and cherish our hybridity.

Part III explores the question of what a productive tension of otherness in immigration could look like. In Chapter Five, I describe psychoanalytic work with a patient from the West Indies and explore our respective original experiences of otherness, the "pre-immigration otherness" that gave us the impulse for leave-taking and courting the foreign. Having felt at the margins in our place of origin, home expels us to explore our liminality and otherness elsewhere. The process of settling in a strange land has at its center meeting ourselves: making ourselves home in the foreign as well as in our foreignness. What is the opportunity in speaking oneself in a new language: American English accented in Creole and German/Greek, respectively? I examine how issues of longing, ambiguous belonging, and outsiderness play out between my patient and me, complicating notions of both immigration and psychoanalysis. I elaborate on how moving away from home may be the only way to give contours to an opaque sense that something is not quite right, an attempt to become intelligible to ourselves and others.

Dino Koutsolioutsos, a psychotherapist and political writer, offers us an autobiographical exploration of his otherness in gender and sexuality, within the context of his migrations from Greece to Switzerland, to the United States, and back to Greece. He observes the ways that sexual otherness can only exist in relationship to other people and is a dynamic, relational concept, fated to change in time, place, and context. The symbolic and concrete journey of leaving our place of origin and moving to a place of choice can both facilitate and further complicate the experience of otherness and the process of becoming. The author examines the particular ways his moves and life changes were a means of resistance to, as well as a tool for acceptance of, his otherness, a process he experiences as ongoing.

Part IV is entitled *Native Language, Foreign Tongue: Speaking Oneself as an Immigrant.* The first contribution is by Jeanne Wolff Bernstein, a German-born psychologist and psychoanalyst who settled in the United States for close to four decades and now lives and practices in Vienna. She describes the return to her native tongue, spoken now with the bi-focal attention of an outsider. She experiences the structuring power language exerts upon our deepest emotions, longings, and desires, drawing on Lacan's concept of "I is Other": The "I" is structured by the Other who is both most intimate and most foreign to us. Jeanne Wolff Bernstein speaks to the freedom of the foreigner who can play within and between languages, as the one location she has come to consider home by now is the place of the eternal stranger lost in translation.

Irene Cairo practices as a psychiatrist and psychoanalyst in Manhattan. As a Buenos Aires native, she spent her teenage years in Europe. In Chapter eight, she examines the role and function of foreign, native, and adopted language in the analytic relationship and process. She shares two clinical case examples in which the analytic dyad met in a third language—English, a second language for both patient and analyst. She focuses on the moment in treatment when the patient suddenly spoke her own mother-tongue, foreign to the analyst, and with it ushered into the room previously unexpressed, conflicted feelings about the analyst. Irene Cairo asks: "How does the patient create a bridge to me through the language that actually is foreign, and not available to me?" She explores the role of difference and separation from the analyst, as it emerges in this unbidden use of the patient's maternal language, concluding: "The foreign language was an unarticulated message, a measure of our difference, a music (harmonious or dissonant) of the analytic moment."

Part V explores the significance of names and name changes for immigrants. "Names, Name Changes, and Identity in the Context of Migration" was written by Pratyusha Tummala-Narra, an Indian American immigrant and analytic psychologist who teaches and practices in Boston. She carefully examines intrapsychic, interpersonal, and social implications of parents' choices of names for their children and the re-naming process in childhood, adolescence, and adulthood among first- and second-generation immigrant-origin individuals. Pratyusha Tummala-Narra addresses the manifold facets of identity that can be discovered through the naming and re-naming process with special attention to the normative process of settling into a culture (i.e., acculturation), as well as the social stressors of immigrant life, such as intergenerational conflict, traumatic stress, and discrimination. Examples of her work with immigrant-origin patients illustrate the importance of attending to names as both intrapsychically and contextually driven. She concludes: "Names (further) indicate a sense of pride, desire for belonging, and imagining new possibilities of hybrid identities."

Part VI looks at the effects of trauma on the immigration process. Dori Laub, a psychiatrist and psychoanalyst and the deputy director of the Yale Genocide Study Program, is a Holocaust survivor from Romania who first lived in Israel after WWII and then moved to the US. Chapter ten, entitled "On Leaving Home and the Flight from Trauma," is a personal, social, and psychoanalytic reflection about his journey from being a perpetual refugee, who maintained an inner exile, to finding an emotional home in his relationships with others who shared his experiences. He reflects on the collective blind spot of the psychological effects of the Shoah on many survivors and his own disavowal of his past. His experience as an analysand, and later on his encounters with other Holocaust survivors, helped him emerge from his inner exile. He also speaks to the ways that being an immigrant and a trauma survivor inform and enrich his work. Dori Laub reaches the conclusion: "For an analyst to do his work, he must reside in his own emotional home." For him this means keeping cultural perspectives, stemming from his background and history, and his new home in discourse with each other, as well as finding an emotional home in relationships with others who share aspects of his past.

Part VII explores the role of mourning and melancholia in the complicated process of settling in. Lama Z. Khouri, a social worker and psychoanalytic therapist who came as a young adult to New York City from Jordan, explores the trauma and loss of pictures of an old life that cannot be brought back. In "The Immigrant's Neverland: Commuting from Amman to Brooklyn," she shares her experience of working with a group of Arab adolescent boys at a school in Brooklyn, New York. To investigate the melancholy and mourning of the immigrant, she draws from the fairy tale of Peter Pan and his suspension in the limbo of Neverland, longing to return home when there is no home to be found. Khouri explores the experience of alienation and loss of shelter through the dialectic tension of idealizing or denigrating the old country in the context of hostility and xenophobia toward Arabs and Muslims in the current social and political climate in the United States.

Part VIII, with the title *Forever an Immigrant? The Immigrant in Older Age*, looks at the question of whether immigrant identity is a static and lasting condition. Eva Hoffman, a writer of several non-fiction works, and professor of Literature, grew up in Poland before emigrating in her teens to Canada and then the United States. For the last two decades, she has been living in London. In "Out of Exile: Some Thoughts on Exile as a Dynamic Condition," she explores the question of the immigrant's identity as an "existential location" and asserts that our relationship to our experiences of relocation does not remain static. She notes that it is seductive to define ourselves in reference to our place of departure and assume the position of the outsider: "The exilic position is isomorphic with exactly those qualities, which are privileged in a certain vein of post-modern theory: marginality, alterity, the de-centered identity." It assumes that our life before and after is immune to evolution, yet we live in a perpetually mobile, nomadic, and heterogeneous world, which changes the categories of native country, foreigner, and alien.

Eva Hoffman asserts: "The strong contrasts between home and elsewhere, the native and the stranger, have given way to something less polarized and more fluid. In a sense, everyone's subjectivity is becoming hybrid."

The essays in this volume form an elaborate tapestry of the multilayered experience of immigration. We aim to convey the complexity and the contradictions of the immigration process: the tension between loss and hope, future and past, the idealization and denigration of the other/stranger, and what it takes to tolerate the existential dialectic between separateness and belonging. Through these personal accounts, we hope the stories of immigration come to life and become accessible to the reader. These essays bring into focus where and how "our minds meet" (Aron, 2001) in the analytic dyad and how we are changed by immigration and psychoanalysis.

References

Ainslie, R. (2011). Immigration and the psychodynamics of class. *Psychoanalytic Psychology*, 28(4), 560–568.

Akhtar, S. (1999). *Immigration and identity*. New York, NY: Jason Aronson.

Aron, L. (2001). *A meeting of minds: Mutuality in psychoanalysis*. London/New York, NY: Routledge.

Grinberg, L., and Grinberg, R. (2004). *Psychoanalytic perspectives on migration and exile*. New Haven, CT: Yale University Press.

Hoffman, E. (2000). Wanderers by choice. *Utne Reader*, July-August: 46–48.

Ipp, H. (2010). Nell—A bridge to the amputated self: The impact of immigration on continuities and discontinuities of self. *International Journal of Psychoanalytic Self Psychology*, 5: 373–386.

Jacoby, R. (1983). *The repression of psychoanalysis*. Chicago, IL: University of Chicago Press.

Khouri, L. (2012). The immigrant's neverland: Commuting from Amman to Brooklyn. *Contemporary Psychoanalysis*, 48(2): 213–237.

Kuriloff, E. (2013). *Contemporary psychoanalysis and the legacy of the Third Reich*. New York, NY: Routledge.

Lahiri, J. (2003). *The namesake*. Buena Vista, VA: Mariner Books.

Laub, D. (2013). On leaving home and the flight from trauma. *Psychoanalytic Dialogues*, 23(5): 568–580.

Lobban, G. (2013). The immigrant analyst: A journey from double consciousness towards hybridity. *Psychoanalytic Dialogues*, 23(5): 554–567.

Makari, G. (2008). *Revolution in mind: The creation of psychoanalysis*. New York, NY: Harper Collins.

Modaressi, T. (1997). A Life of Wonder. Accessed 7/1/2014 at: http://articles.baltimoresun.com/1997-05-03/features/1997123094_1_modarressi-language-of-babies-iran.

Said, E. (1994). Intellectual exile: Expatriates and marginals. Quoted in Bayoumi and Rubin (Eds.), *The Edward Said Reader*. New York, NY: Vintage, p. xiv.

Said, E. (1999). *Out of place: A memoir*. Vintage, NY.

Toibin, C. (2009). *Brooklyn*. New York, NY: Scribner Publishing.

Part 1

Immigration as Psychological Opportunity

Chapter 1

Only What Is Human Can Truly Be Foreign

The Trope of Immigration as a Creative Force in Psychoanalysis

Francisco J. González, MD

Until recently, there was a relative paucity of work on immigration in the psychoanalytic literature. What might have been seen as uncanny irony—given the remarkable diasporic movements of psychoanalysis itself—has increasingly been recognized as the effect of the cultural repression or dissociation of our psychoanalytic history (Jacoby, 1983; Kuriloff, 2010, 2012; Makari, 2008; Yi, 2014a; Yi, 2014b). Indeed, writings on the subject have recently burgeoned (Ainslie et al., 2013; Boulanger, 2004; Harlem, 2010; Tummala-Narra, 2009), as evidenced also in the production of this volume of essays. The predominant tendency in this developing literature has been to see immigration largely as a psychologically damaging process, a traumatic event that poses unprecedented difficulties and usually leaves irremediable scars in its subjects. Such analysis has been necessary, to not only ameliorate suffering but also initiate a process of remediation for the dehumanizing tendencies of xenophobia, whose principle mechanism is the erasure of the histories of (subaltern) Others.[1] Little in evidence is an accounting of what immigration produces, how it generates and creates. The displacement necessarily occasioned by immigration—especially when forced by economic deprivation or political oppression—is unquestionably a tremendous challenge to subjectivity, but it is also the fertile ground of creativity, the strange place where something new can come into being.

Consider this poem by Wislawa Szymborska, who won the Nobel Prize for Literature in 1996, called simply *Psalm*:

> Oh, the leaky boundaries of man-made states!
> How many clouds float past them with impunity;
> how much desert sand shifts from one land to another;
> how many mountain pebbles tumble onto foreign soil
> in provocative hops!
>
> Need I mention every single bird that flies in the face of frontiers
> or alights on the roadblock at the border?
> A humble robin—still, its tail resides abroad
> while its beak stays home. If that weren't enough, it won't stop bobbing!

Among innumerable insects, I'll single out only the ant
between the border guard's left and right boots
blithely ignoring the questions "Where from?" and "Where to?"

Oh, to register in detail, at a glance, the chaos
prevailing on every continent!
Isn't that a privet on the far bank
smuggling its hundred-thousandth leaf across the river?
And who but the octopus, with impudent long arms,
would disrupt the sacred bounds of territorial waters?

And how can we talk of order overall?
when the very placement of the stars
leaves us doubting just what shines for whom?

Not to speak of the fog's reprehensible drifting!
And dust blowing all over the steppes
as if they hadn't been partitioned!
And the voices coasting on obliging airwaves,
that conspiratorial squeaking, those indecipherable mutters!

Only what is human can truly be foreign.
The rest is mixed vegetation, subversive moles, and wind.

This song is full of inexorable movement—birds, clouds, insects, fog, dust, octopus, and pebbles—all scrambling over, ignoring, and disrupting the territorial lines established by the imperious humans. And while Szymborska issues a deeply humanist call to what binds us together, the poem is couched in the ironies of one who has lived through what tears us apart: upheaval, war, and totalitarianism. You can hear the lament in it. What a funny thing, Szymborska seems to be saying, these useless and impossible boundaries that attempt to separate and divide, but are nothing if not full of mole holes and the diffusion of clouds.

At one level this message is simple enough: There is no natural division of the land, no essentialist state or border, between Palestine and Israel, between Turkey and Iraq, between the United States and Mexico. The land itself knows nothing of its partitioning, and it is we—humans in boots—who do the dividing. But she also alerts us to something more complicated and painful: the layering inherent in the world, the way a single place contains the simultaneous flow of separate registers. The ant making its way past the guard on the ground occupies the same place as the robin bobbing up on the roadblock and as the squeaking mutter of human voices high overhead, adrift on the airwaves obliged to carry them. There is a childlike delight in the cartoon of pebbles provocatively hopping onto foreign soil, oblivious of their transgression, but by the end, this animistic world is reduced to "mixed vegetation, subversive moles, and wind" and what we are left with is the echo of something deeper down, saturated with histories, closer to our very subjectivities: "only what is human can be foreign."

Man-made states—whether these be political or psychic—can only be bounded leakily, only contingently demarcated. There is *always* something blowing across the border from the other side, something smuggled in whether by privets or the human *coyotes* paid exorbitant sums to ferry Mexican families across the Arizona border. And more mysteriously still, we are repatriated daily in the nocturnal ships that transport us from that foreign country of our dreams. Our aching humanness, the inheritance of separation and division and loss, is soaked with foreignness. As Rilke (1923/2009) reminds us in his first *Duino Elegy*, "we are not really at home in our interpreted world." None of us.

But these displacements, as well as being the wellsprings of grief, are also the engines of poetry. Crossing the border undoubtedly makes enormous demands of any who undertake the journey; this demand is, above all, a call for creative transformation. Residence in the new requires innovation.

It is from this place that I begin to think about immigration: not with a sense of the otherness of the immigrant, but by way of the very foreignness constitutive of each of us as human beings and the call such foreignness makes of us for improvisation. We are all immigrants in this sense, all "strangers to ourselves" as Julia Kristeva (1991) concludes in her meditation on the foreigner.

Most psychoanalytic papers on immigration tend to conceptualize the terrain—perhaps inevitably—in dichotomies: there-and-then vs. here-and-now, the old country vs. the new, mourning vs. melancholia, assimilation vs. isolation. It is well established that faced with literal transplantation, the immigrant must steer between the Scylla of adaptation to new cultural ground that promises survival by assimilation but threatens a deracinated soullessness, and the Charybdis of an encapsulating nostalgia for a never-attainable paradise lost that ends in the withering victimhood of melancholia. What this subject can hope to achieve is biculturality.

Perhaps we have become nostalgic for a time in which the old country could be clearly demarcated from the new, one without the temporal displacements and simultaneities of our multicultural postmodernism. What counts as the old country is no longer so clear. An American ex-pat living in Europe misses good Mexican food; while an undocumented Mexican repatriated to a border town opens a Chinese restaurant (NPR, 2014).

The days of simple biculturality are gone. For one, we now take seriously the fragmenting inflections of other fault lines: the ways that class, gender, sexuality, race, and ethnicity, for example, rupture the supposed homogeneity of given national cultures and bridge subcultural groups. Take the case of numerous gay immigrants from Latin America with whom I have worked: Many feel more at home with their sexuality in the United States than they ever did in their country of origin, and not just in terms of White American "gayness." Immigration has in many cases facilitated the discovery of a queer identity *in Spanish* through participation in a multinational Latino gay community that was not available to them back home. But neither is this to be romanticized as an uncomplicated story of emancipation. Socioeconomic status, education, race, and the poisoned legacies of colonialism and civil war split and multiply cultural identities along complex lines. Nationalized identity is refracted through the improvised, multinational subcultures of Latino gayness: a formation more complicated than simple biculturality. Indeed, by postulating an *other* culture, usually premised on nationalistic identity (including national language), biculturality can obscure the fractures extant in any native culture, furthering the fiction of a uniform national character.

This is brought home in any theorizing about immigration, since it must contend with the extraordinary variability of immigrant experience under the specificity of manifold conditions, as a number of writers have noted (Akthar, 1995; Antokoletz, 1993; Brody, 1973; Grinberg and Grinberg, 1989; Lijtmaer, 2001). The variables are manifold: the freedom or constraint regarding timing of departure or choice of a destination; the reasons for leaving; whether there are language differences, and if so, how divergent; the available resources (or lack thereof) to cushion the transition; the traumas that might aggrieve it; how beneficent, facilitating, persecutory, indifferent, or harsh the States involved might be; whether one is classed as a refugee, a dissident, a criminal, an ex-patriot, or a national treasure. Add to this dizzying array the complexity of socio-demographic status: whether the migration is made alone or in a group of strangers or a family or with the remnants of one, and the determinations of age, gender, sexuality, class, educational level, race, and ethnicity. All of these factors, to name some of the more obvious, make for radically different, indeed practically incomparable, immigration experiences. The war-torn Sudanese refugee who emigrates to Israel and the wealthy ex-pat American who chooses to live in London can be fitted under a shared rubric of "the immigrant" only with considerable force.

If there is an irreducible specificity for the immigrant, so is there a dense layering of place in the contemporary metropolis. The relatively ensconced Chinatowns and Little Italies of old have become a patch-quilt of Little Koreo-Pakistans, of Afro-Cuban, Dominico-Chicanotowns, perhaps bordered by a Hmong or Quechua community. We see saris while shopping for good harissa at the Syrian market to put on our chorizo and eggs. You can no longer assume that a conventional family is comprised of one race or one culture. Red-blooded, blonde-haired, American couples adopt babies from Africa and Ecuador.

Increasingly we live in a mosaic, a land of hybrids. As Guillermo Gomez-Peña (1992), the internationally recognized performance artist of the borderland, writes:

> The bankrupt notion of the melting pot has been replaced by a model that is more germane to the times, that of the *menudo chowder*.

According to this model, most of the ingredients do melt, but some stubborn chunks are condemned merely to float. Vergigratia! (as quoted in Bhabha, 1994, p. 313)

Homi Bhabha (1994) goes on to elaborate the hybridity of contemporary identifications for the cultural subject of the new world. Plural and in flux, these identifications (which we can contrast to the fixity and singularity of the term *identity*) are grounded neither in the monolithic past of the old country nor in an assimilationist accommodation to the new, but rather in some intermediate zone that elaborates the "incommensurables" of cultural difference, what will not blend into the melting pot, what refuses translation:

> Such assignations of social differences—where difference is neither One nor the Other but *something else besides, in-between*—find their agency in a form of the 'future' where the past is not originary, where the present is not simply transitory. It is, if I may stretch a point, an interstitial future, that emerges *in-between* the claims of the past and the needs of the present. (p. 313)

This kind of thinking resonates with my own experience, a result in part of how young I was when my family immigrated. My parents, strongly sympathetic to the Cuban revolution of 1959, became embittered when Castro established a communist state and left Havana for Mexico City with their two young children in 1962 before immigrating to the United States almost a year later. I was almost four, just old enough to color my newfound ability to speak with the lilting rhythms of the Mexican capitol. Once landed in the US, I witnessed at close range the tribulations and triumphs my parents experienced in reestablishing themselves: hard work and perseverance triumphing over the occasional humiliations of xenophobic misrecognition. We took up Americanisms. My mother dutifully learned how to make turkey and packaged stuffing when I came home from school crying because everyone but me had shared in the incomparable feast called Thanksgiving. My grandparents came over a few years later to live with us and kept close to the old ways, getting by with a little phrase-book English and *cafecitos*, and over the years there were waves of cousins, some entering easily with visas, by plane, others more harrowingly on small make-shift rafts, via the refugee camp in Guantanamo. My grandfather tended the backyard with his machete; we danced salsa in the living room at family parties and ate a lot of *picadillo* and *plátanos fritos*. Still, I hardly remember learning English—it poured into me like the pink Slushees at the neighborhood "ice house" (which I later learned to call convenience store). And while my closer friends occasionally ran into markers of my cultural difference (my mother, who still struggles with her English, once told a neighborhood kid that we couldn't come out to play because we were eating a *snake*, rather than a *snack*), for the most part the social worlds of school and play were made in America. In a number of ways, the inflection of immigration on my cultural difference was not too much more externally pronounced than the traces of otherness (due to more distant migrations) in the lives of my Chicano or Jewish friends.

More than a severance of old country and new, for me the trace of immigration, divided institutional public life from the life of the family, braiding the strands. Or more analytically, it constituted an Oedipal crossing of a cultural kind, from the dream-memories of a primal world—Cuba, I used to say, was the body of my mother floating in the Caribbean—into the bilingual secondary processes of the United States. If Oedipality has to do with the construction of thirdness, then crossing borders began the construction of that point in the triangle from which I could start to *situate* my cultural identity, nationality, and language, not as something essential and natural, but as one position among very many.

Then I started visiting relatives in Cuba, developing relationships to the people (and the places) there, and they in turn came to visit here. The otherness I felt in Spanish was marked more by differences inside of the language and within each country than by the contrast with English and between countries. My Spanish did not sound like the relaxed Tex-Mex Spanglish of the Mexicans and Chicanos I grew up with in San Antonio, but then neither was it the slang-filled Cuban pell-mell of my cousins when I visited the island as an adult. These differences were much more marked than those between Spanish and the English-speaking suburban world of "los Americanos." At home, generational language switching became the norm: the siblings routinely speaking English to one another while always speaking Spanish to the older generations in the same conversation. Eventually, I moved to California and became "Latino," a category of cultural politics that attempts to buck the US government by excising the hegemonizing influence of Spain evident in its official designation, "Hispanic." In the big tent of Latino Spanish speakers in San Francisco, my Spanish grew and flexed, taking on the hues of Mexicans from the capitol, Chileans, Colombians, and Central Americans. I became both more and less Cuban in this mosaic, more knitted to other Spanish-speaking immigrants, and more specifically recognized as *Cubano*. My cultural identity fractured and multiplied: inflected by my gender, my queerness, my profession, my paycheck, my whiteness. This proliferation and dismantling and reconfiguration of cultural identity: what could be more American?

And so, from this position and with this history, I take up the idea of what immigration has to say to us through the lens of psychoanalysis, both as a clinical practice and as a theoretical discipline. Rather than focus on *the plight of the immigrant* as patient, strung between the discreet poles of old and new country, old and new identity, I consider *the location of immigration* in psychoanalysis, strung as a productive tension between the irreducible specificity of any immigrant's experience (what can never be generalized) and what this illuminates about how we can theorize psycho-cultural process for all of us. Psychoanalysis itself, after all, shares a great deal with the hybridized and hybridizing immigrant, for the improvisation of new cultural forms lies at the heart of the analytic enterprise. What is (counter)transference as useful clinical praxis if not this?

Following Bhabha's (1994) temporal notions concerning hybridity, I want to sketch out some ideas about the "interstitial future" of psychoanalysis: one—as he writes of the agency such social difference can take—"where the past is not originary, where the present is not simply transitory," taking each moment in turn as it turns on the theme of immigration. I begin with a (re)conception of immigration as a story of origins in Freud. In the next section I move to a conception of the present, which immigration teaches us is anchored by place. I end with a reflection on what gets lost in translation and what is found or made specifically in that losing, which illuminates how the immigrant helps make the new.

I - On the Migration of Origins

The force of the migratory trope permeates the psychoanalytic enterprise, troubling the very question of where one is from. But, as Homi Bhabha (1994) writes: To be unhomed is not to be homeless ..." (p. 13). Like the quintessentially analytic notion of *Nachträglichkeit* (or deferred action or *après-coup),* immigration posits a new place from which to start.[2] To be sure, the very concept of *Nachträglichkeit*—whose own evolution as an analytic idea was propelled by psychoanalytic migrations and the process of translation—is essential to a psychoanalytic conceptualization of immigration. Indeed, the idea of *Nachträglichkeit* began as a reference to a kind of "retranscription" (Freud, 1896, p. 207) in which psychic material is translated from one register to another. It is precisely through the retrans-lations of a relatively commonplace German word, *nachträglich* (literally, "later, after, following") into English ("deferred action") and later into French ("après-coup"), that the latent seeds of an extraordinarily potent theoretical construct are developed, partly through uncovering and partly through creation (Faimberg, 2007; Laplanche, 1991; Thomä & Cheshire, 1991). Translation here acts as a kind of incubator. By producing iterations, translation both amplifies embryonic potentials in the term and accretes new meanings through the nuanced associations possible in second languages (see Bernstein, this volume).

Immigration itself inaugurates a process of *nachträglich* signification, opening new origins in ways that perturb a too-easy demarcation between *back there* and *here,* rendering these boundaries leaky, permeable, and teeming with life. The immigrant, like the analysand, finds herself in a strange situation, forced into innovation, called upon to make a new start.

Indeed, the theme of migration is much more seminal to our discipline than first meets the eye. The rich equipage it carries stitches through the analytic fabric in profound ways: in ideas about cultural history and cultural difference, about language(s) and the movement across boundaries, and about the discontents and pleasures of civilization. It is almost impossible, in fact, to conceive of the vibrancy of psychoanalytic theory today without the effects of immigration. From the beginning, migrating analysts transplanted seminal ideas from their birthplace to new cultural ground where they have flourished through transformation, from the early confluence in London that spurred the controversial discussions, to the dispersement on the continent and across the Atlantic in the mid-twentieth century. What we recognize today as the singularities of theory and practice are in fact often the regional inflections that a specific place and culture impart to psychoanalysis as it travels the globe: the Italian slant on Bion, the South American version of Lacan, the Israeli take on relational ideas.

Even in the homeland of psychoanalysis, the Freudian text, we find traces of migratory displacements. The seminal Oedipus myth appears primarily as a paradigm for the structuration of sexuality, but we should not forget that it begins and ends as a story of banishment, repatriation, and exile (Grinberg & Grinberg, 1989). Nor are the concerns of the myth restricted to individual fate: The fortunes of the *polis* are equally at stake: the future of Thebes and the destiny of the House of Laius. The twists of destiny and the cruel hand of the unconscious (are they not the same?) make the hero's return home not one of nostalgic yearning for the homeland finally fulfilled, but rather a macabre tragedy of the *Unheimlich* that ultimately results in Oedipus's banishment. Oedipus begins and ends as an exile: as with dreams, displacement is the prime mover.

Freud's own life was similarly marked. Anzieu (1986) describes his early years, allowing us to discern the formative mark of transgenerational migration. Sigmund's father Jacob was born in Tysmenitz in eastern Galicia, on the border between Poland and Ukraine, a land rife with "class struggle and rivalry between Poles, Ruthenians and Jews" (p. 9). As an itinerant merchant, Jacob traveled extensively, flourished, and brought his family from Tysmenitz to Freiberg, where Sigmund was born. Those early years were lived in a multigenerational extended family, a polyglot Babel of Yiddish, German, and Czech, crisscrossed by diverse cultural and religious influences, which Anzieu describes as the "primal horde" of Freud's childhood: "the proto-group... in which psychical forces and systems of different types, each using its own language, cohabited in a continual process of conflict, alliance and subordination" (p. 12).

An economic crisis made Jacob an immigrant to Vienna in 1859, and he never really recovered financial success. The extended family broke apart in the immigration, and the smaller Freudian clan moved several times in the early years of relocation into ever more cramped quarters as more children came along. Ernest Jones (1953, p. 17, quoted in Anzieu, 1986, p. 16) describes these years as "evidently very unpleasant. Freud said later that he remembered very little of the early period between the ages of three and seven: 'They were hard times and not worth remembering.' He greatly missed the freedom and enjoyments of the countryside."

It seems that the lost early childhood of Freiberg remained for Freud a kind of irrecoverable Eden:

> But he always remembered the meadow near Freiberg, a sloping green carpet dotted with yellow flowers and with a cottage at the top: it was a landscape whose image came to represent his longing for a beloved and long-lost childhood home. As the French literary critic, Bertrand Poirot-Delpech, has so rightly pointed out: 'Exile in one form or another has incited a very great number of creators to live in an imaginary world and to share their dreams with others.' (Anzieu, 1986, p. 14)

It is Jones, once again, who captures the magnitude of the transgenerational impact of migration when he writes of the early move of the Freud family to Vienna: "the ancient march of the family—Palestine, Rome, Cologne, Lithuania, Galicia, Moravia—was resumed, as he himself had to resume it once more nearly eighty years later" (Jones, 1953, p. 14, quoted in Anzieu, 1986, p. 15).

That last migration "eighty years later" is captured in a strikingly textual way in Freud's final work, *Moses and Monotheism* (1939), written over a period of the four years during which Freud was forced into exile by the Nazi occupation. It is a strange and poignant example of the effects of displacement. Strachey (1964) notes the "eccentricity" of the work's construction; indeed, it reads like something torn apart and subsequently stitched together. Two prefaces appear at the beginning of the last of three essays, an eruption of beginnings squarely in the middle of the text: the first preface written in Vienna—"before March, 1938,"—and the second in London in June of the same year. They act as bookends on the interval of Freud's forced immigration, the textual parentheses of his displacement at the very end of life. In the first preface, Freud writes of his fears of a Catholic church hostile to the Moses book and worries that psychoanalysis will be driven into exile through religious repression, but these fears are nullified by the heightened virulence of the German invasion, which drives psycho-analysis out of its natal home not on the basis of threatening ideas, but more nefariously on the supposed dangers posed by racial difference.

The quirky text itself, premised on the historically discounted thesis that Moses was an Egyptian, also circulates around the themes of cultural displacements and exile. Jewish monotheism is posited as a reiteration (through the return of the repressed) of Egyptian monotheism, via Moses's supposed imposition of the cult of Aten on the Hebrews. Whatever one thinks of the veracity or coherence of this work, the ideas presented retain a certain consistency with prominent motifs of the Freudian opus, in which exile (from Thebes or Egypt or the realms of the conscious, for that matter) brings with it the distorted or encrypted but highly significant traces of the lands of origin. As importantly, origins are thereby made suspect. To say that Judaism might actually be Egyptian, is akin to saying that psychoanalytic hermeneutics is the Freudian reworking of a fraught and disavowed Jewishness (Aron & Starr, 2013; Gilman, 1988; Oxaal, 1988; Fuks, 1999), that the Corinthian-raised Oedipus is actually from Thebes, that the hysterical symptom of the body is actually a manifestation of the repressed mind.

Indeed, Betty Fuks (1999) in her brilliant study on Freud's Jewishness, understands *Moses and Monotheism* as a "hypertext," whose metapsychology is founded on the metaphoric displacements of migration. Freud, she writes,

> ... could see that all of them [his patients], independent of culture, ethnicity and sex, were part of the *Diaspora* in a way; that is, if their identities were fixed in the order of the same by some frontiers, they were also, because of their subjective *Spaltung* part of the *Country of the Other*, that which is beyond any frontiers: the unconscious. (p. 9)

The generative skepticism of psychoanalysis is premised on just such a questioning of the origins of things and on the displacements of translation that accompany taking up residence in a new land, whether that land be London, Rome, mythological Thebes, or the realm of waking consciousness after a dream. Migratory displacement thus shadows the very origins of the psychoanalytic project in profound ways: the central tenets of its way of thinking is haunted by transgenerational diaspora and animated by a migratory restlessness that leaves unsettled the question of just where it is that we actually start.

What lies buried in Freud's texts and exemplified in his life became all the more realized in the vast wave of immigration that dispersed psychoanalytic thinking across the globe in the turbulence and aftermath of World War II. The question of immigration then became central to the analytic community, which sprang into action, aiding émigrés organizationally and financially, but also managing the "panicky" reactions provoked by the incoming flood to the United States (see Emergency Committee on Relief and Immigration, 1938a, 1938b; Jacoby, 1983; Kuriloff, 2013; Steiner, 2011). Certainly there was traumatic loss and displacement in these movements but also the work of creative elaboration.

In short, psychoanalysis as a discipline is soaked through with migration from within and without and from its very migratory beginnings. I say migratory not simply because these origins have to do with immigration, but because the origins themselves are moving. Psychoanalytic origins are nomadic. Like the immigrant reconstructing the past from the vantage of the new world, with the trappings and language of a new place, the analytic process places great value in *the present as a moment of origin*, with the (re)construction of a useable past through the phenomenology of what is happening in the *here-and-now* of the transference situation.

The fact that there has been a relative erasure of this history, both specifically (Freud's dissociation of his cultural Jewishness) and generally (the paucity of immigration as an elaborated trope in our theorizing) is bound up with and simultaneously exemplifies just how complex a matter origins are for psychoanalysis. When we fail to elaborate these migratory origins, we court the danger of advancing a universalist and totalizing theory, one that lacks the rich texture of a place.

II - A Place for Now

If the trope of migration serves to both found and confound notions of origin and the past in psychoanalytic theorizing, it anchors the present to a particularity of place. For the immigrant, the sense of *now* is marked most poignantly by *where*, in the difference between this place and that. Immigration gives time a geography and memory a dwelling. Place is a category largely neglected by psychoanalysis, which opts for the much less saturated, less physical, more mathematically abstract and universalized idea of space. Immigration brings into sharp relief what usually remains invisible: place matters.

To better see just how it does, we can start with Winnicott's famous formulation that transitional space is the first location of culture. It is an empty locus, defined by what it is not, which grants it its signature attribute: potential. This is the territory of between: between here and there, between the world of external objects and the inner world of fantasy, emergent from the transition between what is me and not-me, we discover and make the world through culture, says Winnicott (1967). In his description of this "third area" of culture, he invokes the "inherited tradition" as "the common pool of humanity ... into which individuals and groups of people may contribute, and a source from which we may all draw" (p. 370). He thereby signals something both presumably symbolic and temporally past, but he adds a critical rejoinder to this formulation of culture: The inherited tradition is a place of creative exchange only (and he italicizes this in the original) "*if we have somewhere to put what we find*" (p. 370).

This notion of a some*where* to put what we find in culture—rather than a some*one*—complicates our usual notions of psychoanalysis as a highly intricate and nuanced theory restricted to human object relatedness. Winnicott postulates that true "living" must include more than healthy object relationships: It requires play. Play requires a play*ground*, an environment, a setting; it implicates—following Searles (1960)—the material world beyond relationship.

These registers of human and material interaction are, of course, closely imbricated. Winnicott (1967) is explicit that there must be sufficient (human) object relatedness in order to have the *confidence* necessary for play in culture. Confidence is built up out of reliable dependence on an object (the caretaker) who adapts through love and allows the build-up of trust in the environment. What we tend to neglect, I think, is how such play is necessarily an interaction with the embodied and material: the teddy bear or blanket or pacifier that acts as transitional object provides bodily comfort precisely by being sensuous stuff.

If, following Winnicott, we take the location of culture to be this materialized world of the transitional, the experience of the immigrant—who necessarily experiences a radical change of material environment—opens a window on its functioning by demonstrating our psychic reliance on the materiality of the world.

Marion Milner (1952) wrote of the importance of a "pliable medium"—paint, pencil, or clay—that conforms to the imaginative imposition of the naturally creative mind. At times Milner describes this medium as a proxy for a maternal human object, one fully receptive to the child's projections (Milner, 1987, p. 136). But it would be a mistake to ignore the emphasis she gives to materiality here and to think of the pliable medium as merely transparent, a window that directly conveys us to psychic representation. She is deeply interested in the process of externalization, the way patients "threw out of themselves on to the paper, marks which, because of the pliable character of the medium, could take on an infinite variety of shape and thus provide a feedback, a basis for communication, both with the analyst and with themselves" (Milner, 1987, p. 136).

Extending Winnicott's ideas, and (re)marrying them to Milner's, we might say that confidence in loving caretakers promotes faith in the receptivity of the environment, promoting a vigorous use of the pliable media at our disposal. In short, confidence makes possible the projection of our subjectivities into the *material* surround of objects external or marginal to psychic subjectivity (including one's own body, as a material thing outside of psychic "me-ness," and the sonority the body produces that can be shaped into words).[3] These materialized externalizations thereby become symbolic, by being put into play with others, exchanged, or shared. In the absence of dependable loving others, things in the world might seem to refuse our subjective shaping, making the world something alien and persecutory. Reciprocally, the creative processes of externalization into pliable media facilitates the evolution and representation of developing object relationships.[4] Perhaps more accurately, we can say that there is continual flux between engagements with the environment and with human objects, between projecting ourselves into the materiality of the world and putting this subjectivized stuff into play with others.

How Is This Linked to Migration?

To begin with, by taking the materiality of environment seriously, we can mark a useful distinction between transitional *space* and the *place* of culture. Transitional space implies a psychic field of potentiality. It is an abstraction, a domain *between* the object subjectively and the object objectively perceived: the interval or gap or vacancy *between* what is me-extension and what is not-me. Into this abstract potential field, if the conditions are right, cultural production may emerge. Or, to put it another way, potential space is the empty stage on which the play of culture can take *place*.

The notion of place as a particular and materialized environment brings with it the sensuous texture of locality: the specificity of variegated terrains and the colorful sonorities of locution, the particularities of the rhythms and cadence of a region, the specific curve of this street and what this light looks like in winter, the smell of the alfalfa field or the hum of the highway, the taste of bread or naan or tortilla. The texture of a place—its geomorphic vicissitudes and the florid material jungle of its cultural productions—forms a vast and distinct matrix, the environmental surround in which object relationships are embedded.

Post-colonial theory reminds us that "it is precisely within the parameters of place and its separateness that the process of subjectivity can be conducted" (Ashcroft, 1995, p. 392). Considering the dislocation of peoples, the imposition of colonial languages, the global standardization of cartography and chronometry, post-colonial theory problematizes the relationship between a universalist notion of empty space and the local specificities of place. This thinking animates the *topos* of immigration in psychoanalysis, for the process of becoming a subject actually occurs not only in abstract intersubjective psychic space, but also in distinct actual places.[5] Just as the relationship to the particularity of our unique bodies informs the construction of our psyches, so must the extension of our subjectivities into the first not-me objects be affected by their materiality.

In a spatial history of Australia, Paul Carter (1987) writes of place as a palimpsest, inscribed and overwritten through naming in a complex interaction with environment. In tension with a colonialist narrative that might read like a novel, the kind of history Carter is interested in is "spatiality as a form of non-linear writing" (p. xxii). He shows us how a sense of place heaps up, describing his project as:

> ... a prehistory of places, a history of roads, footprints, trails of dust and foaming wakes. Within its domain fall the flight of birds, the direction of smoke, the lie of the land. Against the historians, it recognizes that our life as it discloses itself spatially is dynamic, material but invisible. It constantly transcends actual objects to image others beyond the horizon. (p. xxii)

Carter's classic text, a paean to the power of naming, postulates that place is constructed through a kind of semiotics or poetics, extending Winnicott's notion of the transitional to the grand scale of landscape and history. Psyche is constructed in a delicate imbrication with just this kind of history, a spatial dynamic of the evanescent. What we so early lose is not just the breast. The *objet petit a* of Lacan (1981/1973)—that always already lost object that primes the engine of our desire—may not just be a corporal part-object, but also perhaps a part of the world. And just as a sense of place is built up through layers of descriptive signification, so too is the mind textured by the sense of its place. And when we *place* psychic construction so, the idea of potential *space* becomes less of an algebraic abstraction; it becomes thickened, a little like Carter's Australian interior, whose "map-made emptiness [is] written over, criss-crossed with explorer's tracks, gradually inhabited with a network of names" (pp. xx-xxi). The immigrant comes trailing the particularity of her cultural semiotics grounded in a particular materiality—*as do all subjects*. But the displacement of places in immigration makes this visible.

We can examine this intersection of subjectivity, the material surround, and representation through naming more closely. Consider the simplest Freudian paradigm for cultural play—the famous *fort-da* game in which the child comes to represent (with considerable brio, we might add) his mother's absence by tossing away and retrieving a wooden reel. Freud (1920) reads the pleasure the boy experiences as a movement from passive into active: He can now control the mother symbolically, banish her at will and exult in his command of her return. But the Botellas (2005) add that this game constitutes the entry into representation, adding that the catastrophe we fear is not the loss of the object per se, but rather the loss of representation. This small but significant shift in perspective signals the inter-reliance between confidence in human objects to instill confidence in the world of cultural play beyond human objects and the confidence in culture (via representation) to potentiate our relation to others. Let us here too affirm the great joy of representing through the creative manipulation of the material world (including language), for while the communications inherent in any act of creating may be a way of relating with others (including primary unconscious ones), they become a profound pleasure in their own right. Transitional space becomes human transaction in a material place, for place is where space assumes form.

Immigration, of course, highlights just how profound disruptions to place can be. Because subjectivity and its materialization are so tightly interwoven, migratory displacement can easily send shock waves that resound in psychic organizations, exposing vulnerabilities that are variously understood as pathologies of separation-individuation (Akhtar, 1995) or unintegrated dissociative splits between self states (Boulanger, 2004; Harlem, 2010).

What we lose when we immigrate is not just the organizing specificities of the lexicon and grammar of a language or the myriad networks and particular instantiations of rules and laws (including those of custom, hospitality, insult, temporality, and so forth)—we also lose the ways the words form in our mouths, the smell of a place, the texture of foliage and buildings, whole landscapes of sound, the feel of the air. We lose the pliability of media.

For almost four years now I have been working in a once- or twice-a-week psychoanalytic therapy conducted in Spanish with Rosa, an intelligent and engaging Mexican woman who immigrated to the US to be with an American man. In addition to therapy, I prescribe an antidepressant, and Rosa has struggled on and off with adherence to the medication, which by all accounts has been of great help to her: occasional discontinuations typically result in some emotional instability. We have interpreted these lapses in the regimen as having to do with anxieties about dependence, most especially on a good object in the transference, and this has been fruitful, but not quite sufficient. One day Rosa is telling me about experiences with *curanderas*, indigenous healers who also prescribe medicine. As we explore this topic we realize that one very significant difference between the medicine I prescribe and that of a *curandera* is that Rosa takes my medicine at home, away from the place of our work together: My medicine lacks presence. This enriches our extended discussion on her relationship to something we call *México profundo*,[6] our name for a complex confluence of themes regarding early object relations, politics, the land, indigenous culture, and the sensuous material surround of primary culture. Rosa and I often come to a failure of language in talking about *México profundo*, perhaps language always evokes an absence, and what we are trying to touch is something about presencing. For Rosa, forgetting to take the medicine is a way of remembering. *There,* in the rituals of the *curandera*, giving and receiving medicine take place (literally) together. Here, they operate at a distance.

We can argue that representation always takes place in a constitutive absence: in Freud's *fort-da* game, after all, the boy picks up the wooden reel *because* his mother is away. But, as importantly, representation depends on the use of what is materially present: It requires an actual reel. Does it make a difference if instead of a wooden spool the child picks up a stone *tejolote*[7] or a computer mouse or a bullet casing? Don't the materialities of the primordial cultural surround weave and shape a fabric or backdrop against which we constitute our absences? What is lost in translation is not just a question of content and associative chains of signification, but also of material specificities. Just as our native tongue literally imprints our bodies so that the acquisition of a new language is marked by the physical limitation we know as a "foreign accent," so must primal culture saturate us materially more generally, conditioning and forming all of our registers of perception in myriad complex ways. For the immigrant, the new immediate cultural surround is no longer materially pliable, will not bend to intention and creative impulse. The words will not form; the gestures are misunderstood. And just as confidence in the object world of loving others is necessary to develop the capacity for cultural play, so too is confidence in the artifacts of culture necessary for the capacity of human relating.

Elsewhere (González, 2013), I have written about "desubicación" (literally "disorientation," but also referring to "displacement") as the primary "diagnosis" of most of the Latino immigrants we treat at Instituto Familiar de la Raza, a clinic in San Francisco where I have worked since 1997. The patients are almost exclusively working class or indigent immigrants from Mexico and Central and South America, mostly Spanish-speaking (although there are increasingly Nahuatl-speakers), and usually traumatized by poverty, violence, and immigration. In addition to providing treatment in Spanish, the clinic cultivates a particular environment, using cultural iconography, including *altares* (religious altars) and at times incorporating traditional healers to do *limpias* (ritual cleansing) in the context of conventional dyadic psychotherapy.

I have speculated that under conditions of significant trauma to the social third (Gerson, 2009), the psychological space of the dyad may not be sufficient for healing. Restoration of the social requires work in the social. Provision of a good-enough cultural surround—necessarily a *materialized* one (in art, ritual, language, physical plant, forms of hospitality, food, etc.)—may be required in order for the patient to recover the confidence in cultural forms needed to do psychological work.[8] The enclave provided by such a protected cultural space replicates the material surround of "home," if only transitionally. Trust in the therapeutic environment makes possible trust in the person of the therapist, which reciprocally facilitates the hard work of integration into the new culture, a strange new world full of resistances: the brittleness of a new language that will not flow, the odd vegetables one has no idea how to cook, the alien rhythms. But out of this not-so-pliable medium, at the borderland between immigrant and native, what can emerge is something new.

III - What's Lost in Translation: On the Border with the New

A subject of displacement, then, the immigrant must contend with a new surround and one that will not easily bend to the will of imaginative projection. The wooden reels of the new culture, the gestural idiom and fashion sense, the temporal pace and interpersonal distance, the food, the words themselves are not as malleable as they were back home. And, of course, immigrants bring their own wooden reels, accents, gestures, and foods. These are the "incommensurables" of cultural difference, as Bhabha calls them, the chunks that will not assimilate in the stew of the melting pot. As everyone knows, something is always lost in translation. What is "lost," the element that will not enter the new language, is this remainder of cultural difference—the "incommensurable"—that refuses to melt.

At this frontier—a borderline of difference between incommensurables—what takes place is not just traumatic loss, violent intrusion, and unbridgeable alienation. It is also a doubled site of innovation; the native, as much as the immigrant, must confront an unassimilable otherness. What gets lost in translation is a two-way street.

Pontalis (2002) goes further in marking all language with uncanny mystery and thus elaborates the quality of the link between this resistance to translation and Szymborska's formula that "only what is human can truly be foreign":

> A language does not translate. It can only be shared by those who speak it, live inside it and, being so familiar with it, fail to recognize its strangeness, unless in a dream, a word or isolated phrase reveals this strangeness to them, revealing at the same time that every language, beginning with the mother tongue, is a foreign language. (quoted in Farhi, 2010, p. 489)

What the immigrant reveals then, like a dream operating through the register of the social, is the foreignness inherent in the language of the native.

Evan, who is talented as both an artist and an analysand, is joking with me in the ease and fluidity that comes after more than 10 years of working together. She has received a summons for jury duty, an event that had caused considerable anxiety in the early years of the analysis, requiring me to write a letter that requested she be excused. She now takes it in stride, riffing in mock high-mindedness on the sacred obligations of citizenship and gently satirizing the notion of patriotic conviction. We are enjoying the playful banter, when she asks ironically if I too am not loyal to my country, to which I spontaneously answer, "which one?" The mood takes a more serious turn as we launch on a thread of engagement that will span a couple of sessions. *At least you have an identity*, she says. In having two countries, I have a place of belonging in this one, a cultural location that she feels she lacks. Ironically my immigrant status confers and confirms my American status, while she, without a clear pedigree (*I am a mongrel*, she quips), finds no easy way to locate herself. She does not belong to mainstream American culture, which she first considers stereotypically: the arena of football, consumerism, and apple pie. Room opens up when I suggest that she is not considering how such stereotypic confinement exists in any culture, but she still feels her cultural identity is somewhat unmoored. The outsiderness she felt in her family as a child was most lovingly healed by being "adopted" into her best friend's immigrant Chinese family, where, ironically, she felt much more at home. I have recollections of a few years I lived in Germany, and how I had never felt so American as I did while living abroad. It takes two countries, it seems, to make a cultural identity in one; for it is only at the seam with otherness that one really begins to feel like oneself, though that one-self-ness is always haunted by the shadow of the other.

Holding the (potentially) constitutive place of otherness, the immigrant is thus not only called to produce something new for and in herself in relation to the new culture; she also implicitly troubles the self-same integrity of that culture. *If I am a foreigner*—the immigrant seems to say by her very presence—*then, foreign to what or to whom? Who are you, now that I am here? Who are you, actually?* This, of course, is not so different from the project of psychoanalysis and its ethic of dialogue with what is foreign in ourselves. But the questioning the immigrant opens—implicitly, insistently—can make the natives restless. The reactionary moves we have seen in recent years to secure the border with Mexico bespeaks the anxiety of this interpellation (Althusser, 1971) from the frontier with otherness, as the recognition of difference in the other opens a difference within one's self.

The Border, We Can Say, Is Always Leaky

Laredo, Texas, a frontier city that is 96% Hispanic, hosts the largest celebration in the country in honor of George Washington's birthday; the apogee of this event is the annual Society of Martha Washington Pageant and Ball, a cotillion for the city's wealthy (LatinoUSA, 2014). The extravaganza includes sequined gowns purported to cost up to tens of thousands of dollars and elaborate coiffures, as the daughters of the Mexican-American rich dress as the wives of the colonialist founding fathers. The current celebration (which includes an international bridge ceremony between representatives of Mexico and the US, a jalapeño eating contest, and a Princess Pocahontas parade) is clearly not a simple inscription of assimilationist American patriotism, an uncomplicated narrative of immigrants leaving behind their old country and adapting to the new.

The seeming incongruity of the spectacle bespeaks a deeper history: Spanish kings, the colonizing powers of Mexico, deeded oil-rich land to settlers centuries ago. In 1849, it was the border itself that immigrated, as Mexico ceded land in the Treaty of Hidalgo, making the progeny of Spanish colonizers sudden citizens of the United States. And so, a convoluted braid of colonialism, class, ethnicity, and nationalism gets woven at the border and tangles the founding fathers in it. The quintessential iconographic figure of American patriotism becomes thereby somewhat *fronterizado*, appropriated and remade in the image of the border. George Washington may confer an air of aristocratic power and largesse to the wealthy scions of Laredo, but as the correlate of Spanish royalty in colonial Mexico, he is also hispanicized, made brown, feted with jalapeños rather than cherries. This is a new figuration (Botellas, 2005) in the collective imagination for the father of the country.

What we find here is a *local* incarnation, one determined by the materiality of place and governed by homologies of difference that multiply and refract. We could say that a great deal gets lost in translating George and Martha from Mount Vernon to the Spanglish idiom of the border. The debutantes of Laredo—with names like Gutierrez, Torres, Ramirez—are Daughters of the American Revolution only in the widest sense, heirs of a quintessentially American mélange that has no difficulty in marrying pompadour wigs with *lucha libre*. But in these unlikely crossings, something new gets made. Laredo and Washington may both be cities in the same nation, but the Potomac and the Rio Grande mark the flows of two very different immigration histories. Cultural iconography is fungible, heavily shaped by local histories that complicate the origins of what it means to be an American. The national mythology of New England is troubled by the recognition of México Nuevo: The appropriation of founding-father drag both reestablishes the wealth and power of lineage (First Families rule), while fragmenting the supposed monolith of the country's identity (the southern border is also an origin; Spanish too is the lingua franca). And from these troubled waters rises a new version of what it can mean to be "American," no longer so obviously white, no longer so apple-pie-eating.

Such Border Crossings Occur in the Consulting Room as Well

Working within the context of the American Dream, Ghislaine Boulanger (2004), herself an immigrant, describes working with Juanita, a working-class Cuban woman, struggling with the complexity of scars associated with her immigration. In a mysterious dream that captures this density, the patient encounters Cary Grant on a bus that is traveling too far away for the patient's comfort; she gets off early, at a more familiar place that allows her to get back home. The therapeutic pair comes to see Grant—a working class Joe who transformed himself into an icon of suave sophistication—as a figure for the repudiated parts of the self and what gets left behind in the "imperative to fit in" (p. 367). Boulanger writes that "bridging the gap between two countries and between the self-states that represent these two countries is a dialectical process rather than a forced choice" and takes Grant to be a transference object: "Did she [Juanita] imagine that I, with my British accent, had felt the need to undergo a radical personality change, repudiating my origins?" (p. 367).

What I find fascinating about this example is the triangulation involved in the figure of Cary Grant. In this treatment, the "third" (in Ogden's sense of the word) constructs an analytic object that takes up elements of the analyst (the British accent) and is co-constructed to symbolize something about the patient (her split off Cuban identifications), but the symbolic figure itself is quintessentially American. It is precisely in America that the dream of leaving your working class roots and reinventing yourself takes on mythological proportion; America is the iconic place where repudiation of your origins becomes the catapult to success. Consider our contemporary Cary Grant, Mad Men's Don Draper: His entire identity is predicated on the radical and disowned severance of his past.

What Boulanger and her patient have in common is a homology of difference. Immigration from England and from Cuba are two very different things, and the differences between the two sets of culture are hardly comparable, but both women can organize something with respect to one another through the resonances of immigration. The analytic third inscribes this homology of differences in the cultural third (now more in the sense of Winnicott or Lacan): In an image that belongs to the new country they both share. Specifically, American iconography becomes the container for analytic representation, and the transitional space that is opened here is much more than a bridge of comparison between old and new nationalized self states. The spaces they are standing in—this somewhat deracinated, wild west of reinvention and manifest destinies—is the place of America.

Perhaps as much as having to acknowledge the impossibility of assimilation and what parts of themselves are left behind, Boulanger and her patient Juanita are themselves cultural objects, holding something for all cultural subjects, but especially for those of us residing in these United States. The state and cultural norms demand assimilation of everyone; conformity is the usual price of intelligibility and the ticket to success. All sorts of cultural identifications—not just national ones—can make one an alien.

More specifically, Boulanger and Juanita—in the role of "the immigrants"—serve discursively, as projective social objects that hold a dissociated history of America. The patrols of the national border exert their influence inside us as much as at the frontier, constituting a collective identification that fortifies itself with the exclusion of supposedly unlike others. The US is famously a land of immigrants, but one that infamously dissociates its past.

About six years ago, my partner and I began hosting Robert Burns suppers, a project in hybridity if ever there was one. The Burns supper is a very traditional Scottish celebration, complete with haggis and the occasional bagpiper, but the dinners have been heavily inflected by all manner of cultural twists according to the "incommensurables" of the attendant guests. The whole affair started as something of a whim—which is to say motivated by relatively unconscious currents. We had both attended Burns suppers at critical turning points in our cultural formation while living in Europe; living there had been a way of breaking from the gravitational confines of home, a way to give expression to a foreignness we felt that had little to do with nationality or ethnicity (see Beltsiou, this volume). The Burns supper became a way to sit together at the table of our cultural quirkiness, our delight at crossing borders.

We invited friends with no regard to cultural provenance. In the first year we were surprised to find that several friends turned out to have significant Scottish pasts. One woman brought a detailed family history, tracing her clan's tartan; another guest's parents had actually immigrated from Glasgow (he could do a perfect brogue); a third broke into tears at the bagpipe music, too reminiscent of her father's funeral. Friends whom we thought of as generic white, non-ethnic Americans were revealed to have consequential links, emotional ones, to the "old country." Natives were suddenly immigrants.

Conclusion

The reflections in this essay—on migratory origins, the materiality of place, and the creative border between the immigrant and the native—are anchored in the idea that immigration is a critical category for psychoanalysis and that what it has to teach us is not limited to our work with those from foreign countries. Further, that immigration is one of the generating engines of psychoanalysis, an itinerant discipline whose warp and woof is so often an account of migrations, theory as the embroidery of displacements.

I hope to have opened questions that engage our thinking about immigration in a dialectical manner. One that would have us consider that the psychoanalytic venture is always an immigrant's journey; that deeply buried archaic immigrations are constitutive of the individual psyche without any movement from one land to the other, that the immigrant throws into question the identity of the so-called native and not just her own, that we are all hybrid subjects.

As important as it is to conceptualize how to work effectively with immigrant patients (considering real questions of trauma and dissociation, for example), we must also recognize what and how immigrants and immigration produce and generate. I contend here that the *topos* of immigration is a vibrant animating force in Freud's life and texts, helping to provide one of the recursive patterning fractals of psychoanalysis: displacement and the retrospective revision of origins. Further, I consider that immigration helps us elaborate abstract notions of (transitional) space, supplementing it with the idea of material *place*. Finally, I suggest that the immigrant represents (and sometimes holds) a crisis of identity for the native as much as for herself, and that the frontier of this meeting is a dynamic locus of innovation. It is precisely what does not melt or assimilate, where the medium is no longer pliable, where irreconcilable difference meets, that the new emerges.

Notes

1. Subaltern is Gramsci's (1999) term for those who are subject to the hegemony of the ruling class, those with control over the means of representation. The term is often aligned with the colonized subject in post-colonial studies. Gramsci emphasized the importance of recovering a history of these subaltern classes.

2. Although *immigration* connotes the place one is coming *to*, as opposed to *emigration*, which emphasizes where one is leaving, I think the former term is actually the one that constructs the notion of origin more strongly. The so-called

country of origin, say Cuba, would be constructed rather differently when viewed through the various lenses of life as an immigrant in Angola, Spain, or the United States. For excellent reviews of the concept of Nachträglichkeit, see Faimberg, 2005, 2007; Perelberg, 2006; Thomä & Cheshire, 1991.

3. Milner (1987, p. 99) includes in her description of the pliable medium "the 'stuff' of sound and breath, which becomes our speech."

4. Milner's treatment of Susan, largely through her drawings, is an excellent example of this. See Milner, 1969; Farhi, 2010.

5. Leavitt (2013) writes about the importance of materiality in all psychoanalytic process in her idea of the "thinking surface."

6. *Mexico Profundo* is the title of an anthropological study by Guillermo Bonfil Batalla (1996), which links the culture of the rural and urban poor of Mexico to the Mesoamerican culture of indigenous peoples, postulating that a Westernized "imaginary" culture has failed to recognize this deeper cultural reality at its peril.

7. A *tejolote* (also called a *temachín* or *muchacho*) is a stone pestle, used with a matching bowl (*molcajete*) for grinding grains and spices in traditional Mexican cooking. The names themselves imply a "masculinized" pestle.

8. For a fascinating description of the recovery of dissociated intergenerational memory, and its relation to bodies and food in an immigrant Italian family, see Caputo (2011). While the essay focuses on the transmission of shame through trauma, it highlights the power of food to carry cultural identity.

References

Ainslie, R., Harlem, A., Tummala-Narra, P., Barbanel, L., Ruth, R. (2013). Contemporary psychoanalytic views on the experience of immigration. *Psychoanalytic Psychology*, 30: 663–679.

Akhtar, S. (1995). A third individuation: Immigration, Identity, and the Psychoanalytic Process. *JAPA*, 43: 1051–1084.

Althusser, L. (1971). *Lenin and philosophy and other essays*. Tr. B. Brewster. New York, NY: Monthly Review Press.

Antokoletz, J.C. (1993). A psychoanalytic view of cross-cultural passages. *American Journal of Psychoanalysis*, 53: 35–54.

Anzieu, (1986). *Freud's self-analysis*. Tr. P. Graham. The International Psycho-Analytical Library, 118: 1–596. London: The Hogarth Press and the Institute of Psycho-Analysis.

Aron, L., & Starr, K. (2013). Psychotherapy for the people. New York, NY: Routledge.

Ashcroft, B., Griffiths, G., & Tiffin, H., Eds. (1998). Post-Colonial Studies: The Key Concepts. New York, NY: Routledge.

Bhabha, H. (1994). The location of culture. New York, NY: Routledge.

Bonfil Batalla, G. (1996). *México profundo: Reclaiming a civilization*. Tr. P. A. Dennis. Austin, TX: University of Texas Press.

Botella, C., and Botella, S. (2005) The psychic work of figurability: Mental states without representation. New York, NY: Brunner-Routledge.

Boulanger, G. (2004). Lot's wife, Cary Grant, and the American dream: Psychoanalysis with immigrants. *Contemporary Psychoanalysis*, 40: 353–372.

Brody, S. (1973). The son of a refugee. *Psychoanalytic Study of the Child*, 28: 169–191.

Carter, P. (1987). The road to Botany Bay. Boston, MA: Faber and Faber.

Emergency Committee on Relief and Immigration. (1938a). Minutes of the meeting in Chicago June, 1938. *Bulletin of the American Psychoanalytic Association*, 1: 65–68.

Emergency Committee on Relief and Immigration. (1938b). *Psychoanalytic Quarterly*, 7: 590–591.

Faimberg, H. (2005). Après-coup. *International Journal of Psychoanalysis*, 86: 1–6.

Faimberg, H. (2007). A plea for a broader concept of Nachträglichkeit. *Psychoanalytic Quarterly*, 76: 1221–1240.

Farhi, N. (2010). The hands of the living God: "Finding the familiar in the unfamiliar." *Psychoanalytic Dialogues*, 20: 478–503.

Freud, S. (1896). Letter from Freud to Fliess, December 6, 1896. The Complete Letters of Sigmund Freud to Wilhelm Fliess, 1887–1904, 207–214.

Freud, S. (1920). *Beyond the pleasure principle, SE, XVIII*. London: Hogarth Press.

Freud, S. (1939). *Moses and monotheism, SE, XXIII*. London: Hogarth Press.

Fuks, B.B. (1999). Vocation of exile: Psychoanalysis and Judaism. *International Forum of Psychoanalysis*, 8: 7–12.

Gerson, S. (2009). When the third is dead: Memory, mourning, and witnessing in the aftermath of the Holocaust. *International Journal of Psychoanalysis*, 90: 1341–1357.

Gilman, S.L. (1988). Constructing the image of the appropriate therapist. *In Freud in exile. Psychoanalysis and its vicissitudes*: Eds. E. Timms & N. Segal. New Haven, CT, and London: Yale University Press.

Gomez-Peña, G. (1992). The new world (b)order, *Third Text*, 6: 71–79.

González, F. (2013). El Entorno Cultural, la Práctica Indígena, y el Campo Terapéutico Extendido. Unpublished published paper given at IARPP, 11th International Annual Conference, Santiago, Chile.

Gramsci, A. (1999). Selections from the prison notebooks. Ed. & trans. Q. Hoare and R. N. Smith. London: ElecBook. www.elecbook.com. Transcribed from edition published by Lawrence & Wishart, London, 1971.

Grinberg, L. & Grinberg, R. (1989) Psychoanalytic perspectives on migration and exile. New Haven, CT: Yale University Press.

Harlem, A. (2010). Exile as a dissociative state: When a self is "lost in transit." *Psychoanalytic Psychology*, 27: 460–474.

Jacoby, R. (1983). The repression of psychoanalysis: Otto Fenichel and the Freudians. Chicago, IL: University of Chicago Press.

Jones, E. (1953). *Sigmund Freud: Life and work. Volume 1: The young Freud, 1856–1900*. New York, NY: Basic Books.

Kristeva, J. (1991). *Strangers to ourselves*. Tr. L. S. Roudiez. New York, NY: Columbia Univ. Press.

Kuriloff, E.A. (2010). The Holocaust and psychoanalytic theory and praxis. *Contemp. Psychoanal.*, 46: 395–422.

Kuriloff, E. (2012). History means interpretation. *Contemp. Psychoanal.*, 48: 367–393.

Lacan, J. (1981/1973) *The seminar of Jacques Lacan, Book XI: The four fundamental concepts of psychoanalysis*. Tr. A. Sheridan. New York, NY: W. W. Norton & Co. Orig. published 1973.

Laplanche, J. (1991). Specificity of terminological problems in the translation of Freud. *Int. R. Psycho-Anal.*, 18: 401–406.

LatinoUSA (2014). Laredo celebrates George Washington, in photos. May 2nd. http://latinousa.org/2014/05/02/laredo-celebrates-george-washington-photos/.

Leavitt, J. (2013). Superficie, spazio e artefatto: la presenza materiale della memoria. *Rivista Psicoanal.*, 59: 549–571.

Lijtmaer, R.M. (2001). Splitting and nostalgia in recent immigrants: Psychodynamic considerations. *Journal of the American Academy of Psychoanalysis*, 29: 427–438.

Makari, G. (2008). *Revolution in mind: The creation of psychoanalysis.* New York, NY: Harper Perennial.

Milner, M. (1952). Aspects of symbolism in comprehension of the not-self. *International Journal of Psychoanalysis*, 33: 181–194.

Milner, M. (1969). *The hands of the living God: An account of a psycho-analytic treatment.* London: The Hogarth Press.

Milner, M. (1987). *The suppressed madness of sane men: Forty-four years of exploring psychoanalysis. New library of psychoanalysis.* New York, NY: Tavistock Publications.

NPR(2014). "From Pancho Villa to Panda Express: Life in a border town." http://www.npr.org/blogs/parallels/2014/03/26/294357174/from-pancho-villa-to-panda-express-life-in-a-border-town.

Oxaal, I. (1988). The Jewish origins of psychoanalysis reconsidered. In E. Timms & N. Segal, Eds., *Psychoanalysis and its vicissitudes.* New Haven, CT, and London: Yale University Press.

Perelberg, R.J. (2006). The controversial discussions and après-coup. *International Journal of Psychoanalysis*, 87: 1199–1220.

Pontalis, J.B. (2002). *En Marge des Jours.* Paris: Gallimard.

Rilke, R.M. (1923/2009). *Duino elegies and sonnets to Orpheus.* Ed. & Tr. S. Mitchell. New York, NY: Vintage Press. Duineser Elegien originally published in 1923.

Searles, H. F. (1960). The Non-Human Environment: In Normal Development and Schizophrenia. New York, NY: Int. University Press.

Steiner, R. (2011). In all questions, my interest is not in the individual people but in the analytic movement as a whole. It will be hard enough here in Europe in the times to come to keep it going. After all, we are just a handful of people who really have that in mind .... *International Journal of Psychoanalysis*, 92: 505–591.

Strachey, J. (1964). Editor's note to "Moses and monotheism." Standard Edition. Vol 23. London: The Hogarth Press and the Institute of Psychoanalysis.

Szymborska, W. (2000). Psalm. From Poems: New and Collected 1957–1977. Tr S. Baranczak and C. Cavanaugh, p. 148.

Thomä, H., & Cheshire, N. (1991). Freud's Nachträglichkeit and Strachey's 'deferred action': Trauma, constructions and the direction of causality. *International Review of Psychoanalysis*, 18: 407–427.

Tummala-Narra, P. (2009). The immigrant's real and imagined return home. *Psychoanalysis, Culture & Society*, 14, 237–252. DOI:10.1057/pcs.2009.9.

Winnicott, D.W. (1967). The location of cultural experience. *International Journal of Psychoanalysis*, 48: 368–372.

Yi, K. (2014a). From no name woman to birth of integrated identity: Trauma-Based cultural dissociation in immigrant women and creative integration. *Psychoanalytic Dialogues*, 24: 37–45.

Yi, K. (2014b). Psychoanalysis's cultural dissociation meets ethnic minorities: Reply to Kimberlyn Leary. *Psychoanalytic Dialogues*, 24: 52–55.

Part II

The Effects of Immigration on Self-Experience

Chapter 2

Nell—A Bridge to the Amputated Self

The Impact of Immigration on Continuities and Discontinuities of Self

Hazel Ipp, PhD

(Edited and expanded version of article previously published in *International Journal of Psychoanalytical Self Psychology*, 2010, 5: 373–386.)

The thick Afrikaans accent crackled through my answering machine. Immediately I tensed, froze, hearing little more than the startling guttural tones. The bare bones of the message filtered through. An Afrikaner wanting to enter therapy with me: me, the South African, English-speaking, protesting other, who, by definition, would be pitted as the natural enemy of the Afrikaner. Suddenly the 30 some years since I had left my homeland collapsed and I felt catapulted back into that world of divisiveness, hatred, pain, suffering, horror; a world of angst and terror. The feeling was powerful, visceral. In those next moments I became painfully aware of the alarm and reflexive feelings of hatred and rage this accent triggered for me. Of course I would not respond to this message, let alone even contemplate being this woman's therapist.

By way of some clarification here, South Africa's apartheid system, although most heinous in terms of Black and White segregation and the bitterly cruel oppression of all those designated "non-Whites," also permeated many other aspects of the nation. South African Whites were essentially divided between English- and Afrikaans-speaking people, whose segregation, although not legally enforced, was sociologically organized in terms of geography, schooling, and cultural and political alliances. Exposure and, hence, familiarity with each other was severely constrained. We lived with an abiding sense of mutual negativity, each group dominated by stereotypical thinking about the other. In essence, the Afrikaners were the architects of the apartheid system and controlled the country politically, whereas the English were perceived, for the most part, as the opposition—the White renegades who, through their "revolutionary" tactics, could endanger the country, wresting the Afrikaners from "their rightful place of religious covenant." The stage was set for mutual facile generalizations, stereotypical aspersions, and role rigidity.

Within this context, this phone message mystified and anguished me. Being approached by an Afrikaner, so many decades later, catapulted me into a fierce personal struggle to protect myself from feelings and images that had been outside my immediate awareness for so long that I could not know then how much they had been coursing through and impacting my very being, in critical ways.

Before returning to the clinical material, I want to underscore how often we analysts have to struggle to maintain the dialectic between certainty and doubt, particularly when we are most deeply impacted, most anxious, most disrupted, most uncertain. Certainty offers blind comfort, a place to stand, particularly at our most fraught moments. Doubt is more complex. By doubt, I refer to the disruption of social categories, the state that alters our sense of the familiar that permits and creates a necessary perturbation of our semiotic systems. Inhabiting this position of doubt enables the holding of several possibilities simultaneously, of wrestling with not knowing. It enables us to interrogate our beliefs and our need to believe what we believe in relation to another whose very being, or so we believe, pits us against ourselves in ways too painful to imagine or to hold. This is hard to do, painfully hard. Yet this challenge is also our opportunity to grow, to learn what we could not know before.

Circling back, several days passed after this first phone call. Again a message requesting I call back. Slightly calmer this time, I could register a little beyond the accent to the polite but desperate edge to the voice. Now, somewhat intrigued, I returned the call. Trying to listen beyond my flood of associations evoked by this accent, I was struck by a woman who sounded smart, thoughtful, and motivated. I decided to meet with her, curious at least as to why she would select me, her seemingly natural enemy, as we were to discover, Nell felt an "enemy insider" was preferable to an "ignorant outsider," an English South African who had long ago fled the land of pain and suffering; also the land of incredible beauty and diversity; one that would always also be experienced with a sense of longing, deep in my bones.

Nell looked the imagined part—tall, beautiful Aryan. A cautious if not frozen air marked her presence. At times, during her narrative, this stance would yield to a smile that radiated such warmth that, I found myself at odds with my deeply engrained expectations of what it would feel like to sit with the enemy. As is the case when one's past comes crashing unannounced into the present, I felt somewhat disoriented. What was happening? Was I crazy? These questions and various manifestations of them would continue to feature in multiple ways as our work together progressed.

Nell's stated reason for seeing me was to address her unhappiness at her recent emigration, to find meaning in this very different land and, failing that, to get help to facilitate her return to South Africa. The latter position was one vehemently opposed by her husband and three children who loved Canada, loved the calm, the predictability, and the feeling of safety that set it apart so starkly from the violence and turmoil they had left behind. Nell struggled with this. While she understood their perspective rationally, she was more concerned with what she experienced here as vacuous. She felt pained by the seeming absence of higher purpose in the Canadian psyche and by the striking lack of passion she experienced amongst the people. She longed for the kind of experience that accompanies feeling fully involved within one's often lunatic country, where one's every breath becomes saturated with highly charged affect and strong opinions, where one is bonded in intensity and purpose with like-minded others and pitted in hateful enmity with those who don't share one's views.

Nell's concerns struck me deeply: How much they resonated with my own early experiences in Canada when, in despair, I felt convinced that Canadians were doomed to put their every energy into some repetitive discussion of the weather (it was awful enough to bear discussing) but seemed to lack the concern or investment or apparent knowledge or interest in developing any deep grasp of issues that tore countries and people apart, of any world events or experiences outside of their borders. How lonely and angry and contemptuous I felt then. How well I could relate to her narrative in the present. Even as I begin to register this resonance I was struck by a nascent "her and me," an almost "we," supposed enemies, bound in commonality of experience and feeling. This was a pivotal moment for me, one that began to dislodge some of my earlier reservations, stirring feelings of curiosity and other nameless sensations that would take time to achieve conscious formulation.

Joining with her I say "I remember those feelings well." Polite but uninterested, she goes on to discuss her feelings of displacement and alienation. Nell's curiosity about my South African experience felt minimal, if not nonexistent, even as I sensed a tacit acknowledgement in her accounts that I knew of what she spoke. It soon became apparent that while Nell was Afrikaans by birth, her politics were not those often reflexively linked with the Afrikaans sensibility. Instead, she had sustained a very active, risky anti-apartheid political involvement through the most perilous of times, not only as a willing and seemingly fearless participant but as a respected student leader operating from within all the organizations I admired most. Another stereotype bit the dust for me. In its dissolution I became increasingly aware of more complex feelings of my own. I felt a deep sense of shame that I had not stayed and fought the battles I so believed in but had been too afraid to engage at deeper levels. I recall how at the time of emigration I had to face the choice that to stay required me to engage more actively and risk the fate of many of my friends: solitary confinement, house arrest, or worse. To remain without active engagement constituted colluding with all I abhorred. Emigration felt like my only choice. Now in this moment with Nell, this choice felt shameful. Doubt was painfully creeping in for me.

Sitting with Nell's bravery, her unfaltering convictions, her abiding sense of purpose, I was, for the first time, starkly confronted with my amputated self—that part of my self that had been left behind, severed, and frozen in a place and space that could not travel with me as I struggled to achieve a new sense of comfort for myself in my adopted country. As we know, the land of our birth continues to reside deep within us long after we have exited. Bridging the experiences of there and here, then and now, is daunting, often impossible. While an abiding sense of self may prevail, and many aspects of self do go forward together to face the novel, punctuating and enriching these new possibilities, something vital is left behind, lost, encapsulated in the complex and multi-layered world in which we grew. Becoming more aware of this dimension of myself (a dimension from which I'd fled and not taken the time to grieve) became imperative if I was to truly sit with Nell and listen to her struggles as these were located within her.

Nell was the younger of two sisters born to a German mother and an Afrikaans father. Much trauma filled the early lives of both her parents. Her mother, having lost her father early in the war, lived a precarious existence with her mother in Russian-occupied territory where they faced many tribulations, most especially the trauma of multiple rapes, endured and witnessed by both mother and daughter. Nell's father lost his mother in early childhood. As the less favoured son, he endured chronic emotional abandonment, general isolation, contempt, and humiliation as his father bestowed his every energy on his special elder son. This brother (Nell's uncle) rose through the ranks in the military achieving a significant status in the deeply feared security forces of the South African government—a branch of the police that had carte blanche to remove or destroy any "element" thought to be harmful to the state. Nell's political involvement achieved a new irony for me in the face of this piece of information.

Nell's older sister was sickly, and it was Nell the family looked to for the realization of their dreams. "I was my mother's face for the world," said Nell as she described a mother riddled with anxiety, who would retreat to her bed for weeks on end leaving the family to fend for themselves even as she demanded unending succour from them. She talked of a father, seemingly gentle, who could explode in rage from time to time; a father who managed his life with compulsive order and quiet self-preoccupation. Other than occasional involvement with extended family and a handful of friends, they led an insulated, isolated life. Nell described growing up with a sense of cautious vigilance, experiencing a youth of endless angst and feelings of alienation, with little sense of her own desires or hopes.

Was this what lay behind the frozen, restrictively cautious air I felt in her presence, behind the careful calibration of her words and the minimal information detailing her experiences, all of which carried hints of so much more? And yet there was that smile, that radiant, captivating smile with the twinkly eyes that spoke to a totally different self state, to a self that could be thoroughly engaged and emotionally present. I wondered how this person had extricated herself from such a restrictive life to enter the world of perilous political engagement that she pursued so passionately. Of course there is an important divide between those who can sacrifice themselves to a cause and those who can only engage at the margins. What was it in her background that enabled Nell's particular trajectory? Her growing years were so seemingly devoid of passion and engagement, so riddled with the vicissitudes of transgenerational trauma, trauma that seemed to keep her family pinioned in a state of terror and hyper-vigilance, that it was hard to imagine her finding this path.

We began to meet three times a week. Increasingly I found myself warming to Nell, feeling a level of comfort and familiarity with her that outstripped our short acquaintance. And yet I felt a growing frustration that I could not establish any real purchase with her internal world. Her accounts of both past and present were offered in more of a reporting style, and in spite of some of the compelling events narrated she remained mostly dispassionate, an observer of her experience, pragmatic, rational. I frequently commented on what I experienced in terms of the difficult stories she recounted and the apparent absence of the kind of emotions I would expect to be present.

"Really?" she would say, and go on with her account. Nevertheless, I ventured forth at times—particularly as my own emotions filtered through in response to her particular narrative.

"How awful that must have been for you." Or "How frightened you must have felt when the police grabbed you." Or "How courageous you were."

An enigmatic smile would greet these efforts at empathic expression, and she would continue in the same almost monotonic, dissociated tone as before. Clearly, her history of trauma was far deeper and more pervasive than I had realized, and I began to understand that these comments felt quite meaningless to her at this time, that they spoke to my experience, not hers, and that I could and should simply listen to her accounts without trying to name their affective underpinnings—at least for now. Instead, I concentrated on immersing myself more in her narrative, attempting through my questions to expand her level of curiosity about her experience, her choices, her own mind.

In struggling to make a decision about a new appointment she'd been offered, she raised the notion of wishing it were part of a specific institution.

H: In what way would that be preferable?
N: I would belong to something known. It would feel more dependable. I would not feel so invisible … just a speck in the larger, undefined picture.

In exploring this further we established that she felt in many ways that she was an invisible part of an invisible family—a family who saw its members only in functional/instrumental terms that had no bearing on comprehensive or recognized selves. Belonging to a legitimate institution carried with it not only the belonging itself but the sense that one was seen to belong—the kind of belonging she felt so strongly in the political groups of which she had been an intrinsic part. A real institution also carried with it legitimacy and protection, or at least the illusion of protection.

At the start of our next session, Nell recounted a dream:

> I was looking after two younger children—I was about eight or nine. They were children of family friends. I had to go back home and for some reason the children got left behind. I felt very anxious right through this dream. I immediately told my mother "You HAVE to call their mother." There is a very powerful sense in this dream of my mother saying "NO—we can't. This is too terrible." She finally made the call, but she was very ineffective: too apologetic with no strategy for working it out. I felt anxious about her call and furious with her. The strong feeling I had is that she did nothing to help resolve it. I felt frightened of their anger. There was this stark moment at the time of her making the call. She should have been resolving it, telling them their kids are fine, just left behind. She didn't. She didn't fix it.

Spontaneously, Nell talks about this dream as emblematic of her relationship with her mother—a mother who could never fix things, who imposed responsibilities on her way beyond her years in which she had no expectation of support or rescue. She associates with her struggle with feeling recognized—for her limitations as well as her strengths. She needs the safety of belonging to legitimate institutions and/or projects where she is appropriately recognized for her abilities, where she can extend herself with the knowledge and security of a safety net that is automatically cast. I note, too, the strength of her affective expression within the dream as well as in the recounting of it. I comment on this. She agrees.

N: I didn't realize how angry I have been with my mother, how horribly unprotected I always felt … how much was always expected of me … how little recognition there was of my own vulnerability. Maybe I never really knew how vulnerable I felt. I think I'm only beginning to realize that now.

I consider the transference implications possible here but choose not to pursue them at this time.

H: Perhaps your not realizing your own vulnerability enabled you to take the chances you took back in South Africa.
N: Maybe. I never felt scared … not ever. That's why I always got the tough jobs. Like when I would have to smuggle people out of the country in the trunk of my car. Everyone always saw me as so calm—unflappable— they knew I could get through the borders or any other roadblocks and appear innocent.

H: And you registered no fear, not even at those times?

N: No—it was exciting actually. I felt alive, involved. More alive than I had ever felt before. Much more alive than I feel these days.

Sitting with her, I resonated with the feeling of passionate engagement, to the sense of aliveness that goes with such risk, but at the same time, I was immediately daunted by the larger fear that eclipses these feelings.

H: Were your parents aware of what you were involved in, Nell?

N: Only superficially. You know, for an Afrikaner to have gone against the government was even more shameful than an English-speaking person. My mother didn't want to know. She felt ashamed. My father—well, he was different. I'm not sure what I mean—there was something in him I sensed that was different from the rest of our family. He took chances with his workers on the farm extending them opportunities and privileges that violated apartheid law. This was very unusual and very risky. I never realized it then, but it's amazing for a man who was so rigid and compulsive about everything else.

H: Perhaps you felt your political involvement would please him in some way, make him proud. Allow him to recognize you in a fuller way.

N: I don't know. I never thought about it. One time I was arrested … it was very serious. I thought I was really done for that time. Suddenly a few days later I was released with no explanation. Seems my father's brother intervened. Of course he made sure my father knew that he had saved me even though I was disgracing the family. My father was instructed to warn me off, to let me know my uncle would never intervene again. My father told me all this but he did so calmly. He didn't instruct me to stop. I didn't anyway.

She paused and then after a while added, Maybe he did feel proud. Even though it would have been humiliating to have his brother lord it over him.

Nell and I continued to move between her feelings of discontent in the present and her longings for South Africa. Rarely during this time did she express as much emotion as she did in the session containing the dream. I continued to wrestle with my own feelings stirred by her accounts, by my growing awareness of aspects of myself I'd left behind along with an emerging clarity that I had made the only choice I could have made. I was not fearless.

Nell began to raise concerns about her marriage, wondering how much her earlier sexual inhibitions were playing a part. These inhibitions were a legacy she felt came from her mother who, raped at the age of 11, repressed any sexual or sensual expression in the family. She wondered whether she had been sexually abused as a child.

H: Does that feel true for you?

N: I don't know—I really don't. I recall something at about age 10.

The image of Nell's mother being raped at age 11 comes to mind.

H: Something like what?

In a more purposeful voice, Nell said, "I think it involved my uncle—you know—my father's brother." She pauses, looking intently at me, seeming to wait for me to jump in. I quietly indicate that I am listening not wanting to direct this more specifically.

N: I don't know if it was just inappropriate flirty behaviour on his part—he was always seductive with his nieces. He just left me with uncomfortable feelings. I felt very self-conscious and awkward around him and avoided any alone time with him. I don't think I can say any more about this now.

After a silence she added, "Strange that this uncle keeps coming up."

H: He does. Seems he was a force that needed reckoning with. Perhaps (I ventured with a somewhat conspiratorial smile) you felt some pleasure later on when he faced embarrassment on account of your political activities.

Nell laughs long and hard. We laugh together. It is the kind of laughter bursting with meaning; laughter containing a tacit understanding of the complexity of motivation along with a shared pleasure at disrupting the enemy. Laughter, too, that stood in stark contrast to the horrors and pain that beset much of what we were speaking about.

N: I never consciously thought about all that before, but as I think about it I think I felt glad that he was so uncomfortable especially since he'd spent so much time making my father feel uncomfortable.
H: And you too.
N: And me too.
H: Makes us think about the multiple layers of meaning of political and personal engagement.

She gets it. Again we laughed together. The feeling of deeper connection was growing, and we have opened new space within which we can explore and experience together.

Some time later I went to present at a conference in Israel. Nell opened our first session after this with "What was it like to be amongst such a traumatized population?"

I was very startled by this, not only because it was the first time she had ever asked me a personal question, but because of the question itself—trauma was a word studiously avoided by her. I also felt somewhat challenged, perhaps defensive about my visit to Israel. The current political climate along with a long history of anti-Semitism amongst the Afrikaners had me on alert.

I answered somewhat sharply, "No different than being amongst the traumatized population in South Africa." Nell looked stung. She became teary. Another first. We sat quietly together until her tears settled. Realizing it would take some time for me to process and understand more of my part in this enactment, I simply said, "I'm sorry if I hurt you with the sharpness of my tone."

N: Your response felt like a jolt—one that brought up many images of many traumatized faces—images I never allow myself to think of. Important images. Images of suffering … images that used to keep me focused on what I needed to keep doing.

H: I wonder if any of those images include you and your suffering?

Nell looked off into the middle distance. Perhaps I've pushed too hard. Perhaps not. After a few moments Nell said, "There's much for me to think about over this next week." She was leaving for a visit to South Africa the next day.

Nell's return from South Africa ushered in a new phase. She felt immediately more emotionally present to me. Raring to go in our first session after the break, she dived right into a vivid and animated account of a breakthrough in relation to her mother. She described her mother sinking into the familiar morass that always served as a signal for Nell to be even more solicitous, even as she had to endure and absorb her mother's escalating tirades that accompanied this space, regardless of how painful and self-erasing they felt for her. This was a topic that had occupied considerable time in our work together, extending to our own relationship where she felt she had to work harder if she experienced me as too quiet or drifting off.

Back in South Africa she was predictably confronted head-on with her mother's controlling manoeuvres. However, this time as her mother began to escalate in her raging and blaming, Nell simply said "I need to go to bed now," calmly kissed her mother, and left the room. She described a feeling of elation, of liberation, of empowerment—like she had shaken off the shackles that had so bound her for so long. Her feelings were palpable, almost electric.

This elation was short lived. The next session Nell arrived looking anxious and distressed. She had just spoken to her father who said her mother had taken to her bed and was refusing food and any engagement. This behaviour was all too familiar, along with the implicit and terrifying threat of suicide it always communicated. The family looked to Nell once again to "fix things." This time she felt even more like the perpetrator of her mother's pain. As she talked, she began to sob. She sobbed long and hard. The intensity of this sobbing struck us both, but somehow it felt like a forward movement.

Quietly, I began to talk about her pain, about her mother's pattern as one that would be expected to follow any self-assertive or differentiated steps attempted by Nell. It was no surprise that Nell's elation at breaking free of an old familiar vice was a signal that mother would retreat to this behaviour again. Could Nell hold her position? Could she support her mother without capitulating? Could she continue on a path that carried the promise of so much more without feeling that she alone could save her mother from herself? These were some of the questions we pondered as we sat together in her distress over the next few sessions.

A week passed, Nell took no steps to "rescue" or undo what she had done; her mother "rallied" once more. Nell brought in another dream.

N: I had a bizarre dream about my mother. My sister and I were standing somewhere. We looked up and there was my mother sitting on a fairground horse in the sky—a very ethereal scene. She was looking very happy, riding into the clouds with her hair blowing beautifully behind her. As she saw us looking at her she said "I'm so tired," and I thought "WHAT? !!!" Then all of a sudden she was coming down in a hot-air balloon—headfirst and at full speed. My sister and I just yelled. She came down with a thud. We just stood there. My sister said 'She must have fallen off'. We just kept standing there—thinking catastrophe, we should rush over. But actually we just kept standing there without moving.

H: Is this dream really so bizarre? It seems to me that you've been working so hard to understand the paradoxical aspects of your mother's words and behaviour. Recently you have begun to feel less responsible for her welfare, even for her life in the sense that it is really not possible to save her from herself. This dream, amongst many other things, speaks to that part of you that recognizes that your life needs to go on and that to do so means you cannot simply keep doing the same dance while remaining hostage to her whims. That is painful, difficult to do, but I think the dream suggests a part of you feels it is possible.

N: My sister has always had a more indifferent attitude to my mother. That's why it always fell to me. But I don't want to feel like that anymore. I think that the dream is letting me know something important about that. I feel stronger. I want to choose more. So much of my life has been about "YOU HAVE TO." My political activities, especially the really dangerous ones, were so often also about "YOU HAVE TO."

I felt some release in this, a little less cowardly about leaving South Africa. Our choices are multiply determined by the complex and intricately woven, textured experiences of our lives that include the transgenerational transmissions of trauma and other complexities that have come before. I had been less governed by "YOU HAVE TO."

At the same time I could not help but wonder about that aspect of her dream that described the stillness of the two sisters (us?) at the end. Was this the signifier of a grieving process (the grieving of mother and mother country) that had become possible for each of us; grieving that upends the "fraught circular insanity of melancholia" (Corbett, 2010, p. 391), grieving that enables the opening of space and permits the possibility of moving forward more comfortably where the dialectics of experience, of knowing, not knowing, and un-knowing, can be tolerated and held in a more sustained way?

Now, as Nell was becoming more integrated and emotionally animated, she was readying to relinquish a vise that, in some respects, had served her and others well but, in other respects, had kept her from being more fully alive and meaningfully related.

As we continue, Nell is very much alive. Her twinkly eyes and beautiful smile are now regularly accompanied by laughter and tears and a sustained range of emotions. Our relationship feels strong and dependable, and in many ways our sense of being paradoxical fellow travellers has offered us a space within which to tackle much together. Whether she returns to South Africa or not is unclear. The option is less compelling, certainly less coercive. Whatever decision is made will more likely emerge from a reflective choice influenced by both agency and desire.

Nell has been my gift. Apart from providing me with the opportunity to dismantle many of my own prejudices and stereotypes, she has enabled me to re-connect with that part of me that I refer to as my amputated self, to grieve my losses and open new spheres of reflective space connecting me with dimensions of myself that had previously been sequestered. Locating oneself within the other, with all the struggles and angst that stimulates, is perhaps the essence of what we need to grapple with as contemporary psychoanalysts as we confront our countertransferential responses and inevitable blind spots.

This indeed is a story about the psyche evolving from the social and the social being infused with the psyche as Corbett (2010) has noted. It speaks to the co-construction of new experience for both Nell and me—experience that permitted the dismantling of old belief systems, an erosion of our defensive certainty along with the other protective barriers our respective biases and convictions had served in the struggle against painful personal reckoning. We have been able, separately and together, to revisit our conflicted separations from our mother country—separations punctuated with feelings of betraying and being betrayed, encoded in feelings of cowardice and shame, along with pride about real feats of heroism, as well as illusions of bravery, laced with much disavowal.

Immigration poses daunting and often enduring challenges. At the same time it can offer unique developmental opportunities. And of course, the psychological phenomena of immigration vary dramatically. Push versus pull factors organize much of the immigration experience and, in turn, impact the sequelae. I did not literally flee from my homeland. I, like count-less thousands of others, chose to leave for complex yet compelling reasons. But in the choosing, I, like most others who leave behind intolerable or dangerous regimes, do not only leave behind the horror and the fear, we also often exchange animating affects on the edge for something seemingly more sanguine, definitely safer. Yet, we miss much. We miss the land of our birth; we miss our deep-rooted connectedness to the sights, sounds, and smells; and, of course, we miss the people who have formed the very fiber of our being—people who carry the sense and recognition of our earlier selves, our history. We move forward, but interrupted. Boulanger (2004) describes such discontinuities in self. Indeed, we miss the passion and intensity of our often lunatic countries, deeply.

References

Boulanger, G. (2004). Lot's wife, Cary Grant and the American dream: Psycho-analysis with immigrants. *Contemporary Psychoanalysis*, 40: 353–372.

Corbett, K. (2010). Mother country: Discussion of Hazel Ipp's "Nell—A bridge to the amputated self." *Inter. Journal of Psychoanalytic Self Psychology*, 5(4): 387–391.

Goldberg, L. (1970). Pine. In T. Rivner (Ed.), *Collected Poems* Tel Aviv: Iachov/ Writers Association.

Straker, G. (2004). Race for cover: Castrated whiteness, perverse consequences. *Psychoanal. Dial*, 14: 405–422.

Chapter 3

Seeing Double, Being Double

Longing, Belonging, Recognition, and Evasion in Psychodynamic Work with Immigrants

Ghislaine Boulanger, PhD

(A shorter version of this essay was originally published in the *American Journal of Psychoanalysis,* 2015, Vol. 75, Issue 3.)

About 10 years ago I ran into my first analyst on the street. We greeted one another warmly and, after exchanging the usual family details, she asked me what else was happening. I told her I had recently published a paper about psychoanalysis with immigrants (Boulanger, 2004).

"Immigrants don't go into psychoanalysis," she replied.

"What does that make me?"

"Oh you're an émigré!" With those words she fitted me snugly into a place of privilege. In this resignification, she had removed me from the classism, racism, and prejudice that so many immigrants face, and, by and large, I have not had to face; she situated me in what I am sure she thought was a glamorous, even enviable, position.

But what about the psychic meaning of that move from my hybrid French-English family and what I believed would be a narrowly circumscribed future in England to life alone in New York City, where I hoped I would find much more freedom? What about trying to fit into a new culture in which, even if I spoke the language like a native, my accent clearly marked me as an outsider, with daily reminders from people who still ask where I come from?

In the months before that chance meeting I had spent many hours deconstructing the unforeseen emotional terms of my passage into American life. I had analyzed a recurrent dream in which, night after night, I overlooked a colleague, a patient, or a friend who needed a place to stay, a place to put down roots. I had come face to face with former selves that had been silenced; I had come to appreciate the lengths to which I had gone *not* to be seen as "other."

I realized that in the course of my first treatment, my therapist had never shown any curiosity about that emotional journey. Apparently, she had never suspected that behind the clinical psychology graduate student, balancing coursework, a relationship, a toddler, and step children, was an uncertain, vigilant, immigrant self, watching interactions carefully to see how to fit in without drawing attention to that self. Indeed, I paid no mind to that self until she insistently announced herself in my dreams. Just as I did everywhere else in my life, I had tried to present myself within my therapist's cultural idiom, and, judging from her response to me, I had succeeded, but at what cost? Druckerman (2013), an American living in Paris, recently wrote humorously about her decision to begin therapy in French and found "it was hard to free associate when I was worried about conjugating the verbs correctly." I did not have to worry about conjugating verbs, but I did worry about sounding too English. I remember once being chided for saying I was *cross* with someone. That did not sound sufficiently angry, my therapist coached me; either I didn't really mean it or I should find less prissy language.

The meeting with my former therapist should not be so surprising. When it took place, you could count on the fingers of one hand the number of psychoanalysts who wrote about the plight of immigrants. Today, our field has taken up this theme energetically. And just in time. The topic of immigration is particularly relevant for those of us who practice in New York, where 37% of the population is made up of immigrants to the United States and, together with their first generation children born in this country, make up more than half the population of the city (Foner, 2013). Looking at these demographics another way, it is clear that clinicians in New York are increasingly likely to treat patients who have immediate experience with immigration or who have been shaped in part by their parents' struggles to adjust to and accommodate the demands of the new world, often while simultaneously trying to remain faithful to old traditions. Further, as the diverse contributors to this book attest (and, I suspect, the potential readers as well) mental health providers are increasingly likely to be immigrants or the children of immigrants themselves.

* * *

For years the unexamined self in psychoanalysis was the gendered self, aided and abetted by psychoanalytic theory dominated by patriarchal ideas and values. More recently, cultural differences have taken gender's place as previously unexamined constructions (for example, Dimen, 2010). As Hoffman (1999) points out, "within the framework of postmodern theory, we have come to privilege exactly those qualities of experience that exile demands— uncertainty, displacement, fragmented identity" (p. 44). But in celebrating this now preferred psychic positioning, we must not underestimate the complex psychic implications that cultural dislocations confer.

Multiplicity provides theoretical tools to consider the immigrant's dilemma without having to settle on one identity or another; today it is possible to embrace a decentered subject with fingers in many cultural pies, to explore shifts in identity and cross-cutting—though not necessarily competing—loyalties, rather than stressing the contradictions that were formerly considered inherent in these shifts and demanding resolution. Furthermore, the relational turn has given immigrant clinicians (and others who have experienced seismic shifts in their identification with different home grown cultures such as Bodnar, 2004; and Bernstein, forthcoming) permission to bring themselves into the consulting room, exploring the interaction between their own uprootedness and that of their patients.

Before this tilt toward multiplicity, psychoanalysts traditionally adopted one of two approaches to those who had immigrated. Either they ignored the topic completely, which is particularly interesting when we recall how many of the early analysts were immigrants (for lengthier discussions on this topic see Boulanger, 2004; Kuriloff, 2001, 2013) or, as I discussed previously (Boulanger, 2004), they conflated mother and country. Akhtar (1995) describes immigrants' attempts to master the emotional demands of immigration as a "third individuation," a further iteration of Mahler's developmental sequence. I find the developmental trajectory earlier analysts impose on the process of acculturation to be confining. As relational analysts, we can draw on Mitchell's (1984) assertion that developmental tasks, such as separation/individuation, and from this I extrapolate the struggle between acceptance by a community and the need to establish a separate identity, between feeling a part of and being apart from, are the projects of a lifetime, not milestones to be checked off on the road to maturity or the path to assimilation.

Assimilation is a construct belonging to a world of discrete categories and forced choices; you belong to one culture or another; you are an insider or an outsider, a member or an "other." Contemporary analysts (Boulanger 2004; Harlem, 2010; Ipp, 2010) conclude that the process of assimilation is neither achievable nor desirable; moving back and forth between self-states identified with different cultures, and eventually living comfortably and consciously in the spaces between those cultural selves, is considered a more realistic goal. Indeed, it is hard to imagine a situation in which assimilation would not come at the cost of dissociation.

In this new climate, a decade or so after my chance encounter with my former analyst, the relational literature is brimming with articles in which psychoanalysts are exploring this topic within a less confining theoretical framework, one that privileges multiplicity, one that facilitates the exploration of subtle shifts in identity, the longing to belong and the sometimes contradictory longing for recognition of a self that had to remain hidden if other selves were to belong. There is a firm understanding that culture plays a constitutional role in psychic development.

For many years I never mentioned the encounter with my first analyst, although it continued to surprise and disappoint me. I rationalized that I had probably never referred to my immigration during the treatment, but her failure to even show curiosity about the topic when I mentioned it, the fact that she dismissed my immigrant status and all I had come to understand about it, with a witticism, did rankle. Then, recently, in a discussion period after a panel on immigration at a professional conference, I described that meeting. I was self-conscious, caught between feeling that I had no right to make a big deal about it, the fear that I could not possibly be understood, that my ongoing sense of not quite fitting in was out of all proportion because, after all, I do not bear the usual markers of immigration as many people in that room did, and as my former therapist in her smug resignification of my status had suggested. I need not have worried; people gasped. We were different ages, races, classes, colors, creeds, and ethnic backgrounds, but we shared a common understanding. We recognized each other. In that moment, we could acknowledge each other's struggle, the inevitability of being seen as apart from a world that many of us felt so very much a part of. We knew the *doubleness* that we all inhabited.

Later that day, I had a much more common experience. As my husband and I got into the elevator I said, "I'm so tired; I wish we didn't have to go out." Picking up on my British accent, a woman in the elevator turned to me and said, "Well, where you come from you should be in bed already." Her comment was an othering, a slap in my psychic face. The implicit interpellation "Stranger, foreigner, alien, you don't belong here, in this time zone. You are not one of us." In her attempt to be friendly, this woman had blundered into my internal discourse about belonging and not belonging, about longing to be seen, yet risking being outed as the Other, about the meaning of recognition and the limits of recognition. Recognized by whom? Under what conditions?

Those of us who inhabit the hyphenated space between cultures are hypersensitive to difference; we constantly straddle the gap between one world and another. For some, that is the gap between their parents' cultural imperative and the larger world in which they live; for those of us who immigrated as adults, it is between where we used to be and where we find ourselves today. We are intimately aware of infinitesimal differences in speech, accent, emphasis in the way a word is said, particular gestures that can give us away or identify us as belonging; we know how to manipulate them, how to appear less alien, how to *perform* belonging.

In the time it took the elevator to descend to the lobby, I engaged in a dialogue with this woman that is worth considering frame by frame because it illustrates my title, *Being Double, Seeing Double*. The constant shift in perspective between two worlds parallels the neurophysiology of the eye. Neurobiologists Martinez-Conde and Macknik (2010) demonstrate that the eye refocuses up to 240 times a minute. Without this back and forth, the world starts to fade, to grow faint, and to disappear. Psychically, immigrants are always refocusing, automatically keeping both worlds in mind. It is not volitional; normally it is not a conscious act, but it is a preconscious counterpoint to just about every social interaction. In a poignant essay, aptly titled, *No Reconciliation Allowed*, Edward Said (1999), who was sent to an

English boarding school by his Palestinian father, describes internally echoing whatever he said in English in Arabic and *vice versa*.

Back in the elevator, I looked at this woman who wanted to put me in my place, asleep in bed in London, and said, "Excuse me?" If I had said, "I beg your pardon," immediately, I would have given myself away, so I chose a much less English expression and made sure to put the correct accent on "excuse" so that it did not sound English—exCUSE me? My would-be interpellator looked confused, "Well, where do you come from?" Again, choosing my diction very carefully, "I said Noo Yawk City."

On that day two events collided that made me once again aware of my competing difficulties and longings as an immigrant. Occupying the margins of nationalities, ethnicities, and genders creates confusion in others, so outsiders often seek to comply by fitting in, but on this occasion I was not prepared to acknowledge what this woman obviously thought was a very clever remark; I was going to stay in the margins. I resisted her need to reduce me to a stereotype. Her misrecognition allowed neither one self-state nor another to step forward; all I wanted was a polite "good evening," or "have a nice dinner," a wholehearted acknowledgement that I belonged there as much as she did.

At the same time, I was thinking to myself, "Well you can't have it both ways. In the morning you were recognized as a stranger among strangers and you loved it; this evening you confuse this poor woman by daring her to call you 'stranger,' posing as a familiar when she clearly knows that you are not." Immigrants know about living on the edge, the liminal space we all occupy all the time, and when we return to our countries of origin, we often find ourselves there too (Tummala-Nara, 2009). As time goes on, if we are fortunate we take the doubleness for granted, rather than being sabotaged by it, effortlessly privileging one self-state over the other. But there is always an echo, a life not being lived—even if it is not a life we want to be living. Every now and then it is affirming to encounter a group of people, just as I did at that conference, who know about the echo.

***

James Baldwin (1956) is quoted as saying that home is an irrevocable condition. It is hard to resist the nostalgia in that statement. Many, but not all, of us who immigrated by choice sought to revoke the original condition of home. We sought a new home, and many of us work with patients who are also seeking to establish new homes, but not always. Some clinicians evaluate and/or treat exiles whose enforced migration resulted from life-threatening political or personal persecution. They seek asylum from the threat of imprisonment, torture, humiliation, or even death. They have left behind families they were not ready to leave. Others, patients and analysts, left their countries of origin on ideological grounds, finding the prevailing political climate at home to be unacceptable (see, for example, Rozmarin,

2009 and 2011; Ipp, 2010; Philips, 2011). Many, documented and undocumented immigrants, came here to find economic stability or educational opportunities for themselves and/or their children (McCarroll, 2009). Many, particularly those Akhtar (1995, 2004) describes, join established groups, finding husbands or wives among those already settled here, ready-made culturally syntonic family constellations. Some of the clinicians who work with these immigrants (Beltsiou, 2015; Lobham, 2006; Ipp, 2010; Boulanger, 2004) came as young adults looking for education and opportunities. Some came as children. The mounting swell of psychoanalytic literature on immigration over the last 10 years covers these conditions and more. The clinical relationships that have been described are fruitful and full of surprising insights for patient and clinician, even when the clinician is not an immigrant (Bernstein, forthcoming; McCarroll, 2009), even when the treatment itself does not focus on the facts of immigration (for a comprehensive and systematic review of this literature see Ainslie, Harlem, Tummala-Narra, Barbanel, Ruth, 2013).

It is implicit in our therapeutic work in general that we seek to provide a transitional home for our patients, a containing environment in which they can explore the roots of the past as they are multiply present in the here and now, bumping up against unrecognized selves, unrealized hopes, and terrible regrets in the process. Time and again we find that the recognition and acceptance the right treatment can provide is transformative, but perhaps never more so than in our work with immigrants who contend with several culturally competing selves in their daily lives and seek one relationship in which they can all be heard and seen.

***

Miriam

This case describes my work with a woman who was not only an immigrant to the United States, she was also the child of immigrants to the country from which she herself had emigrated. We had an opportunity to follow the contradictory and sometimes cataclysmic changes in her sense of self, her terrible fear of not making it, of being revealed as an imposter, not worthy of the life she was leading in America. When I began to work with her, although she excelled at *seeing* double, *being* double did not come easily to her. At least two self-states were engaged in a tug of war; she feared that the winner would take all, and it was not clear to her who the winner would be.

Background

Miriam was referred to me by the mental health clinic at the university where she was finishing up her coursework in the English Department. She was preparing for her orals and getting ready to write her dissertation. Her topic was a deconstruction of Holocaust literature. She was in her mid-forties, married, living in Connecticut with two school-age daughters. Her husband, whom she had met when he was on a year's sabbatical at Hebrew University, was a rising star in Middle Eastern studies at another university. She is a beautiful woman, charming, charismatic, and with such command of English that I had remind myself it was not her native tongue. And most mornings she could not get out of bed to take care of her daughters because she felt so depleted the effort was beyond her.

The incident that had precipitated her seeking me out was a very frightening moment during the previous summer when she suddenly sensed that she was about to have a seizure. In her mid-twenties when she was still living in Israel, Miriam had had a series of *grand mal* seizures that led to surgery to remove a benign brain tumor. For a 27-year-old with almost no social or financial support, it was a terrifying experience. For a while, it was not clear that she would make a full recovery, but she did.

For 12 years, always fearing a recurrence, she took Tegritol, but she was no longer being medicated when I met her. After neurological examinations ruled out an underlying physiological cause for the symptoms she had experienced, it emerged that earlier in the summer her dissertation advisor had rejected the particular direction in which she wanted to take her research, meaning that her dissertation would take at least two years longer to complete than she had anticipated. It was not possible to articulate the horror Miriam experienced at this turn of events; it felt literally life-threatening, throwing into question the identity she desperately wanted to construct, and appeared to have constructed, in the United States. It was only as I came to know more about the ways in which she was continually plagued by memories of the worlds she had left behind that I could grasp the significance of this setback.

Miriam is Israeli, the oldest daughter in a large and desperately poor Mizrahi family[1]. Her parents had joined a mass exodus from their country of origin when her mother, who had entered into an arranged marriage at the age of nine, was 12 and no longer married and her father was 15. They met in the absorption center where they were sent on arrival in Israel, both mourning their mothers who had died shortly after the exodus. Miriam's mother was and remains illiterate. As Miriam put it, in a theme that became significant, "I was seduced into the Holocaust thing for my dissertation because there are no words for my mother's experience. At least the survivors from Eastern Europe had words to describe their experience. In the West you get to refine an emotion when you are talking, with my parents there is no system at work in which to refine an emotion. Everything is always unfiltered. My parents' cultural ego is so limited. My mother isn't reflective; she narrates everything she does, even going shopping; she's so concrete."

Miriam was acutely aware of and able to articulate the vast difference between her parents' meaning system and the one that she and I shared—the one that she demonstrated with such sophistication as she described these differences to me. Yet she was haunted by the discontinuities; they could not exist side by side in the same person. Doubleness was not possible. She was terrified of tumbling back into a world that did not rely on words and their affective valence. There was no way in which Miriam could share her increasingly Westernized thoughts and feelings with her parents. There were no words for the mother's experience, yet the daughter had made words her stock in trade. There was no self-reflection in her family's concrete and repetitive use of "facts" to justify and govern narrow and alienating religious rituals and behaviors, yet the daughter used reflection to analyze and give meaning to her life. Nonetheless, her Mizrahi self felt only too real: "I identify with the woman behind the veil in those pictures from Afghanistan, the sense of being trapped, a girl who never had an education."

When she was growing up, her home was chaotic, the children dressed in hand me downs, her father, frequently drunk, stumbling around the house. Although he was never physically abusive, his behavior was frightening. Her mother loved to cook and gather people around but often was overwhelmed by her children's needs. The extent to which Miriam feared I would be similarly overwhelmed by what she imagined to be a gaggle of patients around me emerged in the first dream she related that she had just before our second session, "I am in your office. There were people in the waiting area and there wasn't enough separation and they kept disturbing us, and you didn't seem to be paying attention to the disturbance. When I pointed it out to you, you seemed to be more interested in the voices than in taking action." In the absence of responsible parents, it had fallen to Miriam to attend to what happened at home. Transferentially, she feared it would be the same with me. I would not be able to protect her from everyone else's needs.

When things got too much at home, her mother would leave to spend time with her family or to go dancing, as her husband, Miriam's father, protested, physically barring the door, appealing to Miriam to stop her. As the oldest daughter, Miriam was the interpreter, she spoke Hebrew, her parents Arabic. She learned the habits and expectations of the dominant Ashkenazy culture that established the norms in Israel; her parents were never comfortable submitting to those norms. To this day her parents look ragged and unkempt; her mother eats with her hands. Miriam was ashamed of them and ashamed of her shame; always on the verge of being ashamed of herself. As a little girl she tried to bathe in bleach to lighten her dark skin. "If I can get people to see my parents as cool and exotic, then they are not embarrassing," she said after one visit from them. But even when this appeared to be the case—her American friends took great interest in this unusual Mizrahi couple—each visit left her utterly depleted. Trying to get beyond her parents, to separate herself from their other-worldliness, was exhausting.

In the secular primary school she attended, Miriam had an Ashkenazy friend who went to ballet lessons; she longed to go, too. Knowing her strictly observant father would have opposed her wish to attend, her teachers and mother conspired to enroll her. This was a significant turning point. "It was then and there, in that ballet studio that I began my underground emotional life, my first infiltration into secular Ashkenazy existence. Since then," she says, "I am well disguised, an infiltrator." I am reminded of Chiang Rae Lee's (1995) description of the "ugly immigrant's truth." "We will learn every lesson of accent and idiom; we will dismantle every last pretense and practice you hold, noble as well as ruinous. You can keep nothing safe from our eyes and ears" (p. 319). Miriam soaked up the Ashkenazy pretenses and practices, she mimicked and idealized. She fell in love with her teachers, she sought their admiration and sought to copy them, she made fast friends with the Ashkenazy children who came from small families. She felt nothing but disgust for large, untidy Mizrahi families with 12 or 14 children. "I remember wanting to take a knife to my mother's belly when she was pregnant with my youngest brother. 'How could you do this to us again?' I thought. 'There isn't enough room; there isn't enough anything." Of that first definitive move away from what she saw as her primitive Mizrahi community to seek acceptance among the Ashkenazim she said, "It was then I began my self-imposed exile from my family." But, at the same time she recognized, "I have lost part of myself."

By the time I met her she had, like her parents, immigrated, this time to the United States seeking acceptance in the world of intellectuals; her PhD was to be a passport into a world she had been denied when she failed to be admitted into an Israeli University. Much of the early treatment was characterized by Miriam's depression where the danger of undoing all the gains she had made felt very real; keeping her Mizrahi and Ashkenazi sides separate was of paramount importance to her. I was overwhelmed by the balancing act she had pulled off and how vividly she spoke about her experiences.

On the day she began treatment, Miriam said, "I have to bring my story to life." She had told her story many times to therapists, to colleagues, and to friends; she had reflected on it; she recounted it with affect, with sadness, disgust, awe, amusement; nonetheless she said it had not come to life for her. Bollas (2009) claims that there is a universal, uniquely human drive for representation. This drive "presupposes the self's belief in a good object, which in turn is based on the self's communications of early infantile states to the mother who, to a lesser or greater extent, has received and transformed those communications" (p. 37). In effect, Bollas is arguing, as many earlier developmental psychoanalysts have argued, that early recognition facilitates the baby's capacity to internalize a good enough mother. Bollas continues, "The pleasure of representation promotes other pleasures; the pleasure of self-discovery, and of being understood" (p. 37).

In some ways Miriam's story was only too alive for her, her past only too present. She needed to be able to tell her story to someone who recognized and understood not just the dramatic nature of the transformations she had undergone, but the psychic cost of those transformations, the ongoing complications of having actively sought all these dislocations. And she needed to internalize the listening other.

Transference

In response to my standard question, asked several weeks into the treatment, about whether the fact that I was an immigrant had influenced her decision to see me, Miriam made it clear she had no wish to consider that possibility; she hadn't *chosen me* she said, she had been sent to me and, in fact, she was not sure I really understood her. She had had an extremely meaningful treatment earlier in Haifa. I was neither as smart, as exciting, nor as well known as the analyst who had treated her there.

Her previous treatment had been significant. For the first time in her life she had she felt seen, she was taken care of and not exploited. I came to know that every other significant authority relationship she entered into had ended with Miriam doing the caretaking, just as she did with her parents. She consistently found narcissistically vulnerable people as mentors, as counselors, as professors, as friends, all of whom eventually turned to her for help. They were never as able, as mature, as generous as she had imagined. Quickly putting her own needs aside, she would turn her disappointment into contempt, "People see me as this huge tit," she complained, but at those moments she felt in charge, all-knowing and all-giving. "I get a good feeling when I equalize a relationship."

I wondered how this pattern would play out with me. Although she accepted my explanation that the treatment was about her not about me; she even admitted that it "kind of" felt good not having to worry about whether I had children or what kind of struggles I was having in my own life; at the same time, something was missing. The early treatment was characterized by her great disappointment in me. I was typical of the "emotional stinginess of the West." She wanted me to be warm, but she found me cold. She wanted me to help organize her material in a way it had not been organized before, but she did not believe I was up to the task.

As I was being assaulted by her early doubts—and my own—about whether I could provide an environment in which Miriam's story would come to life, she had a dream about an aunt who, in her real life, had two children whom she had treated terribly, totally ruining them. In the dream the aunt has given birth to a third baby, a talking baby, and there is another chance for her to raise this baby without ruining her.

"Oh," I thought. "I'm being given another chance!" But I also thought that it was quite a burden for this precocious baby to have to talk her mother through the correct mothering steps. In a series of articles, Grossmark, (2012a, 2012b) has pointed out the danger inherent in what I call the emerging relational orthodoxy, which demands that we treat all patients as if they are able to talk about the intersubjective clinical process, as if they are capable of mentalization. Some patients, and I believed that Miriam was one of these, despite her very sophisticated presentation, have dissociated the regressed and damaged parts of themselves. They may not be ready to talk about the intersubjective process. In doing so the analyst may engage the verbal and competent self and not allow sufficient space for the damaged, concrete, dependent, and regressed self to be truly present as the central focus of treatment.

I was concerned that if I engaged Miriam's highly analytical grown-up self in a discussion about the correct mothering steps in the wake of this dream, which she had found quite delightful, the baby who needed an intuitive mother, a mother who did not need instruction from her little daughter—or no more than the average mother takes nonverbal instruction from her infant—I would indeed be turning her into a surrogate therapist/mother/colleague just as everyone else did, so I said nothing. The dream went unexamined but left a feeling of hope between us.

When she steals my toothbrush in a later dream, then replaces it, she realized she still had to steal what she wanted. And now I was in the dream in person not in metaphor, and I could wonder aloud why she had to steal what she needed from me. "My life is so much more settled than it was in that earlier treatment when I was so volatile. I have fantasies of being cradled and looked at as if by a mother. Coming here is about peacefulness, like wanting to lie down and to take a break, being a child again, I want to be seen by you, and I want to see you seeing me." At this point in the treatment we had worked out our own way of being together in my office where I would sit close to the couch on which she would recline on her side watching me. "I need to connect with you in order to connect with myself," she said, "but I feel so alone, I have done so much alone. I do want to keep the boundaries, but I strive to be fully seen; I feel such desperation to be someone in the eyes of another person, to be seen as valuable."

"At our core," write Fonagy, Gergely, Jurist, and Target (2002) "is the representation of how we were seen" (p. 348). And, of course, when we were not seen, or when the see-er, the mother, was distracted with her own mourning and confusion over her life as an immigrant in an incomprehensible country, we seek in our analyst someone to reflect a view that is consistent with our own experience.

If her story was to come to life for her it would mean trusting me in a different way, allowing me to move from being perceived as a distant, cold, and dull presence to a source of warmth and hope. Then she dreamed about standing inside a bakery in Israel, her mouth watering, waiting her turn to buy the one loaf she wanted in all of Haifa. As she recalled the dream, she laughed, reminding me that I had told her once, after she returned from a trip to France, that *boulanger* means baker. Now I was with her in Israel; she could draw nourishment from our work there as well; I no longer represented the coldness of the West.

Seeing Double, Being Double

In the first year of treatment, Miriam had a dream that crystallized her dilemma "I am driving a car, a silver car. I drift to the right, there is a huge ..." she stuttered, "valley, chasm, cliff. It isn't clear to me how I do it but I leave the car, it drops down into the water below. I am holding on to the footholds in the rocks and I bring myself up to the top of the cliff. I look down and I see the car drifting away in the stream. The roof of the car is still above the water. I have no emotions, I say, 'OK I made it out of there.'"

I asked about her stuttering. "That word has a sense of falling," she replied. "In Hebrew it is *tehom*. Abyss. I can't keep the experience and the word separate." Miriam lived on the edge of that abyss, in danger of being felled by her sense of humiliation, by the abject conditions of her childhood and by her unwelcome yet inescapable identity as Mizrahi. During the day she drove the silver convertible between her suburban home and the Ivy League university she attended. But there was a spectral self simultaneously bobbing along in the water at the bottom of the abyss. She didn't know how she "made it out of there." Night after night, in one dream or another, she fell back into the abyss, into the arms of her chaotic, dysfunctional family, or she replayed the humiliating years in high school where it seemed as if everyone lived in large warm homes with their own bedrooms, and she returned to a crowded, unheated hovel.

During the day she was accomplished and elegant, competent, sought after, a pillar of strength to family, friends, and neighbors. At night she was the dirty little Arab girl, longing to feel deserving but knowing that she would never belong, or a near destitute directionless 20-something. She struggled to make the past and present continuous, but she could not. Abject self states were not dissociated; she could taste the shame, the disappointment and fear of her earlier years; they were a painful reminder of how precarious she believed her present life to be, how easily she could be reclaimed by the past. In our work together, all the contradictions between her worlds, the vast distances she had travelled physically and psychically had to be validated, rather than pushed away. Her current life felt so natural and at the same time so tenuous. She believed it had been bought by her Ashkenazy husband's stability and reputation. Her longtime dream, her fantasy of a life among intellectuals in the West was realized not because of her own abilities, she feared, but because of a chance meeting with a man who was overwhelmed by her beauty and decided to take a chance and marry her.

I asked myself whether the ability to stand comfortably in the spaces between these astonishingly discrepant cultures would develop (Boulanger, 2004). They were not spaces; they were the abyss, the life she was trying to escape, deeply religious, superstitious, rejecting the values of the twenty-first century, the self she felt she had to kill in renouncing her parents' culture.

She was preoccupied with the violence she had done to herself and her family in rejecting her Mizrahi roots. "Last week in my dream I killed someone, and now I am going to be in jail for the rest of my life. I am asking myself, was it worth it?" Indeed, her constant preoccupation with the abyss was a jail sentence. The people she had left felt dead to her, too. "My life feels like a cemetery of people I have left behind."

And yet, inexorably, she moved forward, "I am not worrying about them anymore. By striving to be all I am, these are the consequences. Success is dangerous because it takes you away from who you are. My parents are irrelevant to me. I love my mother, but it doesn't matter whether I speak to her or not. The family that I have made here is in another dimension. Do you remember I used to have the dream that I was the translator for all the aliens? I helped them fit into this planet, and I helped them understand. I am no longer the translator or therapist, but that role kept the ties alive."

She was having recurrent dreams of giving birth to twins and having to give one up. Of babies who were getting another chance with a new mother, or of weddings—an attempt to marry the disparate parts of herself. After seven years in treatment, Miriam was offered the opportunity to return to Israel to teach for a few years. We moved into a termination phase, earlier than I might have wished, but a series of vivid dreams took us forward, repeating earlier themes yet suggesting ways of resolving the discontinuities less definitively.

"I was with my mother and father. My mother was upset because my father had left the house because he was upset with her, and I said, 'That's the way he is; he'll come back.'"

Her associations to the dream spoke to the changes she was making. "In the dream my parents seemed more modern, less in the twelfth century. It's interesting. It's a reversal of what normally happened—she used to leave. She would go to her father's. In the dream, I felt relieved, it felt normal. My father felt more whole. The dream rehabilitates him; he isn't helpless. He was castrated by leaving his country and coming to Israel where he is less than a man. In the dream he takes action, he rebels. I felt so much better after this dream, as if I had been liberated somehow."

I cannot imagine a better example of Freud's contention that psychoanalysis cannot cure ordinary unhappiness (Breuer and Freud, 1896). Miriam was rejoicing in a dream in which she had normal parents who fought in the way other people's parents fight, parents for whom she did not have to feel responsible, parents she could safely leave to their own devices. The following week she again dreamed of her parents looking much more comfortable financially and socially, her mother was eating not with her hands but with a knife and fork. To her dream mind they were no longer so shameful.

Her sense of belonging grew less tenuous. "I was a guest in this family, a very WASPY family. I was treated so well and made welcome. There was another group that wasn't treated like that. I was aware of how well I was treated, but also aware of the discrepancy." This dream came after Miriam had been to a dinner party where she saw a couple whom she greatly admired. She was struck by how enthusiastically the wife had greeted her, "such a wave of love and warmth towards me, it was so comforting. It was a truly heartfelt greeting, a solid recognition and appreciation. Am I in a place where I can accept it now?"

In subsequent sessions, she continued to talk about these welcome changes. "My life has been defined by a struggle to become something I have not been, now there is no struggle, I am smart, knowledgeable, I fit, I arrived. ... After I got my PhD, I had this sense of safety—I thought I have earned my ticket to this club. There is such a huge disparity between my family and me, but I don't feel the need to talk about it anymore. The sense of leaving them behind—it's real. I am leaving them behind. In the dream there is that awareness that I have been singled out. I received very preferential treatment; I was aware that the other people weren't seen."

"I don't have the discomfort of not belonging, it is clear to me that I don't belong. But I'm not ashamed. For the first time in my life I feel I am aligned with culture, with society, with my environment, I have arrived at my place."

In one of our last sessions, Miriam said that she had been wondering if my experience of having left my culture and trying to fit into another one could be compared with hers. "I was thinking of the confusion about belonging and not belonging that you must have felt too." As her narrative came to life in my presence, so had my presence achieved a different meaning for her. *Her* living narrative, her newfound subjectivity, with all its cross-cutting cultural alliances, and the acceptance of her culturally diverse self states, conferred *my* separate subjectivity.

As Miriam's story came to life between us, her narrative acquired temporality, her past was no longer in danger of claiming her present, although it was alive in her memory, not only could she *see* double, she could safely *be* double. To return to Bollas's contention that the pleasure of telling one's story to another leads to other pleasures, "the pleasure of self-discovery, and of being understood." Self-discovery and understanding, this is no more than as psychodynamic therapists we hope to offer all our patients, but perhaps self-discovery and being understood take on additional meaning when we are working with immigrants, whose different cultural selves cry out for a particular understanding and acceptance of cultural as well as personal conflicts. Isaiah Berlin (quoted in Ignatieff, 1998) lived all his adult life as a Russian Jew in the politely and reflexively anti-Semitic and, during most of his life, bitterly xenophobic United Kingdom. He knew only too well the costs of being a chronic other. He concluded one of his essays, "Belonging was more than possession of land and statehood; it was the condition of being understood itself" (p. 292).

Belonging is the condition of being understood. This is, in fact, how I concluded my previous paper on immigration. My message has not changed; I have come full circle. What has changed in these 10 years is that so many others, many of whom I have referenced in this chapter, have added their insights to this fascinating, life giving, painful, sometimes contradictory phenomenon.

Note

1. Mizrahi Jews are those who immigrated to Israel from other Middle Eastern countries, as opposed to the dominant Ashkenazim who came from Eastern Europe. Traditionally the Ashkenazim have represented the political, social, economic, and military establishment in Israel, while the darker skinned Mizrahis' absorption into Israeli society has been fraught with racism and prejudice.

References

Ainslie, R.C., Harlem, A., Tummala-Narra, P., Barbanel, L., Ruth, R. (2013). Contemporary psychoanalytic views on the experience of immigration. *Psychoanalytic Psychology*, 30: 663–369.

Akhtar, S. (1995). A third individuation: Immigration, identity, and the psychoanalytic process. *Journal of the American Academy of Psychoanalysis*, 43: 1051–1084.

Akhtar, S. (2004). Special issue. Immigration and the lifecycle. *American Journal of Psychoanalysis*, 64: 127–192.

Baldwin, J. (1956) *Giovnni's room*. New York, NY: Dell.

Beltsiou, J. (this volume). *Locating ourselves: Immigration in psychoanalysis*. New York, NY, and London: Routledge.

Bernstein, K. (forthcoming). What matters between us: Cultural specificity in the psychoanalytic dyad. *Psychoanalytic Dialogues*.

Bodnar, S. (2004). Remember where you come from: Dissociative process in multicultural individuals. *Psychoanalytic Dialogues*, 14: 581–603.

Bollas, C. (2009). *The evocative object world*. London and New York, NY: Routledge.

Boulanger, G. (2004). Lot's wife, Cary Grant, and the American dream: Psychoanalysis with immigrants. *Contemporary Psychoanalysis*, 40: 353–372.

Breuer, J., and Freud, S. (1896) *Studies on hysteria. The standard edition of the complete psychological works of Sigmund Freud, Volume II*. London: The Hogarth Press and the Institute of Psycho-Analysis.

Dimen, M. (2011). With culture in mind: Psychoanalytic stories. New York, NY, and London: Routledge.

Druckerman, P. (2013). An American neurotic in Paris. Downloaded from www.nytimes.com/2012/11/28/opinion/druckermen.

Fonagy, P., Gergely, G., Jurst, E., Target, M. eds. (2002). *Affect regulation, mentalization, and the development of the self*. New York, NY: Other Press.

Foner, N. ed. (2013) *One Out of Three: Immigrant New York in the Twenty-First Century*. New York, NY: Columbia University Press.

Grossmark, R. (2012a). The unobtrusive relational analyst. *Psychoanalytic Dialogues*, 22: 629–646.

Grossmark, R. (2012b). The flow of enactive engagement. *Contemporary Psychoanalysis*, 48: 287–300.

Harlem, A. (2010). Exile as a dissociative state: When a self is "lost in transit." *Psychoanalytic Psychology*, 27: 460–474.

Hoffman, E. (1999). The new nomads. In A. Aciman, Ed., *Letters of transit: Reflections on exile, identity, language and loss*. New York, NY: The New Press.

Ignatieff, M. (1998), *Isaiah Berlin: A life*. London: Chatto and Windus.

Ipp, H. (2010). Nell – A bridge to the amputated self: The impact of immigration on continuities and discontinuities of self. *International Journal of Psychoanalytic Self Psychology*, 5: 1–13.

Kuriloff, E. (2001). A two-culture psychology: The role of national and ethnic origin in the therapeutic dyad. *Contemporary Psychoanalysis*, 37: 673–682.

Kuriloff, E. (2013) *Contemporary psychoanalysis and the legacy of the Third Reich: History, memory, tradition*. New York, NY, and London: Routledge.

Lee, C-R. (1995). *Native speaker*, New York, NY: Riverhead Books.

Lobban, G. (2006). Immigration and dissociation. *Psychoanalytic Perspectives*, 3: 73–92.

Martinez-Conde, S. & Macknik, S. (2010). *Sleights of mind: What the neuroscience of magic reveals about our everyday deceptions*. New York, NY: Henry Holt & Company.

McCarroll, J. (2009). Analysis of an undocumented Latina immigrant. *Psychoanalysis, Culture and Society*, 14: 225–236.

Mitchell, S.A. (1984). Object relations theory and the developmental tilt. *Contemporary Psychoanalysis*, 34: 473–499.

Philips, T. (2011). Race, place, and self in the experience of a bystander. *International Journal of Psychoanalytical Self Psychology*, 6: 405–426.

Rozmarin, E. (2009). I am yourself: Subjectivity and the collective. *Psychoanalytic Dialogues*, 19: 604–616.

Rozmarin, E. (2011) Chapters 5 & 15 in M. Dimen, Ed., *With culture in mind*. New York, NY, and London: Routledge.

Said, E. (1999). No reconciliation allowed. In A. Aciman, Ed., New York, NY: The New Press.

Tummala-Narra, P. (2009). The immigrant's real and imagined return home. *Psychoanalysis, Culture and Society*, 14: 237–252.

Chapter 4

The Immigrant Analyst
A Journey from Double Consciousness Towards Hybridity

Glenys Lobban, PhD

(Previously published in *Psychoanalytic Dialogues*, 2013, Vol. 23, Issue 5, pp. 554–567.)

In 1974 I emigrated from my homeland, South Africa, to the United Kingdom because I was opposed to Apartheid and I had become very pessimistic about the possibility of working from within to overthrow it. I began graduate school at Leicester University where I lived in a student house with seven English roommates. I hailed from the manicured suburbs of Johannesburg, a city far larger and more sophisticated than sleepy little Leicester. When my British housemates assumed that I had lived in the jungle and questioned me about how I survived in my grass hut, without electricity, among the lions and poisonous snakes, I was incredulous. In fact, almost everyone I met in Leicester barraged me with similar questions. Finally my patience wore out. Exasperated with my housemates, I concocted an African tale for them. I explained how convenient it was to shop in Johannesburg: I just got on my elephant, and he took me to the local market. I tethered him outside at a special elephant tethering post while I shopped, then I loaded all my groceries into the panniers attached to his saddle and rode him home. Imagine my surprise when they believed me, and their chagrin when I told them that I was only joking. A Black South African colleague later confessed to me that his British classmates at Oxford had fallen for a similar story; he told them that he rode a giraffe to school every day. Neither of us was prone to hoodwinking our peers, or dishing out hostile conversational jabs. Why then did we resort to telling these tall tales to our fellow students?

Now, all these years later, I have figured out an explanation for my behavior. This evolved as I reflected on an enactment that occurred in my work with my patient Rachel. I will describe this case in more detail later in this paper, but here are the headlines: I suddenly registered that I was doing something atypical; I was actively siding with Rachel's boyfriend, Juan, and trying to explain his motivations to her. Juan is an immigrant, a Latino man from the Dominican Republic, and Rachel is a White American. I identified with Juan's sense of being an outsider, who was misunderstood and misjudged by Americans, and this blinded me to how Rachel was faring in the relationship; I attempted instead to help her understand and value Juan's "foreign" traits and beliefs. How had my status as an immigrant to North America clouded my judgment, and why had this occurred? The concept of "double consciousness" (Du Bois, 1903/1994, p. 2) provided me with an explanatory framework, which illuminated my experiences as an immigrant analyst. In this paper I invite you, my reader, to be my travel companion, to accompany me on my trek back through the terrain I traversed as I became an immigrant analyst. I intend my description of my personal journey to provide you with concrete data about how it feels to be an immigrant analyst, which I will then utilize to outline a theoretical framework for conceptualizing how the subjectivity of an immigrant analyst is constructed.

Let us return to my elephant still tethered outside that supermarket in Johannesburg. I invented him because I felt angry about being misunderstood and disparaged by my British peers. I was at the receiving end of what Paul Gilroy terms "cultural insiderism" (Gilroy, 1993, p. 3). My fellow students, blinded by the "dazzle of Whiteness" (Gilroy, p. 7) judged Africa from within British culture, privileging what was British and Western. Their assumptions about "darkest" Africa predisposed them to believe a wildly improbable tale about transportation in Johannesburg. My Black South African colleague and I each created our stories about giraffes and elephants in an attempt, albeit unconscious, to speak back to the dominant culture, to resist being viewed as "primitive Africans," and to resist seeing ourselves through that lens. We were trying to use humor to counter what W.E.B. Du Bois called "double consciousness": the "sense of always looking at one's self through the eyes of others, of measuring one's soul by the tape of a world that looks on in amused contempt and pity" (Du Bois). Our mocking stories, laced with veiled aggression, represented a reflexive attempt to resist being interpellated as "primitive" Africans, to undo our experience of "double consciousness."

W.E.B. Du Bois used the term "double consciousness" to denote the subjectivity of African Americans, who lived in a culture where they were viewed as unequal to White Americans. He recounted how, in his "early days of rollicking boyhood," one of the White students in his New England schoolhouse refused to accept a card from him during their game, and at that moment he felt "shut out from their world by a vast veil" (Du Bois). Du Bois was "interpellated" (see Dimen, 2011) by a representative of the dominant culture, labelled as someone who was second-class, unequal to his White peers. Du Bois's self was "simultaneously defamiliarized and reconstituted within the cultural discourse on race" (Bergner, 1998, p. 241). He was caught in the dilemma of "double consciousness," seeing himself simultaneously through an African American lens and a White racist lens. "Double consciousness" has become the "standard shorthand to describe African American subjectivity" (Bergner). Gilroy argues that Du Bois intended the construct of "double consciousness" to "illuminate the experience of post slave populations in general" (Gilroy, 1993, p. 126). In recent years, scholars have expanded its scope to include immigrants to America (Falicov, 2003).

This paper will explore "double consciousness" in immigrant analysts in America. While there are many differences between immigrant analysts in language, class, culture, attitudes toward assimilation, degree of privilege, theoretical orientation, and professional training, nonetheless they all have to grapple with viewing themselves at once through the lens of mainstream culture and through their mother country lens.

A number of immigrant analysts have described their experiences as immigrants (Akhtar, 1998, 2009; Boulanger, 2004; Lobban, 2006; Perez Foster, 1996, 1998) and cases where both analyst and patient are immigrants (Guralnik, 2011; Lobban, 2006, 2011a; Pugachevsky, 2011; Rozmarin, 2011; Suchet, 2010), but none of these papers utilized the concept of "double consciousness" to understand immigrant subjectivity.

An immigrant enters her new country with one set of selves. These are then overwritten and refracted by her experiences with peers, neighbors, colleagues, and authorities in the new culture, and this experience shapes her consciousness, subjectivity, and sense of identity. Psychoanalysis has not yet developed a coherent theory about immigrant subjectivity. I propose that we psychoanalysts borrow Du Bois's notion of "double consciousness," reshape it to accommodate current notions of multiplicity, and use this theoretical framework to conceptualize the immigrant experience. In this chapter I will use this new framework to analyze how my immigrant analyst subjectivity developed during my sojourn in North America and address theoretical questions such as: What is the subjective experience of the immigrant as she attempts to hold two sets of selves, those cut from foreign cloth and those made in her new country? How does it affect the immigrant's sense of self if everyone in her new country is convinced that her foreign bolts of cloth are inferior and their fabric is automatically superior? How can we integrate ideas about the immigrant as someone with a binary self divided into "foreign" and "new country" facets, with a theory that presupposes a multiplicitous self and defines personal identity as something constituted by a variety of different subjectivities which entails "the ability to stand in the spaces between realities without losing any of them?" (Bromberg, 1998, p. 273).

I have been an immigrant analyst in New York for 26 years. I belong to a particularly privileged subgroup of immigrant analysts. I am what Akhtar (1999) terms an "invisible" immigrant, invisible because I am "White," middle class, English-speaking, and did not come as a refugee to America, yet my accent defines me as the "other." Moving to New York to begin graduate school was my "act of hopeful ambition" (Rozmarin, 2009, p. 476), but once here I missed the familiar backdrop of my motherland: the people, landscape, smells, vegetation, sounds, foods, culture, and language, lit by the intense, searing South African sunlight. I learned that immigration and mourning are intertwined (Akhtar, 2009; Grinberg and Grinberg, 1989). I lived with the sense of "chronic absence" (Boulanger, 2004, p. 356) so vividly expressed by Jose Alavez, the Mexican poet: "How far I am from the land where I was born! Immense longing invades my thoughts, and when I see myself as alone and sad as a leaf in the wind, I want to cry. I want to die of sorrow" (Alavez, 2010.) (The novels of Cisneros, 1984; Desai, 2006; Diaz, 2006; Hamid, 2007; Hoffman, 1989; Lahiri, 1999; and O'Neill, 2008 offer compelling descriptions of the complex, ambiguous losses experienced by immigrants to North America.)

I was challenged by a series of experiences of being "othered" and defined via my immigrant status in my early years in New York and these were the building blocks of my "double consciousness." Even today, despite my 38 years of residence in New York, I am identified as "that South African" clinical psychologist/analyst. I am the "other," and I often feel erased or invisible because many Americans have little information about my country or the continent of Africa.

North America portrays itself as the melting pot, where the Statue of Liberty, "the mother of exiles" waits to welcome all the "huddled masses yearning to breathe free" (Lazarus, 1883). I learned firsthand that this cultural ideal is a myth and that blending in is complicated by the fact that certain attributes of race, class, language, and religion are privileged. For example, Whiteness is the "silent norm" (Suchet, 2007, p. 868) in mainstream America, and "Whites" who are born in North America are viewed as superior to all immigrants (Layton, 2004). Immigrants are graded on a continuum of less to more equal, with immigrants of color categorized as the least equal (Eng and Han, 2000). And similar continua exist that privilege middle and upper class immigrants, Christian immigrants, and those whose first language is English (see Bodnar, 2004; Boulanger, 2004; Bushra, 2009; Eng and Han, 2000; Hartman, 2007; Harris, 2007, 2012; Leary, 2007 Lobban, 2006, 2012; Straker, 2004, 2007; Suchet, 2004, 2007).

Because I was an "invisible" immigrant, it was theoretically possible for me to "pass" as an American, but this required me to pay a heavy price. Becoming culturally bilingual was not enough, I was expected to assimilate, to blend in, to abandon my foreign, made in South Africa spectacles and don an American-made pair. I had to disavow a large part of myself and erase all my "foreign" facets if I wanted to try to "pass" as American, yet I continued to feel like the "other" even when I was trying to assimilate. I discovered that joining the American melting pot carried a secret price ticket. First I was interpellated (see Dimen, 2011) as the "other," who was by definition "inferior." Once I saw myself through that "double consciousness" lens and judged myself as "the inferior other" I could go ahead and assimilate, but the prerequisite for that assimilation was a sense of shame about my immigrant selves that were cut from foreign cloth. I tried to maintain my positive view of myself and mitigate the impact of my "double consciousness" by utilizing "alternation" (Falicov, 2003a; 2003b), as a coping strategy. I adapted my behavior to the context I found myself in; I used American English at the local deli and asked for 'tomayto' instead of 'tomahto' on my sandwich, but when I was at home or with "foreign" friends I talked South African English and made jokes about "the Americans" and their weird customs and rituals.

Each immigrant analyst evolves her own conscious and unconscious blueprint regarding how best to integrate her immigrant selves and her "foreign" selves and fold them into the job description "analyst" (Lobban, 2006). My initial blueprint was shaped by my experiences at my New York graduate school 30 years ago. There were four foreign-born students in our class of 20 students; the other three were Latinos. While the faculty at my school paid lip service to multiculturalism, the hidden curriculum was all about assimilation. The message to us immigrant therapists was: Assimilate to North America yourself and learn how to treat North American patients and facilitate assimilation in your immigrant patients. Nobody realized that we may be feeling nostalgia or loss. We were told constantly that we were lucky to be training in North America. The idea that we might "desire to maintain cultural ideals and practices" that originated in our mother country rather than "shed" our culture (Harlem, 2009, p. 273) was never broached; nor were concepts such as "mettissage" (Gilroy, 1993) or "hybridity" (Bhabha, 1994). My program also placed a premium on "Western" values. I had my first lesson about judging and censoring myself when one of my supervisors was scathingly dismissive of my Brazilian patient who believed in spirits, labeling her as "irrational" and "primitive." I realized that my childhood exposure to spiritualism, ancestors, and astrology (Lobban, 2006, 2011b) would "other" me as "primitive" and was not a safe topic at school.

When I had been practicing as an analyst for about 10 years, I began to theorize about my experiences and examine the analyst self I had fashioned (Lobban, 2006). I concluded that I had tried to maintain two separate versions of my analytic self: a "culturally neutral" one for my American patients and my "outsider" self for my foreign and immigrant patients (Lobban, p. 80). I had not yet embraced the concept of "double consciousness" so I lacked an explanation for this split. I now realize that the "assimilated" analytic self I fashioned had its roots in my own disavowed "double consciousness." I tried to neutralize my South African selves when sitting with my American patients because I unconsciously endorsed the idea that the correct way to be their analyst was the American way.

One of the influences on an analyst's theories about her praxis is her personal experiences with her own analyst (Slochower, 2010). As I was writing this paper, I realized that my experiences with my first analyst, Masud Khan, himself an immigrant, were another factor that predisposed me to downplay my "foreign exoticism." I consulted Khan in London when I was 26 and anxious about moving from London to New York for graduate school.

Khan, who was born in Pakistan, deliberately accentuated his "foreignness" and dramatized his exoticism. For example, he told me proudly that the blanket on his analytic couch was woven by Persian virgins in the fourteenth century. Khan purveyed his own version of "orientalism" (Said, 1978) and exploited the British penchant for the exotic, producing himself as the brilliant, mysterious, "oriental" analyst in the purple cape. Initially, I was fascinated by Khan's tales from the Arabian nights, but I rapidly began to despise how he exploited and magnified his exoticism. (I was fortunate that my exposure to Khan was very brief. I learned later that he had seriously damaged some of his other patients and that he was guilty of various kinds of malpractice; see Cooper, 1993; Godley, 2001; Hopkins, 2006). My experiences with Khan impacted my praxis: I also tried take a "culture neutral" stance with my American patients, to downplay my foreign exotic facets, in order to seem as ordinary as possible and avoid being like him.

Despite my best efforts to fashion two analytic selves, the one "culture neutral" for my American patients, the other bursting with "foreign" color, my selves did not fall into a neat binary of "wanna be American" versus "outsider." My foreign selves kept popping out of their straight jacket in analytic sessions with my North American patients. And because mind is organized in a multiplicitous fashion, neither my "foreign" nor my "American" self was a single coherent entity; each was made up of a host of different facets. If we theorize that "double consciousness" shapes immigrant subjectivity and predisposes immigrants to set up a binary of foreign "outsider" selves versus "insider" new country selves, then how can our theory also accommodate such immigrant multiplicity?

All immigrants in North America are faced with the specter of "double consciousness," but the array of particular selves, which each immigrant has in her closet, varies. What accounts for this, and what enables some immigrants to develop a more multiplicitous bi-cultural self while others have a self that is largely fractured and shadowed by "double consciousness"? I believe that the degree to which "double consciousness" is deleterious for an individual immigrant depends in large part on the degree to which she is interpellated as the "inferior other," on how much she is subjected to prejudice by her host country. All immigrants in North America are interpellated as the "other," but because there is a hierarchy of "otherness" in the culture based on class, race, religion, sexual orientation, and language, the content and severity of the interpellations will vary, as will the toxicity of the person's "double consciousness" and the degree to which it pervades her sense of self. A poor immigrant to North America who was not "White" and spoke very little English, who was relentlessly interpellated as the "second class other" would be particularly likely to see herself negatively. She might try to protect her self-esteem and avoid her toxic "double consciousness" by dissociating her "foreign" selves as "not-me" and defining only a narrow band of "American" self states as acceptable, as "me." A different immigrant might have less searing "double consciousness" and judge herself less negatively because her type of "otherness" was viewed more positively by the culture. This immigrant might sort her selves quite differently, keeping most of her self states under the umbrella of "me-ness," no matter her country of origin.

We can think about the immigrant's set of selves as a deck of cards, which can be sorted in variety of ways, where the red cards in the deck signify her "foreign" made selves and the black cards represent her selves that developed in America. If the immigrant felt that at least some of her "foreign" self cards were seen as valuable by her host country, she would use them flexibly and integrate them with her made in America cards. If she felt her "foreign" cards were devalued in her new country she would adopt a binary solution where she tried to escape her "double consciousness" by denying or dissociating her "foreign" selves and highlighting her American selves.

In order to understand and deconstruct immigrant subjectivity and the impact of "double consciousness" we need to understand the way in which the mainstream culture of a particular host country mirrors and evaluates each individual immigrant's "otherness." How an immigrant is interpellated, how her particular "otherness" is graded by her host country, will determine the content and intensity of her "double consciousness" as well as the degree to which she sees herself positively and how freely she can "stand in the spaces" and experience and express her multiplicity. Individual factors that give the immigrant a sense of belonging such as clan, class, linguistic group, and religion, as well as her particular capacity for resilience (see Hollander, 2006) can somewhat mitigate but not erase these cultural messages. If we could imagine a theoretical host country that genuinely welcomed its immigrants' "foreign otherness" and believed that "otherness" was as vital and important an addition to their culture as salt and spices are in cooking, then, in this imaginary realm, immigrants would not struggle with the effects of "double consciousness." Instead they would revel in a panoply of selves of all makes, shapes, and sizes, some grown at home and some grown in their host country, all mixed up in a glorious multicultural, multihued, hybrid "me-ness."

As North America is definitely not yet such a nirvana, an important therapeutic question is how the negative impact of "double consciousness" can be mitigated or "treated." "Double consciousness" often operates subliminally: The immigrant's self-esteem is eroded, and she feels second class but is not aware of why this is occurring. First, the immigrant needs to become consciously aware of her "double consciousness," and she needs to understand that her self-devaluation is rooted in cultural factors. This would make it possible for her to begin the process Butler (1997) terms "resignification," where a person breaks beyond interpellation by reinterpreting and redefining the social category (in this case the category immigrant/alien) to which she is assigned (see Dimen, 2011; Harris, 2009; Lobban, 2011b).

As I worked on this paper and unearthed why I tried to create a binary—two analyst selves, a made in South Africa self for "outsiders" and a neutralized, assimilated version for Americans—I gradually resignified the category "immigrant analyst" for myself. The binary began to dissolve, and my analytic self deepened and became more overtly multicultural. Now I define myself as a "South African-American" analyst and I have a variety of self-facets under my umbrella of "me-ness." To go back to the pack of cards analogy: I can sort my cards creatively and use foreign and American-made self-facets flexibly with all of my patients, irrespective of their nationality. I now also consciously embrace certain South African cultural beliefs such as *ubuntu* (see Suchet, 2007) and understand how these animate my clinical praxis.

It was my work with patients that particularly helped me to understand the complexity of my experience as an immigrant analyst and the legacy of my "double consciousness." I will describe my relationships with two patients and how these shed light on my immigrant analyst identity. My unconscious self-definition as the "outsider" resulted in an enactment that was difficult to unpack in my work with Rachel, an American patient, whom I defined as the "insider." David, a French immigrant, and I developed a relationship that was the mirror image of my relationship with Rachel. We basked in our "outsider" twin-ship as political activists, until our unacknowledged differences tripped us up. In both of these cases, my patient and I came to a deeper, more layered, and multiplicitous sense of "me-ness" once the enactments were unpacked.

Rachel

Rachel and I have been working together for about four years. She is a math teacher in a New York private high school and is smart, attractive, warm, generous, and open minded. Rachel was raised in New Jersey in a conventional, middle class Jewish family. She is one of my most unabashedly "American" patients; a fourth-generation American whose only "foreign" exposure is a few brief Caribbean vacations. Rachel seemed comfortable with my "foreign" origins, although she was not specifically looking for an immigrant analyst.

During our first year of working together Rachel shared a lot of intimate details of her life. She felt close to me and grateful for our relationship. I found her very likeable, but I felt shut out, as if she had put up a glass wall between us. Our relationship felt oddly formal, as if we were doing synchronized swimming together, and it lacked depth. Rachel's modus operandi was to try to be "good" and to dissociate "bad" feelings in order to ensure that other people loved her. She worried constantly about others and their needs. I did not explicitly point this pattern out to Rachel; I just waited for bits of her own lived experience to surface, and I named her feelings when they did pop up. Gradually Rachel became more interested in what she was experiencing. After she noticed the one-sided nature of her relationship with her egotistical White American fiancée, Rachel's frustration and anger at him gradually percolated to the surface, and she ended their engagement.

A year after her breakup, Rachel fell passionately in love with Juan, a very successful computer software designer. His family left the Dominican Republic and came to New York when Juan was 12 years old, but they still referred to it as "home." Rachel experienced Juan as warm, loving, and caring, but she feared that the relationship could not survive. Rachel said: "My parents will go crazy because he's not Jewish and he's a Catholic Latino from the Dominican Republic. My mother will worry that he will make me move there. And him speaking Spanish will be a problem." After an initial honeymoon period, Rachel and Juan got into frequent arguments whenever their two cultures collided. Rachel complained that Juan spoke only Spanish at family events, and she was left her out. She gradually became less committed to being bi-cultural. She told me: "His family should just all speak English, after all they are in an English speaking country."

It was challenging for me to listen to Rachel's negative remarks about "foreigners" and remain neutral. My "double consciousness" radar was being activated, although I had not yet labeled it as such. I found myself identifying with Juan, the immigrant, and his need to withdraw to a separate Dominican Spanish sphere, to salve the wounds he experienced when he was judged by mainstream America. I felt protective of him because he was the "outsider," the "foreigner." I did something I had never done before; I appointed myself Rachel's cultural consultant/couple's therapist, and I tried to explain to her why she should not take all of Juan's actions personally.

Six months after she met Juan, Rachel was distraught about what had happened at Juan's birthday party. "It was Spanish, all Spanish, all over again," she said tearfully. "From the time we arrived Juan spoke Spanish and never once translated for me or tried to include me. He wants me to stand by his side all night, silent and bewildered. I felt like I did not exist, as if I was something he owned, like the watch on his arm." As I listened to Rachel it suddenly dawned on me that she had legitimate complaints about Juan. In my haste to identify with Juan, I had been blind to his enactments, to his tendency to render Rachel, the white American, "foreign," to make her feel like the outsider. I was so fixated on finding a hybrid solution for Rachel and Juan that I could not see how stuck they were in their "doer-done to" pattern (Benjamin, 2004). Once the penny had dropped, I explained to Rachel how my "foreigner" status had blinded me to the ways in which Juan's needs for special treatment and attention had contributed to their problems. Rachel was enormously relieved to hear that she had legitimate reasons for complaint. She was not angry with me for failing to see her perspective, which did not surprise me, given her tendency to disavow or dissociate negative feelings.

Rachel and Juan had needs that were the opposite sides of the same coin, and these kept tripping them up and causing misunderstandings. They could not step out of their particular positions, which were shaped by cultural and familial patterns. Rachel was an American insider, but she actually felt like an outsider within her family. She had always felt shut out by her mother and unable to get her to focus on her needs. Every time Juan spoke Spanish exclusively to his friends and family, Rachel's sense of being excluded was reactivated, and she felt desperately lonely. The cultural roots of Juan's reactions to Rachel were very clear. He felt excluded by mainstream American culture because he was from the Dominican Republic and did not speak perfect English. He heard Rachel's protests about his speaking Spanish as an injunction from the majority culture to speak in English. She was asking: "Let me in." He heard her yelling: "No Spanish allowed here." Juan wanted to show Rachel his foreign selves so she could know more of him, but Rachel felt dismissed at the occasions spent with his Spanish-speaking family, and assumed that Juan wanted to shut her out, that his real intimacy was reserved for his family. Similarly, when Rachel invited him into her world and urged him to spend more time with her family, Juan felt that she was saying that his world, his culture, was not good enough and should be shunned.

Things did not really improve with Juan and Rachel. She ended their relationship one night after she felt particularly betrayed and shut out by him. She felt relieved and heartbroken. The next day she had a nightmare that terrified her: "I was on a beach in Brazil with Josh my ex, but then he was Juan. Someone yelled and we looked up and a huge tsunami was coming towards us and everyone ran. We climbed these metal stairs that went up high, to nowhere in particular. They were three stories high and just sitting on the beach. The water passed under us and we were safe, but then Juan disappeared. I realized that I was locked into the beach area by a barbed wire fence, and someone was after me. There was a little opening in the barbed wire, so I climbed over the fence and escaped into this really poor favela neighborhood. A Black man told me he would help me hide me from the person who was after me. He locked me into a closet in his office and said he would return at 2 p.m. the next day to get me. I trusted him, trusted that he would return and let me out, and help me to safety, and protect me."

Rachel commented that the dream was "very dramatic and exotic, not my usual kind of dream." She felt that the tsunami was "my feelings for Juan, that threatened me and stirred me up and I only just survived." Being alone in that foreign place made her feel "unprotected, unrecognized, unimportant, so afraid." The staircase was "safe temporarily, but it went nowhere, like my attempts to get Juan to really love me and not criticize me like my mother does. I didn't see the person who was after me; I just knew they would attack me." Her rescuer was "not Brazilian, maybe some kind of African." When I pointed out that I was some kind of African, and we had a 2 p.m. therapy appointment she laughed saying, "I guess it's you; I notice your 'English' accent, but I never see you as 'foreign' or 'African'; I just think of you as 'different' like I am 'different' from my parents." Through her dream Rachel shared a set of feelings she had tried to exile; her painful loneliness, her battle to tame her critical self, and her abiding longing for recognition. Apparently she was now prepared to risk the ensuing tsunami of feelings if she brought these self states back from exile.

I believe that the turning point for Rachel in this treatment came when I acknowledged to her that I had over-identified with Juan, which blinded me to her perspective. Before, Rachel always judged herself according to her mother's criteria and she kept finding herself wanting. When she finally felt seen and recognized by me, this helped her to register and solidify her own perspective, to begin to use her own criteria to judge herself. She could then allow some "not-me" states to become "me" and embrace some "different" dissociated facets of herself.

It was salutary for me when I bumped up against my identification with the pain Rachel's "foreign" boyfriend felt when he saw himself through a "second class," "outsider" lens. I was forced to see that I too had donned made in America spectacles that distorted my view of myself, that I also suffered from "double consciousness." Once I had processed these feelings I stopped trying to keep my pile of "South African" selves rigidly separated from my "American" selves, and my sense of "me-ness" expanded. I began my work with David while I was just beginning my process of resignification.

David

David is an intense, intelligent, 38-year-old French Jew who moved to the United States with his parents and two younger sisters when he was 22 and enrolled in a Master's program in political science. By the time we met, David was an investment banker. David's social world was very French-focused, cushioned from America. He interacted mainly with other upper-middle-class French people who lived in New York, spoke French, and identified themselves as Europeans. His voice mail message was only in French, and he read French newspapers daily. "It is so interesting to have a foreign therapist; I know we will be an excellent match," said David. "My previous therapist was an American, and she was never really interested in my life in France; she focused more on my problems adapting to my graduate program here." I was genuinely interested in David's life in France and his immigrant experiences. In addition, I felt a particular affinity for David because, like me, he was political and "left wing." This sense of affinity grew as the treatment progressed and turned out to be a double-edged sword, as will become evident.

David's father was a very successful art dealer in France who decided to move his family to the United States 16 years ago in order to expand his business. The move was stressful for David and for his sisters, but they all tried valiantly to adapt and did not complain to their parents. Initially, David's father's business prospered and the family lived luxuriously. About four years ago, David's father's business failed because he made some impulsive investments. The father retreated into a state of high anxiety and depression, and David's idealization of him crumbled. We explored David's relationship with his father and his intense feelings of rage, protectiveness, and disappointment. David had chosen investment banking as a career because he unthinkingly adopted his parents' aspirations for material wealth, but he hated his job. Six months into treatment, David suddenly decided to quit his job, live on savings, and volunteer as an organizer for Barack Obama's presidential campaign saying: "I was blind to my own wishes and needs for too long; I must honor them now."

His exposure to the Obama campaign made David more interested in issues of race and inequality in the United States. In France, David's upper-middle-class privileged status had shielded him from direct contact with the less privileged. His work with the Obama campaign stimulated David's interest in political activism, which in turn led him to become curious about my experiences in South Africa during Apartheid. Because I know that I would not enter treatment with a South African analyst unless I knew that she had actively opposed Apartheid, I feel that my patients are entitled to answers to their questions about my position on Apartheid. These questions are asked rarely, and once I answer, the topic of South Africa generally fades into the background. In David's case his interest in my politics persisted, and we developed an ongoing dialogue about exile, homeland, and immigrants' nostalgia. David joined an activist political group that opposed inequality, and he shared his excitement about his experiences with me. David reminded me of my younger activist self; I began to feel a sense of emotional kinship with him as he grappled to define his political self, even though I knew intellectually that we were very different in class, religion, and nationality.

I take the position (Lobban, 2011d) that analysts should treat political content as something valid in its own right and not see it as merely symbolic, a metaphor for personal conflicts. (A similar position is taken by Dimen, 2004a, 2004b; Geffner, 2004; Harris, 2009; Jacobs, 2004; Layton, 2006; Samuels, 2004; Walls, 2004.) When David expressed his excitement about his experiences on the Obama campaign trail, I assumed that he was exploring genuine questions about how a society or culture changes, as well as questions about how he could change himself. Our exchanges about politics were compelling because David and I validated each other's political identity. I was not consciously aware of how much they also served to minister to some of my wounds derived from "double consciousness" or even that these wounds were smarting. Mainstream culture in North America frowns upon and sidelines the left wing activities of "real" Americans (Layton, 2006), so being a left wing immigrant is even more socially invisible. When I described how and why I fought Apartheid to American friends, in an attempt to show them my political self, I often experienced disapproval or disinterest. David's avid interest in my activism in South Africa brought my political self back to life and it made me feel not only that he and I were connected, but also that we were very similar.

At this point in the treatment, an event occurred that pierced this veneer of similarity and forced me to acknowledge our differences and David's "double consciousness" wounds. David's sister, who lived in San Francisco, had a very serious episode of major depression. Her friend called David and his parents to tell them about the hospitalization. Immediately, David took on the whole burden of his sister's illness. He flew to California, met with her psychiatrist, and got her to agree to remain in the hospital. Meanwhile his parents, who adore their daughter, waited in the wings in New York. I was mystified by David's family's response to this crisis. This forced me to see that David and I came from very different cultures, despite the fact that we were both immigrants and political. In my White, English-South African family, the burden of care would have rested firmly on my parents' shoulders, and we would all have believed that they bore responsibility for digesting their children's pain. When I asked David why his parents did not fly out to San Francisco, he explained: "That is my job. My role in my family is to keep everything smooth at home, to protect my parents from stress and pain."

I asked David why he had the job of protecting his parents, how he got it, and whether it had occurred to him that there were other ways to organize the roles in a family. David's parents were second generation Holocaust survivors, and David came to realize that their trauma had impacted their parenting style and was implicated in why they allowed/expected him to parent them. He said: "From the time I was a very young child in Paris I tuned into my parents' moods and knew that they both felt deep pain that could not be spoken. I felt their fragility, and I knew it was always my duty to protect them." Like so many French Jews, David's family had sustained major losses during the Holocaust. His grandparents on both sides escaped from Paris just before Hitler invaded France and waited the war out in England and Switzerland. They returned to Paris in the late '40s. Many of their relatives in France and Europe perished at the hands of the Germans. David's parents were both born in Paris shortly after the war. They met in 1968 when they were students at the Sorbonne and bonded because of their similar family histories of loss, exile, and survival. David's parents and grandparents never discussed how they felt about these Holocaust traumas. David, the third generation survivor, took on and digested the intergenerational pain for his family (see Guralnik, 2011). He tried to fix his parents and care for them, but he did not consciously connect their "fragility" to the Holocaust trauma they had suffered. Once this became clearer to David he also accessed some of his dissociated anger about being what he termed "the perpetual caretaker." David was able to tell his parents that he was angry that they had given him responsibility for his sister's care and that he was handing her case back to them.

Once David had explored his rage at being designated the perpetual caretaker he was able to identify other ways in which he had protected his parents. He realized that he tried to conceal his feelings about incidents when he was "othered" by mainstream American culture. David recalled his feelings of shame and humiliation when he first arrived in New York and a salesman in a store made him repeat his request for a particular item numerous times and complained that he could not understand David's accent. David explained: "We were supposed to be happy and love it here, no problems, so how could I upset my parents and tell them, or even admit to myself, that the American students at my graduate school treated me as second class? I wanted to stand by my father. He needed our move the United States to be seamless." David, the dutiful son, had to become the successful and well liked immigrant who effortlessly adjusted to America, so he dissociated his longings for France, and the painful self-doubt engendered by his immigrant "double consciousness."

David's "double consciousness" began to percolate up into consciousness as his need to protect his parents dissipated. One day he arrived at his session totally distraught and furious. He was first in line for a job at a local non-profit organization, but they decided to hire their second choice, an American, to avoid having to apply for a work visa for David. "I felt like an outsider in America. I guess these kinds of things happened to me often in the past, but I denied they were happening," said David. He was interpellated as a "foreigner," and he then experienced himself through that lens, as imperfect, insufficient, less desirable than an American. "I was just not good enough, I guess; it made me feel second class. I think they actually did prefer the American guy; they felt he would fit in better with the agency's clients than I would with my accent."

Unlike David's parents, I was willing to acknowledge that immigration is a difficult business, and this helped him to access and process his own stressful experiences as an immigrant. Once he could forgive himself for failing to assimilate perfectly, his self-confidence improved, and he began to come out from the within the walls of his French enclave and interact more with Americans and America.

In these two cases, both my patient and I experienced a change, an expansion in our sense of personal identity as the treatment progressed. In the case of Rachel, my American patient, my "double consciousness" impaired my ability to function effectively as her analyst. When I registered that I was over-identified with her boyfriend, I could begin searching for an explanation and my behavior changed. This also enabled Rachel and me to move to a different register. She felt recognized, her sense of self-esteem and pride in herself expanded and she focused less on pleasing others to gain their acceptance. In the second case, David, my French patient, and I shared our journeys as "political" immigrants in the treatment and were initially cushioned by our "twin-ship." Later, when David's sister became depressed, we discovered that though we were both "foreign" we were very different. Once I acknowledged our differences I could register my own and David's "double consciousness" wounds and help David move towards resignification. Ironically, when we confronted our cultural differences we were able to see a new similarity, that both of us had tried to deny or downplay our "double consciousness" and our shame at being "othered."

These cases show that "double consciousness" casts its shadow on immigrant subjectivity in North America. Mainstream culture sees the immigrant through a negative prism as "less than" a White American, and immigrants use that same prism to view themselves. On a more positive note, these cases demonstrate that the effects of "double consciousness" can be mitigated. Resignification is possible once the immigrant becomes aware of his or her "double consciousness" and processes the negative feelings associated with it, and this yields a less binary, more multiplicitous sense of me-ness.

One could argue that all analysts are metaphorical immigrants. We are all legal aliens journeying into our patient's private territory with the green card she issued. An immigrant analyst should not assume that the fact that she and her "foreign" patients are all immigrants exempts her from bringing her travel papers to their sessions or guarantees identity between her experiences and those of her immigrant patients and ensures that she can speak their languages. Similarly, an American analyst should not assume that she needs no green card for her American patients, that their culture is an open book to her, because she might then be blind to variations of class, region, ethnicity, gender, and religion. All analysts of immigrants, and all immigrant analysts, should pack a strong set of binoculars in their luggage and be on the lookout for sightings of "double consciousness" in themselves and their patients as their journey unfolds, and American analysts should keep a careful eye on the ways in which they buy into the "America is best" message and hold that mirror up to their immigrant patients.

I hope that this paper has shown that our selves don't fall into any neat binaries of nationality and our experiences of, and responses to, "otherness" are extremely variable. Because all patients are multifaceted and multiplicitous, one cannot make any assumptions about the mix of nationality or cultural background that will yield a productive therapeutic alliance between a particular analyst and patient. All we analysts can do is tread lightly in our patients' private territory and try to register our assumptions about them, ourselves, their culture, and our culture. We can then attempt to learn the particular languages spoken in our patients' domains and collaborate with them to develop a lingua franca.

References

Akhtar, S. (1998). *Immigration and identity: Turmoil, treatment and transformation.* New York, NY: Aronson.

Akhtar, S. (2009). Friendship, socialization and the immigrant experience. *Psychoanalysis, Culture and Society,* 14: 253–272.

Alavez, J.L. (2010). Cancion Mixteca. *New York Times* Editorial, "San Patricio," March 17.

Benjamin, J. (2004). Beyond doer and done-to: An intersubjective view of thirdness. *Psychoanalytic Quarterly,* 63: 5–46.

Bergner, G. (1998). Myths of masculinity: The Oedipus complex and Douglass's 1845 narrative. In C. Lane (Ed.), *The psychoanalysis of race.* New York, NY: Columbia University Press, pp. 241–260.

Bhabha, H.K. (1994). *The location of culture.* London: Routledge.

Bodnar, S. (2004). Remembering where you come from: Dissociative process in multicultural individuals. *Psychoanalytic Dialogues,* 14: 581–603.

Boulanger, G. (2004). Lot's wife, Cary Grant and the American dream: Psychoanalysis with immigrants. *Contemporary Psychoanalysis,* 40: 353–372.

Bromberg, P. (1998). *Standing in the spaces: Essays on clinical process, trauma and dissociation.* Hillsdale, NJ: The Analytic Press.

Bushra, A. (2009). The strangeness of passing: Commentary on paper by Christopher Bonowitz. *Psychoanalytic Dialogues,* 19: 442–449.

Butler, J. (1997). *The psychic life of power: Theories in subjection.* Stanford, CA: Stanford University Press.

Cisneros, S. (2009). *The house on Mango Street.* New York, NY: Vintage Books (Original work published in 1984).

Cooper, J. (1993). *Speak of me as I am: The life and work of Masud Khan.* London: Karnac Books.

Desai, K. (2006). *Inheritance of loss.* New York, NY: Grove Press.

Diaz, J. (2007). *The brief wondrous life of Oscar Wao.* New York, NY: Penguin Books.

Dimen, M. (2004a). The return of the dissociated: Discussion. *Psychoanalytic Dialogues,* 14: 859–865.

Dimen, M. (2004b). Something's gone missing. *Psychoanalytic Perspectives,* 2: 57–64.

Dimen, M. (2011). Introduction. In M. Dimen (Ed.), *With culture in mind: Psychoanalytic stories.* London: Routledge, pp. 1–7.

Du Bois, W.E.B. (1994). *The souls of Black folk.* New York NY: Dover Publications, Inc. (Original work published in 1903).

Eng, D.L. & Han, S. (2000). A dialogue on racial melancholia. *Psychoanalytic Dialogues,* 10: 667–700.

Falicov, C.J. (2003). Immigrant family processes. In F. Walsh (Ed.), *Normal Family Processes,* 3rd Edition, *Growing Diversity and Complexity.* New York, NY: Guildford Press, pp. 280–300.

Geffner, A. (2004). Political identity: A personal postscript. *Psychoanalytic Perspectives,* 2: 65–73.

Gilroy, P. (1993). *The Black Atlantic.* Cambridge, MA: Harvard University Press.

Godley, W. (2001). Saving Masud Khan. *London Review of Books,* 23: 3–7.

Grinberg, L. & Grinberg, R. (1989). *Psychoanalytic perspectives on migration in exile*. New Haven, CT: Yale University Press.

Guralnik, O. (2011). *The dead baby*. Paper presented at T.R.I.S.P. Conference, New York, NY.

Hamid, M. (2007). *The reluctant fundamentalist*. New York, NY: Houghton Mifflin Harcourt.

Harlem, A. (2009). Thinking through others: Cultural psychology and the psychoanalytic treatment of immigrants. *Psychoanalysis, Culture and Society*, 14: 273–288.

Harris, A. (2007). The house of difference: Enactment, a play in three scenes. In M. Suchet, A. Harris & L. Aron (Ed.), *Relational Psychoanalysis. Volume 3: New Voices*. Mahwah, NJ: pp. 81–95.

Harris, A. (2009). The socio-political recruitment of identities. *Psychoanalytic Dialogues*, 19: 138–147.

Harris, A. (2012). The house of difference, or white silence. *Studies in Gender and Sexuality*, 13: 197–216.

Hartman, S. (2007). Class unconscious: From dialectical materialism to relational material. In M. Suchet, A. Harris & L. Aron (Eds.), *Relational Psychoanalysis, Volume3: New Voices*. Mahwah, NJ: pp. 209–225.

Hoffman, E. (1989). *Lost in Translation: A Life in a New Language*. New York, NY: Penguin Books.

Hollander, N. (2006). Negotiating trauma and loss in the migration experience. *Studies in Gender and Sexuality*, 7: 61–70.

Hopkins, L. (2006). *False self: The life of Masud Khan*. New York, NY: Other Press.

Jacobs, T. (2004). Roundtable discussion: Is politics the last taboo in psychoanalysis? *Psychoanalytic Perspectives*, 2: 5–37.

Lahiri, J. (1999). *The Interpreter of Maladies*. Boston, MA: Houghton Mifflin.

Layton, L. (2004). Dreams of America/American dreams. *Psychoanalytic Dialogues*, 14: 233–254.

Layton, L. (2006). Attacks on linking: The unconscious pull to dissociate individuals from their social context. In L. Layton, N.C. Hollander, & S. Gutwill (Eds.), *Psychoanalysis, Class and Politics: Encounters in the Clinical Setting*. New York, NY: Routledge, pp. 107–117.

Lazarus, E. (1883). The new colossus. Retrieved from http://en.wikipedia.org/wiki/The New Collossus.

Leary, K. (2007). On the face of it—difference and sameness in psychoanalysis. *Contemporary Psychoanalysis*, 43: 469–473.

Lobban, G. (2006). Immigration and dissociation. *Psychoanalytic Perspectives*, 3: 73–91.

Lobban, G. (2011a). Wounded by war. In M. Dimen (Ed.), *With Culture in Mind: Psychoanalytic Stories*. London: Routledge, pp. 25–30.

Lobban, G. (2011b). White or not. In M. Dimen (Ed.), *With Culture in Mind: Psychoanalytic Stories*. London: Routledge, pp. 81–86.

Lobban, G. (2011c). Resignification road. In M. Dimen (Ed.), *With Culture in Mind: Psychoanalytic Stories*. London: Routledge, pp. 155–161.

Lobban, G. (2011d). Political interpretations and political passion. Paper presented at IARPP Conference, Madrid, Spain.

Lobban, G. (2012). Troubling whiteness: Commentary on Harris's "The house of difference." *Studies in Gender and Sexuality*, 13: 224–230.

O'Neill, J. (2008). *Netherland*. New York, NY: Random House.

Perez Foster, R. (1996). The bilingual self. *Psychoanalytic Dialogues*, 6: 99–121.

Perez Foster, R. (1998). *The Power of Language in the Clinical Process: Assessing and Treating the Bilingual Person*. Northvale, NJ: Jason-Aronson.

Pugachevsky, O. (2011). Forbidden to be. In M. Dimen (Ed.), *With Culture in Mind: Psychoanalytic Stories*. London: Routledge, pp. 149–154.

Rozmarin, E. (2009). Living in difference: A commentary on Annie Stopford's "Leaving Home." *Contemporary Psychoanalysis*, 45: 467–479.

Rozmarin, E. (2011). Dori: Oh thy seer go fly thee. In M. Dimen (Ed.), *With Culture in Mind: Psychoanalytic Stories*. London: Routledge, pp. 35–40.

Said, E.W. (1978). *Orientalism*. New York, NY: Random House.

Samuels, A. (2004). Politics on the couch? Psychotherapy and society—some possibilities and some limitations. *Psychoanalytic Dialogues*, 14: 817–834.

Slochower, J. (2010). Our theories, our selves: Commentary on paper by Ruth Gruenthal. *Psychoanalytic Dialogues*, 20: 78–83.

Straker, G. (2004). Race for cover: Castrated whiteness, perverse consequences. *Psychoanalytic Dialogues*, 14: 405–422.

Straker, G. (2007). A crisis in the subjectivity of the analyst: The trauma of morality. *Psychoanalytic Dialogues*, 17: 153–164.

Suchet, M. (2004). A relational encounter with race. *Psychoanalytic Dialogues*, 14: 423–438.

Suchet, M. (2007). Unraveling whiteness. *Psychoanalytic Dialogues*, 17: 867–886.

Suchet, M. (2010). Face to Face. *Psychoanalytic Dialogues*, 20: 158–171.

Walls, G. (2004). Toward a critical global psychoanalysis. *Psychoanalytic Dialogues*, 14: 605–634.

Otherness in Immigration

Chapter 5

Seeking Home in the Foreign
Otherness and Immigration

Julia Beltsiou, PsyD

This is where our story begins: An immigrant patient reaches out to an immigrant analyst, and the two meet in the uncharted land of psychoanalysis. Exploring, mapping, creating a place for us. As we encounter each other, we move back and forth between our countries of origin and our chosen home, back and forth between past and present.

Entering psychoanalysis and moving to a foreign place have in common that we imagine the world we enter, but we do not know what we will encounter. We move into the foreign in order to discover the foreign in us. We cannot know who we will become, but we know that we want to feel something true and authentic. We play the role of analysand or immigrant in order to become (Baranger, 1993). I argue for a complex, multidimensional understanding of the subjectivity of immigration. I lay out how issues of longing, ambiguous belonging, and outsiderness play out between my patient and me, complicating notions of both immigration and psychoanalysis.

Reading Each Other: Intelligibility

"Hi Julia; this is Sam. I am interested in starting psychoanalytic psychotherapy. I was wondering if you are available for a consultation?" Sam seems to know the land of psychoanalysis. He sounds smart and casually friendly, and I feel curious and drawn in as I listen to my voicemail. I sense that I would enjoy working with him. I cannot place his accent: India? His area code is from a nearby university town. He has a British first and last name, which—thanks to British colonial history—leaves many possibilities open as far as his nationality is concerned. As I listen to Sam's voice, I am trying to find him and make him recognizable to me. Where is home for Sam?

From our first moment of contact, questions of belonging, similarity, and otherness are part of our mix. "Who is this person?" we commonly wonder when we first encounter a new patient. For the immigrant analyst (and patient) there is an extra layer of trying to find each other through the social signifiers we grew up with, as we meet in the liminal space of cultural meaning-making of a third place we both moved to. Immigration teaches us that the construction of self is culturally mediated, always fluid and indeterminate.

Forever foreigners, we are—and at the same time are not—equipped to read and communicate social cues. The differences between ourselves and others create ambiguity, which in turn promotes vigilance in our interactions. We inhabit a place of actual and psychic tension between un-belonging and belonging, as well as recognition, invisibility, and stigma (Goffman, 1963).

There are many ways to think about the experience of immigration. One vantage point is to think about the challenge of cultural intelligibility. The social and political vectors of gender, race, and class influence how others see us and ultimately how we experience ourselves. In Butler's words (2005), we need to be recognized as viable subjects. If who we are does not conform to cultural norms that make us acceptable to others, we are rendered illegible, illegitimate, and unreal and ultimately do not matter. We bring with us our histories of recognition, mis-recognition, and non-recognition in our places of origin. As immigrants we face anew the question of what others perceive when they encounter us. Migration and psychoanalysis have in common that they hold the excitement and vulnerability of our desire to be seen and to be known.

In my first meeting with Sam, I encounter a lanky and congenial man of color who grew up on one of the British Caribbean islands. He wears dark-rimmed glasses and is a postdoctoral fellow at a university. As I listen to Sam, I notice the ways he has thrived and has substantial strength. Sam is engaged in his field of study and is well credentialed from prestigious educational institutions; he has worked his way into a position of cultural capital (Bourdieu, 2001) by obtaining a doctorate.

Sam is processing the break-up of his first marriage. He was recently divorced from his wife, with whom he grew up. This adds to his feeling of being unsettled, and he feels unsure of his place in the world. Sam has come to therapy to sort out questions of belonging. He is anxious and ashamed that in his mid-thirties, his life is not more "in place": His position at the university is temporary, and so is his work visa, making his immigration status and professional future in the US uncertain. He wonders what kind of place he can make for himself in the world. Our work begins: writing the story of Sam's migration.

Blind Spots and Bright Spots

In her paper "Bright spot," a variant of "Blind spot." (1993), Marianne Goldberger looks at moments in our work as analysts when we feel we "know exactly what our patient is talking about" or conversely cannot see an aspect of our patients' experience at all. Goldberger examines these moments of over-identification, "bright spots" and "blind spots," both of which lead to not being able to see something our patient is trying to let us know about. There are bright spots of connection between Sam and me. We are the same age, so we share the context of being members of the same generation. We both left our home countries, as young adults with a vague sense of un-belonging, to study in the US. Here, we felt a greater degree of freedom and possibilities to grow and embarked on the difficult process of making a life and home in a foreign country. The people we met and teachers we learned from during our studies in the States have informed our interests and ideas about life. We have worked hard to obtain doctorates in the US educational system, which has offered us professional recognition and a sense of belonging in an academic community. Last and not least, having been trained to think about ourselves, and the world, in a questioning manner has offered us a particular way to find anchoring inside.

Sam had a protected and devoutly Christian middle-class upbringing in a family of predominantly ethnic Indians in his home country. We share the doublings of multiple moves and interminglings: my experience as a Greek national in Germany, his Indian ancestry in the Caribbean. His mother, born in another country, cooked foreign food at home. In Germany, my mother introduced me to a mix of Mediterranean cuisine and her newfound delight in the crunchy northern European organic food culture. We both have felt out of place where we came from, and also—in different ways—in the places we moved to. We both have worked hard to prove our value in the eyes of others, to fit in, and to seek a place where we can feel ourselves.

As to our differences, I find myself "leaning in" to grasp the intricacies of Sam's experience. Our differences as immigrants are an important and complex part of our work, which I will explore shortly. I grew up in Germany, in a provincial yet progressive university town, as the daughter of a recent immigrant Greek mother, who raised me mostly by herself. While Sam had a middle-class upbringing in a poor, economically unstable country, I grew up struggling financially in a prosperous and highly industrialized country. In the same way that I moved to the US on a student visa, my mother came to Germany to study at the university and to develop as a person in a cultural environment that offered women a much greater degree of freedom than she could have ever known in the Greek mountain village she grew up in. This parallel process between my mother's choice to come to Germany and my choice to immigrate to the US is both meaningful and not uncommon amongst children of immigrants. Immigrant families often carry intergenerational patterns of migration. My mother gave me a sense of the power and potential of moving to another country.

My Outsiderness/Sam's Outsiderness

Our respective racial and ethnic experiences in our countries of origin are discrepant from how we are seen and experience ourselves in the US. Race and culture have different connotations and must be reconfigured after our migrations. In my case, migration offered relief from my experiences of stigma: Coming to the US in the early nineties, with white skin and equipped with a student visa, with enough money to get by, and my European citizenship, I was welcomed and greeted mostly with an interest and acceptance that gave me a sense of possibility and hope.

For my dilemma of bi-culturality, I found it easier to fit in while living in liberal and multicultural cities like San Francisco and New York, than I did in Germany or Greece. I escaped the negative connotations of being what Germans call an *Ausländerkind*, or "foreign child," a term that connotes, from the perspective of the German insider, a perpetual outsider status. Growing up in Germany, I felt the tension of never quite belonging—a foreign last name was an important signifier that turned us into perpetual *Ausländer*.

As a teenager I felt simultaneous anger and shame about the ways that some people around me—neighbors, parents, and teachers—had limited expectations for me and did not seem to value who I was. I developed the sense that I had something to prove, and ultimately I chose to become a professional in a country—the USA—where being a white, Western European immigrant more often carries cachet than stigma, and where a foreign-sounding last name does not render you a foreigner. I encountered many teachers, mentors, and peers—some in Germany but mostly in the US—who saw "something" in me, taught and encouraged me.

Paradoxically, it was in the US that I could feel for the first time that who I am is irrevocably connected to German culture, even though my family of origin is decidedly Greek. For me, feeling myself to be German-Greek, but only "somewhat" German, has resulted in my feeling, and being seen as, connected to a complicated historical legacy, something I will speak to more at a later point.

Even though I was born in Germany, and absorbed German as my first language (I am not fluent in Greek), I still encountered a strong ideology of foreignness living in Germany. My experience of immigration highlights the ways in which different cultures can feel more or less permeable for an outsider. In addition to this, markers of outsiderness vary from culture to culture, e.g., having a Turkish last name carries more stigma in Germany than it does in the US. Skin color, however, is an obvious marker: otherness signified by race is not easily dissolved.

For Sam, outsiderness is an integral part of his experience. His ancestral trajectory bears the imprint of oppressor and oppressed: Several of Sam's ancestors came from colonized India as part of the Indian diaspora to the Caribbean island he grew up on, a place that bears its own particular history of slavery. Each move carries new meanings of race: He was regarded as lighter-skinned, which signified his higher social class. When Sam moved to the US, he joined the first world as a brown member of a developing country. Here, he is perceived as a black man, a signifier that colors his experience as he travels in predominantly white academic circles, but of course Sam does not identify with being perceived as African-American, or even black for that matter.

Sam came to the US for the first time at age 11 with his family, when they vacationed in Florida. It was on this trip that he was introduced for the first time to an experience intimately familiar to many people of color in the US. When his family went shopping at a Walmart, Sam temporarily lost sight of his parents. As he walked through the aisles looking for them, a shop worker grew suspicious and asked him to leave the store. Scared and alone, Sam waited outside the store, looking through a window for his parents, who eventually spotted him. Eleven-year-old Sam realized then that "being black means something different in America."

Sam's and my experiences of pre- and post-migration class, culture and race are multilayered and complicated. Understanding how this comes up between us is at the heart of our process: Two years into our work, Sam tells me, "I feel worried about the green-card interview," referring to his recent interracial marriage to his US-born, white wife. I had received my own employment-based green card less than a year earlier, after being on temporary student and conditional work visas for 15 years. Obtaining permanent residency in the US was a fretful, long, arduous, and often nonsensical process. My anxious hope in being permanently rewarded for following the rules surfaces in my reply to Sam: "Your relationship is legitimate; that will count for something." Sam laughs: "You have some faith in the state!" This is one of the moments in which Sam points out to me that my trust in fairness, based on my experiences (and anxieties), is something he is not given to share: "America is not a fair place!" he exclaims. His anxiety goes beyond the absurdities involved in getting a green card: The interview represents a moment where the legitimacy of his interracial relationship is at stake.

We encounter moments between us like this many times in our work. Sam tells me: "It matters that you are an immigrant, too. And that you share similar academic experiences. Education offers a common ground with my colleagues and with you. You do not share the experience of discrimination based on skin color. So, I feel understood by you, but just 99%." "That's a lot!" I respond with some surprise, laced with the unease that comes with privilege and the pain of inequality. "Tell me about the 1%?" "There is always a limit of feeling at home, even with you," Sam explains. In moments like this in our work, Sam faces the loneliness and alienation he feels at so many moments in his life. It is also a moment that captures how closeness and distance are constantly being negotiated in our relationship and how optimal closeness is an ongoing theme in Sam's life.

Sam's experience in percentages evokes the 99% vs. 1% symbolism coined by the Occupy Wall Street movement to critique inequality. We both know that there are things I have easier access to than he does. This is one of the many moments between us in which we are simultaneously linked and unlinked: We both have felt the dread of immigration problems and yet speak to each other across the gulf of difference based on our respective races, of what we can expect from others (i.e., America).

At the same time, these moments of felt asymmetry between us, such as his pointing out my "faith in the state," are the sites of growth in our psychoanalytic migration. In these moments of mutual vulnerability, Sam is able to speak from a place of separateness and point out that his experience is different from mine and that I cannot understand him/his position fully. Alongside my shame, I am determined to understand him. Amidst our differences, we have been able to create our own particular analytic third (Ogden, 1994). This third has enabled us to examine difference and alienation, stigma and recognition. Sam is able to hang in there with me, and he is able to move. Our analytic migration has moved into a new kind of home within belonging and unbelonging.

Immigration and Otherness

The late Iranian immigrant, novelist, and psychiatrist Taghi Modarressi (1992) had the following thoughts about otherness and immigration:

> *On the plane from Iran to the US, a strange idea kept occurring to me. I thought that most immigrants, regardless of the familial, social, or political circumstances causing their exile, have been cultural refugees all their lives. They leave because they feel like outsiders. Perhaps it is their personal language that can build a bridge between what is familiar and what is strange. They may then find it possible to generate new and revealing paradoxes.*

I feel it is no coincidence that this thought occurred to Modarressi while on an airplane, between places, leaving the past, moving into an unknown future. Up in the air we—the immigrants—inhabit a limbo that holds the truth that no place will ever feel like home again, at least not in an unquestioned way. We move through liminal spaces like airports and airplanes, hotels and waiting rooms. It is here where the boundary resides between you and me, where we stand in the spaces of me and not-me, where home and not being at home intersect. The crossing of borders is both exciting and frightening, as we transgress by separating from the familiar and entering into new relations. We cross internal boundaries, into a netherland/twilight zone, toward an unknown place.

During his studies, Sam critically examined his religiosity from the safe distance of studying another and taking an academic stance toward the beliefs he grew up with. Just like immersing ourselves in another culture helps us to realize and examine the assumptions we previously absorbed unknowingly, Sam's migration led him to question what he was taught to believe in church and at home, and he is agnostic now. What strikes me about the academic field he chose to study is that it was guided by his experience of otherness and led to more pronounced feelings of alienation. Ethnically, racially, and in terms of his religious background and current beliefs, Sam stands out among his White colleagues (this is true in academia in general, but extreme in his particular field of sub-study). For the first two years of our treatment, and after several years of trying, Sam could not obtain a tenure track position in his field. Sam's students give him strong reviews, he has many collegial friendships, and he has gained respect and acclaim for papers and published articles. Still, Sam was not being invited to join or to stay, somehow he was not the "right fit." During these first years of psycho-therapy, Sam spoke to me about feeling adrift, "out of place." Coming to the US and his studies allowed him to see and feel himself more clearly, but he also feels the pain of it, an old pain that goes something like this: You cannot be different if you want to belong.

Clearly, his early experiences of unbelonging triggered powerful feel-ings when he encountered visa troubles and difficulties finding a tenure-track job. I was careful in exploring the psychodynamics of his situation as I did not want to blame him for getting himself into a difficult situa-tion. Given the inhospitable external circumstances he faced, I was also worried that exploring the psychodynamics would encourage his percep-tion that he had more agency than he actually did. I knew firsthand how out of control it could feel to be a non-resident alien. I remembered how much I doubted myself during the long period where my life and status in the US were tenuous and uncertain. Sam's choices in trying to find an academic position that would sponsor a visa and ultimately a green card were not really choices, at least not as freely made as choices with a capital C.

As Sam explored his experiences in the workplace and interviewed for different academic positions, he was able to notice the costs of trying to fit into an environment where he would not meet many like-minded people. In other words, his sense of where he could belong and enjoy being became more realistically grounded. I sensed in our work that he was able to leave a place of hiding (from himself and others) and reveal parts of himself that helped others to recognize him and see what is love-able about Sam.

For more than a year of our treatment, Sam and I had Skype sessions. Sam had taken a visiting professorship in another state, and when he was "home" he stayed with his then girlfriend, now wife, in another city, too far for commuting in for our appointments. I found myself being flexible to enable us to continue treatment. It fit Sam's needs: He could move and stay connected. Because of technology, there can be analytic work and also migration.

Strangers to Ourselves

It is ironic that migrating evokes a more pronounced feeling of the original experience of alienation: By migrating we confront ourselves with the heart of our loneliness and the anxieties associated with it. We seek out an experience that catapults us into an existential crisis and, we hope, produces catastrophic change (as it is conceived in dynamic systems theory, Goldberg, unpublished paper). Having felt at the margins in our place of origin, home expels us to explore our liminality and otherness elsewhere. We leave because we sense that there is an important part of us that we cannot experience where we come from. In our chosen foreign land we can explore the foreign life within us. Maybe that's what they call culture shock (Garza-Guererro, 1975): Our strange-ness in plain view, unobstructed by the curtains of familiar conventions and customs.

Away from home we encounter in us what Freud calls the "uncanny," in German *Das Unheimliche,* which literally means "un-home-ly" but idiomatically signifies something "scary" and "creepy." Freud understood it to be an instance where something can be familiar yet foreign at the same time, resulting in a feeling of it being uncomfortably strange. In a foreign land we have the opportunity to make ourselves at home in the uncanny, *heimisch im Unheimlichen* (Freud, 1913).

Moving away from home may be the only way to give contours to our opaque sense that something is not quite right, an attempt to become intelligible to ourselves and others. We bring with us early experiences of unbelonging and solitude, and complex feelings about connection. As we enter a culture and add to its hybridity (Bhaba, 2004), we long to see ourselves reflected in others, to find those words with which we can speak of ourselves and others, to make ourselves intelligible. Yet, joining a place of a multiplicity of cultures and subcultures is paradoxical in its aim: We want to both fit in and go unnoticed, be seen and go into hiding. We join and resist at the same time.

Sam's sense of placelessness and unbelonging is pervasive—especially in the early years of our work—and emerges in many moments in his life. At the same time, Sam is very skilled in forging connections and appearing to fit in. Sam has become part of an urban bohemian academic subculture, yet his history and background are vastly different from many of his peers, who have a similar taste in fashion, music, and literature. The liberal and hip downtown academic I encounter in my waiting room shares with me some academic interests and liberal values. His journey from a conservative religious background in a poor Caribbean country seems "more worlds away" than my trip from a provincial and liberal university town in Germany. Essential aspects of who he is and where he is from do not readily meet the eye and remain hidden, maybe for good reason.

Leaving as a "Choice"

Sam and I chose to leave where we came from; we are not refugees who escaped situations of war or disaster or political, religious, or social persecution. The distinction between voluntary and forced migrations describes important differences in the social reality and psychological experience of leaving home and settling in a foreign place, which are expressed, for example, in the different meanings articulated by calling oneself an exile, expatriate, or immigrant. In reality, most migrations are somewhere in between—involving necessity but also a degree of choice. Understanding what psychic, familial, and social forces push us out of our place of origin is an important part of making sense of ourselves over time. Also, the minute we start to think about differences between forced and "voluntary" migrations, we realize that they are not entirely separate phenomena. Voluntary immigrants have the option to stay, yet leaving even when we are not forced out may still feel like a psychological necessity.

Both Sam and I crossed oceans and borders in search of something we wanted: Our migrations were fueled by desire for something we could not quite grasp. In our search for home, greater freedom, and belonging, we have come to know the (often unwelcoming) realities of immigration, visa stamps, border controls, work permits, and expiration dates. There is a dialectical tension in becoming an immigrant that I keep coming back to throughout this paper: As we reach for freedom from the constrictions of our old home, in our new home we turn into foreigners entrapped by the state.

Feeling at Home and Courting the Foreign

Choosing to leave home entails moving away from early objects, including experiences in the broader community of the "mother country" or "fatherland." If culture is a potential space (Winnicott, 1971) between mother and infant, child and world, then our sense of home is a psychological extension of our sense of family. We feel we belong when we feel recognized and connected with others. Longing for home is longing for intimacy that feels right, a moment when we experience a match between our environment and ourselves (Madison, 2009).

So, when we leave our place of origin and family ties in favor of becoming a stranger in a strange land, it is because we seek out a new object, a more facilitating environment (Winnicott, 1965). We take a leap of faith as we mobilize ourselves for a move from the familiar to the unknown. Our move is as much concrete as it is internal.

I believe there is a particular strength in us migrants who decide to leave and seek: As we move we take the freedom to separate as much as we take the freedom to find. We are Balint's "philobat": drawn to the possibilities of the unknown as we move away from the limitations of familiar objects (Balint, 1959, p. 29). Madison, a British existentialist psychologist describes the "existential migrant" as someone who expresses and actively seeks out fundamental experiences about existence by choosing the strange and foreign over the familiar and conventional. In his interviews with immigrants Madison found that migrations are almost always solitary (2009, p. 155). Alone in a foreign environment, we inevitably move through internal places of separateness, loneliness, strangeness, and otherness and can actively explore existential questions about belonging.

As we leave we seek. Leaving may be a way to turn passive into active (Freud, 1922), as we search for an alternative to feeling confined by place. Moving presents an active and worthwhile struggle for a greater sense of freedom. It can be an attempt to transform our relationship to people and places from near or far to optimal distance (Balint, 1959; Mahler, 1975) or better put, "optimal closeness" (Akhtar, 2009). Leaving home for a place far away opens up potential space (Winnicott, 1957; Ogden, 1985) to experience ourselves in a new way and examine the past with just the right amount of distance. By moving into a new world we get to inhabit and develop different sides of ourselves.

Speaking Ourselves in a New/Old Language

Much has been written about the deep affective resonance of one's first language, the "mother tongue." Conversely, expressing oneself in a foreign language may feel freeing, exciting, and emotionally rich in a previously unformulated way. Different aspects of myself come alive in my adopted language than in my first language. In my case, my first language was not my mother's tongue. As is not unusual for recent immigrants—my family focused on adapting to and finding a place in German culture. As a child I felt the pain of our foreignness in Germany and refused to learn Greek. My mother's German was not fluent when I was born, and I know that the tonality of Greek has a deep, pre-verbal resonance for me, yet one that I cannot fully grasp.

Standing between two cultures and not feeling quite at home in either one, I chose to explore the question of belonging in a third place and came to the US as a young adult. It is not uncommon for bicultural people to emigrate to a third country. I have met many first-generation Germans (Turkish-Germans, African-Germans, Chinese-Germans), who were attracted by the greater cultural diversity in the US and so eventually settled in New York and other US places. There is even a term for this world wide phenomenon: "third culture kids," individuals who do not feel at home in either their parents' home country or the country to which their family migrated. Many of us connect most deeply with other cultural nomads—their tribe in the third culture.

My German mind seems to run a more logical, structured course, although the longer I live abroad, the more I seem to stumble for words and grasp for coherence. Then again, German is also where my sarcastic humor comes out and where I anticipate that the person with whom I am sharing it is in on the joke. English has been the language that over time allowed me to meet myself, and others, in a more open and accepting way. English is an alternative place to my German and Greek selves.

We find our optimal distance/closeness in the way we use our native tongue and adopted language. Speaking ourselves in a foreign tongue, with different sounds, semantics, and visceral experiences of speaking offers an alternative to an old way our affect is carried and may give us sufficient distance to bear to speak certain things.

Three years into our work, Sam spoke about his relationship to his native language. He had just re-married and had begun feeling more settled in his life in the US. As Sam tried to envision a cross-cultural family, he grappled with how his Caribbean self would be part of their life together. This is complicated by the ambiguity of his cultural identifications:

> "This strength of feeling Caribbean comes from my migration. When I grew up, it was less clear to me that I was Caribbean. I did not feel that I belonged because I was not typical. I felt out of place in the wider culture, Brown not Black, part of a puritan Christian religious group, middle class in a country with many poor, a few rich, and very few in the middle. We spoke English at home, not Creole, not even the middle-class local dialect. But once I left, I would come home during breaks from school and find myself speaking Creole with my friends."

Who speaks through Sam when he speaks Creole? Even though he did not speak it at home with his parents, it has deep resonance for him. His Creole self came to him long after he left home, as a way of bonding with his old friends. Is Creole a protected space that the White world cannot enter, a way to finally resist the British colonizing of his mother country? Speaking Creole fits into his adult experience of being from the West Indies, and at the same time it is a part of himself he comes into contact with later on, as he revisits his original home and his Caribbean self. It is an enigma how the multiple languages we absorb signify different registers of our experience that lie dormant and emerge at different moments and times in our lives. And sometimes claiming a part of ourselves involves immersing ourselves more deeply in a part of our culture (e.g., religiosity, language, food) than we did earlier in our lives.

In a similar way to Sam, it took leaving Germany for me to feel more German. I will always have an accent in English. I have no intention of losing it; my accent is part of who I am. It helps that having accented English is met in the US with less stigma than my mother's Greek accent was in

Germany. My accent is not always easily placed: People assume more often that I am from France or Italy than guess that I am German. I like the opaqueness of the origins of my accent, name, and looks, as this actually captures my cultural identity, which carries in it ambiguity.

When asked where I am from, I explain that I grew up in Germany as the daughter of Greek immigrants. People often respond in ways that unsettle me: "So you are really German, since you were born there." Well, no. For example, I did not have German citizenship or even German permanent residency until I was in my mid-twenties, shortly before I left to come to the US. The real loneliness of the immigrant is revealed when people who, when met with our foreignness, try to place us in clear-cut categories that do not capture who we feel we are.

"Growing up Greek in Germany—that must have been difficult," is a comment I have heard many times. Hearing this question makes me uncomfortable, because the more I have come to embrace the part of me that has been irrevocably shaped by Germany, the more I sense that my values are very different from what I suspect is behind the question I am asked. It invariably seems to me to carry the assumption of pronounced German xenophobia, intolerance, and hostility. Lately I find myself replying sharply with something like "Oh, yes? Difficult? How so?" I am trying to get more of a sense of the ideas that lie behind this question. Germany's Nazi past and the Holocaust are beyond frightening, yet some of the projections I encounter now feel so black-and-white that they seem simply wrong as a picture of present-time Germany.

My reaction to these negative opinions about Germany is very complicated, because I am and am not implicated in its history. My family did not live in Germany during the Second World War; I inherited a different intergenerational family history. Yet I grew up going on field trips to concentration camps and was taught about "civil courage" and the responsibility of the German nation and every person to make sure that fascism never rises again. While my own experience in Germany was very complex, I am wary of perpetuating stereotypes of Germany as a xenophobic and intolerant nation. The Germany of my youth, and especially the Germany of today, is full of paradoxes when it comes to how multiculturalism and diversity are lived and understood. More importantly, my own German-ness is complicated. It is simultaneously self-conscious, affirmative, and sensitive to judgment. I, too, feel the shame, responsibility, and compassion that several generations of Germans carry as we try to process and respond to the trauma of the Holocaust in ourselves and in others.

In the act of sharing with you some of the complexity of my German identity, I feel the riskiness of this kind of exploration. I am opening myself up to something that is partially unknown and potentially censorable. It is unclear what kind of history I am stepping into.

Multiple Migrations

Sam has made multiple migrations: cultural, intellectual, religious, and developmental. First, he came to the US from the West Indies; he was raised in one religion, then chose to study another religion while at university; he turned from a devout religious youth to an agnostic adult; he got married at a young age to a woman close to his family culture, then got divorced. Locating and anchoring himself in the context of these complex changes— migrations that were both choices and psychological necessities—has been the core of our work together.

Understanding where we come from and what we carry is a slow-moving process full of enigma. As Sam and I unpack his experience of himself in the world, I am in for continual surprises. Just when I thought I had some understanding about Sam's childhood, he mentions a new detail about his life that surprises me. Initially Sam placed his experiences of misrecognition and stigma primarily in his post-migration life in the US. Then, after almost four years of working together, another layer in Sam's experience of outsid- erness emerges, when he shares that his mother grew up in another, nearby country and cooked foreign food at home. The significance of this detail had not occurred to him. Other memories surface gradually, memories that speak to his feelings of shame and invisibility when he was growing up, based on differences in socioeconomic status, shade of skin color, religious affiliation.

"Did I ever tell you about the time when I participated in a game of hide and seek? I must have been 10 years old and had been invited to a birthday party of a girl in my class, whose parents were wealthy. I felt out of place in their fancy home. We kids played hide and seek, and I found a closet upstairs to hide in. I waited … and waited. At some point the mother discovered me by accident and told me that they stopped playing that game a long time ago! I hid too well and had been forgotten. I am not sure if I wanted to be found or disappear."

The paradoxes in Sam's cultural identity resonate with me on a deep level. I know the curious push and pull of wanting to belong while at the same time distancing myself from the larger culture around me. Somehow I always find myself belonging from afar, from a place of un-belonging. Growing up in Germany, I alternated between yearning to have blonde hair, blue eyes, go by the name of Susanne, and ride horses and on the other hand playing with questions of culture, assimilation, and stigma in ironic moments of rebellion. At age 14, my best Turkish-German girlfriend and I walked into a wedding-gown showroom. With fake Turkish accents and energized by our desire to subvert stereotypes, we explained that the Turkish men to whom we had been promised wanted to see pictures of us wearing various wedding dresses. We proceeded to pose for each other as child-brides, standing on little stools wearing large clouds of wedding gowns. We secretly relished the effect we had on the shop assistants who stood by with pity and horror on their faces. As we dressed up and tried on an exaggerated form of a familiar stigmatized role, we enjoyed the send-up about people's racism. This is in the spirit of Homi Bhaba's idea (2004) of seizing the stereotype and playing with it as an act of rebellion.

Holding the Tension between Ambiguous Loss and Opportunity

What stands out in the psychoanalytic literature on immigration is the central focus on mourning and the complications of separating from the past and adapting to a new place (Akhtar, 1999; Levy-Warren, 1987). Underlying this focus on mourning and displacement is the assumption that we once belonged. This narrative is seductively simple in that it leaves out the complexity of our feelings about our place of origin. It presupposes that we once felt at home. Yet it is often a feeling of un-belonging that propels us to leave home to find our place in the world. Somehow we got the notion that away is better and life is elsewhere. We leave just as much by conscious decision as by unconscious motivation. We carry our relationships with our parents and home culture in us and react to it in the choices we make all of our life. Migrations from one place to another are internal migrations, developmental migrations that involve both a push into the world and a pushing away of painful and constraining bonds. The need to separate, cutting off, or pushing away early objects by moving far away is an act of resistance and self-preservation at the same time.

By exclusively focusing on loss and displacement, what is left out of sight is that we also experience excitement about change and growth that propels us forward. That excitement entails transference to place, which may be idealized, and the existential quest expressed in moving to a strange land. It is the nature and fate of this romance with a foreign place that particularly interests me.

This brings to mind the centuries-old phenomenon of artists, academics, and non-traditional people flocking to cities, cultural epicenters offering a bohemian way of life and subcultures allowing for belonging and a creative exchange. These places of greater diversity allow you to be an outsider; you can be seen and hide yourself at the same time. This part of the immigrant's story may be messier and more difficult to untangle. It may take us many years away from our place of origin to grasp why we had to leave and what we lost.

Immigration involves multiple realms of loss, both real and imaginary. At least temporarily, we lose a sense of agency over our surroundings, lose the comfort of the familiarity of our everyday life, lose our language, and lose the support of family networks. Our losses are intertwined with the opportunities and change immigration brings, which makes them less clear-cut and turns them into ambiguous losses.

What makes our experience of loss complex is the melancholy and nostalgia we experience when (mis)remembering a past we idealize. Nostalgia is our yearning for an imaginary past we never had, imagining that a lack we feel now was once fullness. Settling in the foreign necessitates mourning the home we lost and the home we missed. In dealing with loss, nostalgia is both our poison and our cure. It is part of our attempt to establish links between our old self and new self, continuity of our life story in the face of cultural rupture.

There is a dynamic tension between rebelling against not being recognized and becoming trapped in it, between feeling invisible and feeling stereotyped. It is easy to collapse into hiding and resign ourselves to not being seen. Sam and I circle around this theme over and over again. While he is more and more able to tolerate and even feel comfortable in the position of belonging and at the same time not belonging, he also tries to understand the ways that he gives up on himself:

s: My daughter will grow up here, grow up American; she will grow up in the way my wife grew up.

J: Do you feel like there is no room for your culture in your marriage, in your new family?

s: Yes, I do feel resigned to having to live an American life.

J: What about the idea that you could add something West Indian to your family life—socializing as a family with West Indian friends with kids, cooking Caribbean food, sharing music you like with your daughter and wife?

s: I don't know why I don't feel that I can add my way to the mix.

J: I remember this coming up when you looked for jobs—that there was no way to be part of anything without renouncing most of yourself. There must be some truth to this, to immigration as a kind of loss and the loss of trying to belong while feeling different, but I wonder why it feels so absolute for you?

s: Right now I just feel the loneliness of being different.

Immigration Problems

Choosing a country to settle in signifies creating a life for oneself and taking charge of one's destiny, yet immigration difficulties can create just the opposite experience: a Kafka-esque nightmare that leaves us at the mercy of external circumstances. Worrying about visas and green card petitions is a common situation we experience more intimately than we ever cared to. The imagined good parents, our sought-out facilitating environment, now turn rejecting or, even more confusing, both welcoming and rejecting.

The country where we have forged intimate bonds, found mentors, where we consummated adulthood, is also the place that might not invite us to stay. Our legal status is a hard fact, devoid of symbolic notions of where we feel we belong. The non-resident alien's encounter with the law holds terror, as it points out to us that we are not individual agents, but subjects of the state (Althusser, 1971).

In my experience, not knowing if I could dwell where I wanted to settle concretely recreated an old and familiar experience of ultimately not belonging and not feeling welcomed. Call it repetition compulsion: I had chosen a life situation that let me, the non-resident alien, struggle over and over again with the question of where I belonged.

Some of us cannot feel the extent of our desire unless we can be sure that we are wanted and thus maintain a casual relationship with our foreign lover, the USA (or Spain, or Japan). Alternatively, we may pursue the elusive object of home with single-minded passion and work hard to gain acceptance in a society that can feel like an exclusive country club (with rules of admittance that change all the time and are indecipherable). I vividly remember times I was afraid that my life in New York would come to an end against my will. That scenario brought up a level of dread and panic that could be completely paralyzing, which I learned to manage over time by keeping it out of awareness. For example, a few years ago I received a call from my immigration lawyer. In typical New York style, I was sitting in a taxicab in Manhattan heading to a professional meeting. I listened to the voice of my lawyer informing me about a glitch in my green card petition and the possibility that the application could be rejected. As I gazed through the window of the taxi, the street scene no longer looked like the backdrop of my life. My chosen environment seemed to recede from me—or did I withdraw from it? Either way, at that moment (which luckily passed), my life in New York was something I could not take for granted, and I felt already no longer part of it.

The transitory nature of a work visa makes it very difficult to plant roots. Not being able to decide how long we can stay in our chosen country brings to surface our narcissistic struggles, depressive anxieties, and our complex relationship to dependency and control. We may feel grateful and simultaneously taken advantage of and trapped by an employer who has agreed to sponsor a temporary work visa for a job with high turnover and modest compensation. When we ask about green-card sponsorship, we are often met with suspicion by our employers, and we might feel our wish to stay in the country indefinitely is dubious and our need to belong hardly legal. Some of us take a friend up on the offer to marry, just to stay in each others' lives, and for the next few years we navigate the emotional and practical complexities of this commitment. The realities of the process of immigration can be a high price to pay for what during these times can feel like an impossible dream.

Conclusion: Going Forward, Going Back

Sam and I continue to work together. After a period of uncertainty and feeling adrift, Sam's life has become much more settled: Sam married his American girlfriend in our third year of treatment. He and his wife welcomed a baby into their life, an American citizen by birth. They bought a house and experience the joys and stresses of parenthood. Sam now has a green card and has secured a tenure track position within an interdisciplinary department of a university. He teaches a diverse student population and feels that the department is a good fit for him. These life changes for him coincide with my own marriage and first child, markers of settling into the foreign in a more permanent way.

Since we started treatment more than four years ago, Sam's life has moved in the a direction of feeling himself more clearly and seeking out what he needs to be if he is to be at home with others. He loves the way his wife appreciates him, how she recognizes things about him that he also values in himself. He talks about his collegial and neighborly relationships—the ways in which he is able to reach out to people and connect. He seeks out faculty of color in his department to find out more about their experiences at their shared work place, and to support each other. We continue to circle around his pain and the questions it carries. In a recent session, right after his parents came to visit him and his wife in their new home and met their grandchild for the first time, Sam recounted a dream:

s: I was walking through the town of Cambridge, England, where I lived—with my parents and siblings who came to visit me there. (Sam did live in Cambridge many years ago). As I show them my life in this place, they don't seem as impressed as I want them to be. I told you last week how pleased I was that my parents were impressed with my life here, our home, and the town we live in. Maybe this dream is telling me that on a less conscious level, I feel that really they are not so impressed by my accomplishments?

j: I could see that. I also wonder if your family members visiting you stand for a part of yourself. Maybe your roots are visiting you and letting you know that there are other values and experiences you care about, values that are different from the assumed superiority of colonial values, the markers of success that Cambridge and your life here stand for.

s: I can follow you intellectually, but emotionally it is just all so confusing.

This condensed exchange highlights two aspects of our work: Sam expressed pride and happiness about his current life but was also tentative, and this dampened his feeling of excitement about his accomplishments. He quickly moved from feelings of pride to feelings of inadequacy. I pointed out to him that he may also feel that the family life and culture he grew up in has value in its own right. I interpreted his feelings of melancholia, as missing his roots. In the session following this one, Sam told me that he found it hopeful to think that a part of him values something about his place of origin that is very different from the markers of success he has been aspiring to. I am sharing this exchange because certain feelings and themes keep re-emerging in different forms at various times in our treatment. Making links between past and present, here and there, is an ongoing part of our work together.

A few years ago, on my way to visit my mother in Germany for Christmas, I decided to visit Heidelberg for a day. I had studied psychology as an undergraduate there and I had not been back since. Memories of the past kept surfacing: I saw myself as a young woman walking the streets of an idyllic and provincial, academic, quirky, and also conservative town. I needed to visit Heidelberg and reconnect with this younger version of myself. I yearned to feel a part of myself that feels lovely and lost, a simpler story of my life. I had booked a room online in a new boutique hotel right near the house I had lived in when I was a student there. When I arrived at the hotel, I was given the key to a tiny room in the attic with a beautiful view over the roofs of the old city of Heidelberg. I had a drink with an old friend who remarked that the building the hotel was in used to house student services. That night, my first night back in Germany, as I was drifting into sleep, I gazed into the night sky through the skylight above me. At that moment it suddenly came to me that I knew this very same room! As a 20-year-old, I used to volunteer at a student-run hotline called "Nightline." I used to sit in the attic of the same building, which then housed student services, late at night, looking out of this very same window as I counseled distressed students on the phone. A sleep on memory lane.

Visiting Heidelberg for the first time in many years, I revisited the life I chose not to have, the life I had just before something big happened: pre-immigration Julia. Immigration can be something longed for, and yet it is inherently traumatic. In an uncanny twist of fate I found a hotel that I knew from the inside out—unconscious knowledge was clearly guiding me.

Returning to Heidelberg was the new/older me revisiting the old/younger me. Yet the nostalgia that brought me back was the longing for a home I never had. I never felt at home in Heidelberg; it was there that I gradually realized that I needed to leave not just my hometown, but Germany, even Europe. In nostalgia, we mourn the home we had as well as the home we missed. I revisited in Heidelberg my nostalgic fantasy of belonging and confronted the painful knowledge I had then already, that I, the *Ausländerkind*, never belonged.

When we leave home, life in the new world transforms us, and we cannot return to our old life unchanged. As Martin Buber (2014) said: "All journeys have secret destinations of which the traveler is unaware." Who we are and where we belong has become even more complex than we anticipated when we set out for an exciting trip. In my experience the process of acculturation is not as linear as the stages that Akhtar describes in his book "Immigration and Identity" (1999). I see the ups and downs of settling in as taking the form of a spiral, which we hope is slowly evolving. I do believe that psychoanalysis has a particular draw for the ones of us who are sorting out questions of belonging. While the history of psychoanalysis is one of diaspora, migration, and exile, the process of analysis is the search for an anchor inside. Analytic love can offer asylum in the face of homelessness and ultimately generates a new understanding to come home to. Edward Said (2000, p. 295) ends his memoir with the words: "I actually prefer being not quite right and out of place." Maybe coming home is befriending the fact that belonging is neither total nor constant, as we learn to inhabit our in-between spaces and come to settle between places.

References

Akhtar, S. (1999). Immigration and identity: Turmoil, treatment, and transformation. Northvale, NJ: Jason Aronson.

Akhtar, S. (2009).*Comprehensive Dictionary of Psychoanalysis*. Karnac Books, London.

Althusser, L. (1971). *Lenin and philosophy and other essays*. Trans. Ben Brewster. New York, NY: Monthly Review Press, p. 119.

Balint, M. (1968/1979). *The Basic Fault*. New York, NY: Brunner/Mazel.

Baranger, M. (1993). The mind of the analyst: From listening to interpretation. *International Journal of Psychoanalysis*, Vol. 74: 15–24.

Bhabha, H. (2004). *The Location of Culture*. New York, NY: Routledge.

Bourdieu, P. (2001). *Masculine domination*. Stanford, CA: Stanford University Press.

Buber, M. (attrib.). *Wikiquote*. Retrieved October 19, 2014 from http://en.wikiquote.org/wiki/Martin_Buber.

Butler, J. (2005). *Giving an account of oneself*. Bronx, NY: Fordham University Press.

Freud, S. (1919). The 'Uncanny'. *The Standard Edition of the Complete Psychological Works of Sigmund Freud, Volume XVII (1917–1919): An Infantile Neurosis and Other Works*, 217–256, Hogarth Press, London.

Freud, S. (1922). Beyond the pleasure principle. New York, NY: Norton & Co., 1961.

Garza-Guerrero, A. C. (1974). Culture shock: Mourning and the vicissitudes of identity. *Journal of the American Psychoanalytic Association*, 22: 408–429.

Gerson, S. (2009). When the third is dead: Memory, mourning, and witnessing in the aftermath of the Holocaust. *International Journal of Psychoanalysis*, 90: 1341–1357.

Goffman E. (1963). *Stigma: Notes on the management of spoiled identity*. Upper Saddle River, NJ: Prentice-Hall.

Goldberg, P. *The analytic frame: A reconsideration*. Unpublished Paper.

Goldberger, M. (1993). *"Bright spot," a variant of "Blind spot."* Psychoanalytic *Quarterly*, 62: 270–273.

Grinberg, L., and Grinberg, R. (1989). *Psychoanalytic perspectives on migration and exile*. New Haven, CT: Yale University Press.

Hoffman, E. (1989). *Lost in translation*. New York, NY: Penguin Books.

Lahiri, J. (2003). *The Namesake*. New York, NY: Houghton, Mifflin, Harcourt.

Levy-Warren, M. H. (1987). Moving to a new culture: Cultural identity, loss, and mourning. In J. Bloom-Fesbach & S. Bloom-Fesbach (Eds.), *The psychology of separation and loss: Perspectives on development, life transitions, and clinical practice* (pp. 300–315). San Francisco, CA: Jossey-Bass Publishers.

Mahler, M.S. (1975). *The Psychological Birth of the Human Infant*. New York, NY: Basic Books.

Mahler, M. (1979). Selected papers of Margaret S. Mahler. New York, NY: Aronson.

Madison, G. (2009). The end of belonging. Self-published, London.

Modarressi, T. (1992). Writing with an accent. *Chanteh*, 1: 7–9.

O'Neill, J. (2008). *Netherland*. New York, NY: Vintage Books.

Ogden, T. H. (1985). On potential space. *International Journal of Psychoanalysis*, 66: 129–141.

Ogden, T.H. (1994). The analytic third: Working with intersubjective clinical facts. *Int. J. Psycho-Anal.*, 75: 3–19.

Said, E. (2000). *Out of place*. New York, NY: Vintage Books.

Toibin, C. (2009). *Brooklyn*. New York, NY: Vintage Books.

Winnicott, D.W. (1957) *The child and the outside world*. London: Tavistock.

Winnicott, D.W. (1965). *The maturational processes and the facilitating environment*. Madison, CT: International Universities Press.

Winnicott, D.W. (1971). *Playing and reality*. New York, NY: Routledge.

Chapter 6

Migration in Search of Sexual Identity

Dino Koutsolioutsos, MFCC

In the seven decades of my life, I have travelled through internal migrations of sexual and gender identities, as well as external migrations through cultures and countries, at times dictated, coerced, or voluntary. Belonging to a family or a culture has remained elusive in my life, enveloping me in personal isolation. It has been misery and freedom, vulnerability and strength, as lonely and as free as a person of the world.

My severe case of gender confusion in early childhood set the stage by disengaging me from my family, mentally and emotionally, as well as physically, at times. I wanted to be a girl, but the world wanted me to be a boy. With my one single conflict of gender identity I found myself outside my own family, outside my own culture, outside society. As a toddler, I became a person in "no man's land." At the age of three, four, and then five, I had to learn to fend for myself and by myself, because nobody seemed to be on my side, absolutely nobody. Surviving—I decided as a pre-schooler—necessitated absolute secrecy and constant lying, in order to juggle the two worlds that I found myself in. There was the world of appearances, where I was the third child and youngest son of a middle-class family in Athens, Greece, and my inner world. This inner world was my secret sanctum, where I knew that I could not be who I wanted to be, a girl, and where I had to integrate—or at least manage—my personal desires and needs with the cultural dictates of my family and Greek society. Inside of me, I wanted to be a girl. Outside, in real life, this private me was a monster, culturally, socially, and even religiously. I had to learn how to survive this terrible bind. This entailed, I decided early on, some sort of subterfuge, every second, every day, and every year of my life. It also entailed all sorts of migrations, internal in my sexual and gender identities, and external, coerced or voluntary, through various cultures of home and country.

My life's journey developed as an internal travelogue of gender and sexuality, from gender-confused child, to gay monster, to struggling straight married man, to liberated gay man, to, once again, gender questioning older man, as ever in lust, if not love, with straight men. The history of my sexuality fits all the letters in the acronym LGBTIQ, except one, the L for Lesbian.

My life's journey also entailed external, physical migrations that I will discuss in this paper. I spent a lifetime trying to find and also escape myself, through deed and creed, to no avail. In this essay, I will try to understand any interconnections that may have existed between and among all these internal and external migrations. I fled my state of otherness, which remained a cause of fear, pain, and doubt in my life, by changing myself and/or changing the others I was with, by migrating to another place, to another person, to another identity, or to another culture. My internal migrations were at times helped or hindered by personal psychotherapy. I was in personal therapy four times, from 25 to 50 years old, the first two times demanding desperately to turn into a straight man, the last two needing help to find happiness as a gay man. In all four, I managed to resist, avoid, or ignore gender identity. Instead, the therapeutic experience helped me where I was at the moment, to move on to another place with more hope. It also allowed me to lose track of deeper issues of my life. My collaborations with my therapists tended to lead me to a place of more comfort but further away from the terrors within.

Two Years Old

At the age of two, I developed early symptoms of poliomyelitis. My father sent me with my mother to the United States, where I was treated and cured and returned healthy to Greece after six months. This journey was deeply stressful for both my mother and me. We were without my father, and my mother was a deeply clingy woman prone to hysteria and narcissism who did not speak any English. While in the States, I had also developed a testicular hernia, which made my left testicle grow gigantic with fluid, and I had surgery back in Greece.

Upon our return to Greece, with me physically healed, I exhibited for the first time significant signs of gender confusion. I acted like a girl in every which way, and with the onset of fluid speech, I spoke of myself in the female gender. My mother had left for the States with a two-year-old boy who was physically sick and had returned with a healthy child that acted like a girl and wanted to be one. For a long time, my family took my girlish behaviour in stride and seemed to accept me as this boy/girl. The family household was full of women, with my mother, my four-year-older sister, our governess, and a live-in maid. My father's business already had moved away from Athens, and he would come home only for the weekends. My five-year-older brother was the only other male at home.

Sometime between the age of three and four my father decided that I could not go on acting like a girl. He had become terrified of my gender-wayward ways and laid down the law. This is when the hammer came down on me, that I was going to be a boy, or else … This "else" I understood at that pre-school age was death, extinction. I took the parental threat very seriously and the interdiction to be final and existentially absolute. Either be a boy or cease to exist. There was no third choice.

This early terror became fixated on my father, who, in every other way, was a loving and caring parent. But when in puberty I labelled myself gay, this similar "dirty" secret maintained the wall between us. The emotional split had occurred early on and never healed until he died. It took years of raging and crying bouts in my therapeutic process to come to terms with the lack of connection between us, to accept the love that my father had bestowed on me, nevertheless, and to open myself up to the terrible unmet need for his parental love, support, and protection at the time when I had needed him most.

The Transgender Child—Preschool Age

My earliest memories, in my pre-school years, are centered on my doll, playing in secret with it as often as I could, fantasizing that I was a princess waiting for the prince to come and rescue me from various escapades. These precious moments I played with my doll, as a pre-schooler, were the rare times of day that I could be myself, a girl, in relative secrecy from my family. The rest of the day, I had to conform to who I was supposed to be, or else. ...

These earliest memories are also highly symbolic of my later life, hiding behind something, anything, to experience a few moments of being myself, away from the world, which would not tolerate my otherness. This deep sense of existential danger that my otherness brought to my life, practically from the get-go, I internalize to this day, as evidenced even by the 12 months of personal torment trying to write this essay.

My secret play with my doll was also highly emblematic of my status outside social convention, as I understood it to be. I felt and still feel outside society, a virtual outcast. This has made me, to some degree, an asocial person, someone who, as I experience myself outside the given social norms, also feels less obliged to abide by them, whenever necessary and possible.

There was a dark, painful and deeply scary side to this split reality of my life, but there was also a very important, positive, strengthening side, which was character forming. I was forced and able to handle two different and separate worlds, the outside world of superficial gender conformity that my family espoused and imposed upon me, and the inside world of my personal reality of being a girl. It felt empowering to be able to juggle these two opposing worlds in my little life. It also gave me a sense that I possessed a special knowledge, which has accompanied me throughout my life: Life is not always what it seems, and realities can hide in various layers of existence. In a weird way, I felt sorry for, or even looked down upon, the poor simple folk in my family who thought I was a boy and who believed that everything was as the appearances indicated. It provided a life-saving counterbalance to the terror I experienced of being found out, to the shame of hiding who I really was, and to the chilling loneliness and isolation I felt within my secret space.

My life-long migrations have taken place within this critical dichotomy: Finding myself outside social norms, striving to integrate myself in them, or trying to find different sets of social environments that seemed less punishing or forbidding, I would end up experiencing myself, again and again, falling quite short of full social integration. Being outside society provided me early on with a sense of amazing power, to weigh against the terrible isolation I also felt. Extreme emotional pain can produce a certain amount of narcissistic self-adulation, a trait and an experience I witnessed fully in the hysterical narcissism of my mother.

The limits of conventionality, within the culture of my family, were surprisingly ambiguous to me and therefore quite confusing. In Greek society, any type of aberration from the patriarchal heterosexual norm was considered at that time as simply monstrous and antisocial behaviour. Within the immediate household of my family, on the other hand, which was peopled by women and dominated by my mother, there reigned a lax application of the strict societal dictates of gender conventions of Greece in the mid-twentieth century.

The Conforming First Grader—In Exile

At the age of six my family placed me in a boarding school in a suburb of Athens. My first and second grades in that school were sheer hell. Though I have no direct recollection, I felt rejected and ostracized by my family, unloved, exiled, and thrown away. Nevertheless, by the time I entered first grade I had mastered all necessary acting skills to pass easily as a normal little boy, conforming to the social stereotypes of behaviour I had been ordered to comply with. Life at the boarding school was very harsh, both because of my young age and because of the low quality of that enterprise. I felt scared, abandoned, and terrified of not making it and being punished, not for wanting to be a girl, but purely for not being able to follow the school rules. At that young age, I had moved from a family space, where I was cared for but did not feel loved or understood, to a school environment, as punishment, where I felt neither loved nor cared for.

If the above picture of my boarding school life seems overly grim, almost tragic, it is because it was. By the end of the first year, life had become so unbearable that I made cold, silent, secret, but long-term plans of ending my life, if it continued to be so hard for another few years. The suicidal ideation was real and, though devoid of any immediate plans or means, was serious, sober, and aimed for the long term. Of course, these suicidal ideations remained deeply secret inside me, as was the rest of my existential misery. I had long ago realized, rightly or wrongly, that there did not exist a single person in my family, let alone in the world, whom I could trust to help me.

On the other hand, surviving the first two grades in that boarding school proved to me that I could somehow survive on my own, without a family, an actual orphan. I would chance to say that the seeds of my future voluntary migrations, as well as my lifelong loneliness, were sown during that period.

Interlude as the Family Invalid

In third grade I was erroneously diagnosed with TB of the spine and was given a high probability of becoming a life-long paraplegic. I was ordered into a strict treatment regime of absolute immobility and bed rest at home with every-other-daily injections of antibiotics. When my four-year-older sister left our boarding school for another, I was left alone to fend for myself "in hell," and I developed a debilitating lower back pain. My mother took me to several doctors in Athens, who all reassured her that it was not a big problem, just an old injury that had healed and left a slight scar in one of the vertebrae of my lower spine. My mother, though, needing drama and looking for an excuse to bring me home against the strict orders of my father, finally found a doctor that gave her the most severe diagnosis imaginable, completely unsupported by evidence.

So, I was instantly transformed into an invalid paraplegic, in bed at home, with a live-in nurse to share my bedroom and with the serious prospect of never walking again in my life, but with the total attention, care, and concern of my family. This new life was the exact opposite of the life I had experienced in the previous two years at boarding school. Whereas I had felt harshly ostracized for my gender identity confusion by my family, I felt prized for my identity as an invalid. This made the new physical prison of my absolute bed rest more tolerable, if not emotionally rewarding.

With a private tutor, I completed the third and fourth elementary grades in my bed at home, and at the end of that second school year, I was suddenly pronounced completely healthy and my diagnosis erroneous. Just like that, I was walking free again to join the world. I have hardly any negative memories from that period of my life, other than, of course, the threat of never being able to walk again.

Whereas the two years of boarding school had pushed from the surface my gender confusion, the two years of being an invalid completed that process, by providing both my family and me a much bigger problem to fight against, one for which (medical) remedies existed and one that provided us a common goal. The concern about my medical condition diverted attention from the "original sin" of gender confusion.

From Family Exile to Family Divorce

Beginning with fifth grade, my parents placed me in a boys' boarding school, against my objections, where my brother already was and a much higher quality institution. This time my experience was the exact opposite. I quickly made friends with the kids in my class, and I quickly got used to the rules of the school. Before long, I was enjoying myself so much in school life with all my friends that my life at home, in comparison, became less fun and more boring. I am sure that the difference between spending the previous two grades bedbound at home allowed me to deeply appreciate being able to walk and run and play sports with classmates in fifth grade, my first year of freedom, so to speak. I preferred staying at school on weekends, rather than going home. My connection with my family had, in many ways, been irrevocably hurt during the first two years of elementary school. As I was finishing sixth grade, my friends in the second boarding school were becoming my family and the boarding school my home, and both of those elements made me happy. At home with my family was sheer boredom. Half a century later, the very same friends I made those early years of my life constitute a tight, terrific social network that remains the most important social support I have.

The Gay Little Monster—11 Years Old

My sexuality burst into my life with a bang in summer camp between fifth and sixth grade and left me with no doubt that at the age of 11 the only objects of my sexual desire and interest were adult men. It was a single event that identified my sexual orientation once and for all. I spent the entire time in camp clearly lusting after the body of my gym teacher, who was half naked in the gym shorts he wore all day long. One day in the sea, during our daily swim, I started wrestling with him in the water, ostensibly wanting to dunk him under, but in reality, using this excuse to touch and hold his half naked body. In the few minutes of our tussle in the water, I had an orgasm, for the first time in my life, without him becoming aware of what was going on.

My sudden realization forced me to place myself, lacking any other feedback from family, friends, or society, into the scarcely known but deeply detested category of faggots, synonymous at the time in the cultural and personal consciousness with "monsters." I was terrified. As a measure of the terror about my sexual identity, that of a gay little faggot, I never masturbated throughout childhood, until the ripe age of 19.

Throughout elementary school, the more I became accustomed to my boy persona, the more the female side of me retreated from my consciousness and transformed itself increasingly into a memory, a history, rather than an inner reality. In the first boarding school, the terrors of my daily school life had outshone my struggles with my gender by far. The two-year hiatus with the threatened fate of a life-long paraplegic had done the same, while in the second boarding school, the opposite took place. My integration into the boys' society solidified the boy in me and pushed back from my daily consciousness my earlier need and conviction to live as a girl, so much so that it became more of a memory, a history, an aberration of my early life.

In Love with Adult Men

Throughout my elementary and secondary school years, I never developed any romantic or sexual interest in boys, or girls, my age. This reality aided my full social integration in school life with my classmates without the intrusion of sex or romance. Instead, those interests, lust and love, were exclusively fixated on adult men, including the much older students in my school, classmates of my brother, who were juniors and seniors in high school. I developed a real crush on a buddy of my brother who was very friendly with me, though not in a sexual way. I pined for him for years, until he graduated and went to college in the USA. My brother, five years older, was another object of sexual attraction to me, once he became a young man.

I became sexually aware of my brother the month after I returned from that fateful summer camp. I was 11, and he was 16. That month of September, we shared a bedroom in a beach hotel where we vacationed as a family. Sleeping half naked in our beds, because of the summer heat, I became aware of his almost manly body. He was a star athlete in our school, and fresh from my experience with my gym instructor, I immediately eroticized his male body, though we did not get along with each other as brothers. When he was asleep, I would very lightly, so as not to wake him up, touch his half naked body, and smell his skin. It was a blissful erotic experience for me, fraught with all the anxiety of being caught.

This sporadic experience continued for the following three years, until he graduated and left for college in the USA. It was furtive and did not occur often, as we were in boarding school most of the week, and only shared our bedroom at home on Saturday nights, if at all. I still feel deeply ashamed as I am sharing this reality in this book. I consider it a measure of my character, and of my desperate need to indulge in my forbidden sexuality, that I engaged in such an aggressive, aberrant sexual behaviour toward my older brother.

Although I am firmly against sexual violence toward children by older adults, my personal experience puts a wrinkle, I believe, in the general understanding of children's sexuality. I spent my entire puberty and teenage years craving desperately sexual and romantic contact with older men, never having any interest in my peers, and I felt deeply deprived of it. I was not a sexually abused child in any way that I can imagine or remember. Yet, here I was sexually molesting, so to speak, my older brother. Many years later, when I finally had come out as a gay man to my family at 29, I initiated a talk with my brother about my behaviour, as I felt guilty. He cut me short, not wanting to discuss the past. It left me guessing that to some degree he had at some point become aware of what was going on but had never brought it up.

My aberrant behaviour speaks volumes about the sense of lawlessness I felt already as a child. I was not a normal human being but a monster, as defined by the established social norms and therefore could initiate sexual behaviours toward my gym teacher and my brother. I wonder if I would have acted this way had I not felt like a sexual and social outcast, but instead been accepted by my family and the society I lived in. I offer this not as an attempt to make excuses, but in an effort to understand human behaviours that are outside the norm.

In the years from puberty through my teens, my female side was latent but very potent. The role I instinctively gravitated toward was that of the girl who longed for the strong prince to love her and take care of her. As a teenager in boarding school, I was secretly in love with some young adult men who were wiser, stronger, and able, in my mind, to protect me and take care of me.

A Young Man with No Future—in Athens or in Zurich

As a teenager, and throughout my college years, I saw no viable future for me as a gay man, nor could I function sexually with a woman and hope to have a normal family life. Career plans meant nothing to me since there was no place for me in society. I was desperate to go to college abroad to escape the risk that my family and friends in Greece would see through my straight pretence and discover my gay reality.

I left to study civil engineering in Switzerland with a huge sigh of relief. It was my first self-directed migration. I was running away from a life that was becoming more of a nightmare as I was getting older and expected to engage in sexual and romantic affairs with women. I fled Greece in the hope that this problem would vanish or somehow get resolved. However, in Zurich, I quickly reconstructed my Athenian prison by joining a tight social group of Greek classmates, and I continued the same charade, that of a faggot trying to pass as straight. The label "faggot" may seem harsh, but it accurately depicts how I saw myself at the time. I believed my problem was my homosexual orientation. I understood my female identity to be an indication of homosexuality. I understand now that I chose to be a faggot rather than a woman, the lesser of two social disasters, or evils, if you will. I escaped to Switzerland to survive, but I continued to bury the more important problem of my gender identity.

My First Straight Affair

At the age of 22, I had my first wonderful, and short-lived, affair with an American woman my age, who was touring Europe. It was a breakthrough of sorts. I was able to perform sexually, but it felt like a performance, albeit a successful one. I remained racked with doubt and fear that I might not be able to perform the next time, and my real sexual interest still focused on men. When the woman returned home, our relationship transformed into a friendship, and I remained in a bind between gay reality and straight wishful pretence.

"I am Dying Inside"—Jungian Therapy

At the age of 24, my emotional dam finally burst open. My long-term isolation became intolerable. I started feeling that "I was dying inside." I opened the telephone book and picked a name blindly and started therapy with an old, wise Jungian psychiatrist. I begged him, while sobbing throughout my first session, to help me become straight, and he wisely agreed to try, knowing full well it was impossible. His lie was therapeutically helpful. I stayed with him for nine months, doing dream therapy three times a week. I had to write all my dreams in German, and then type all my associations about them and bring them to therapy to discuss. It was an exhausting and painful experience that produced results. As I kept analysing my family life in my dreams, the reality of being gay started to feel a little more tolerable. Without clearly understanding my process, I was exploring myself and my life in the company of a person whom I trusted and respected, and who in turn accepted me as I really was! I was getting inadvertently adjusted to the idea of being homosexual, as much as I was consciously hoping and aiming for the opposite.

I would experience the same paradoxical process in my second therapeutic experience in primal scream therapy, but much more consciously at that point. The dichotomy of the process pushing in a direction of accepting my homosexuality while my initial desperate goal was to become straight was true of this first therapeutic relationship, as it was for the following one in primal therapy. It speaks to the generally accepted fact that the most important factor for a positive outcome in psychotherapy is a positive therapeutic relationship between therapist and client. Here I was, a desperate young faggot, wanting to escape my horrible fate and instead gaining greater self-acceptance. I was able to show myself fully to a therapist I trusted, without feeling rejected or punished, instead feeling accepted and respected.

After nine months, I fled the Jungian psychiatrist, telling myself I needed to study for my final diploma exams, and I could not handle both. The emerging self-acceptance of my homosexuality that was slowly progressing through therapy was coming increasingly in conflict with my continued terror about my attraction to men and my need for secrecy. Final exams for the civil engineering diploma were approaching, and it felt impossible to struggle through both major stressors. Without calling, because of shame, I never went back one day, leaving the psychiatrist with a debt of 35 Swiss Francs, the cost of the last session.

The Gay Sex Neophyte—The Split Life

A year after I left therapy, I had taken but failed my final exams for the diploma in Civil Engineering, and a couple of months later my father suddenly passed away from a brain haemorrhage. For many years I felt guilty that my scholastic failure had possibly caused his death. A couple of months after his death, I started having sex with gay men. Flunking my exams had shown me that there was no future for me in a profession I hated and did not understand. It was a tremendous loss but also a kind of painful freedom. I had to choose another career and another lifestyle, closer to my real needs.

It was no accident that I would open myself to sex with men the moment my father died. He had been the main symbol of social interdiction in my life, and the main male symbol at that. I had no possibility and no obligation any more, to confess to him who I really was, and no chance of being rejected.

Soon, I created a whole secret world of one-night stands, short affairs, and buddies in the gay world, which I kept firmly separate and secret from my official "heterosexual" life. I met several terrific gay men who fell in love with me and whom I turned down, as I still could not contemplate living as a gay man. I was consciously looking for the impossible: to fall in love with an older straight man who would marry me and rescue me from my life. This lasted for two years until I finally completed my degree. I started looking with continued dread and anxiety into the future, wanting but not daring to study psychology as a career path.

The Last Hetero Effort—Migration to USA—Primal Scream—Marriage to Lena

At 28, I decided to flee my life once more and emigrate from Europe to the States. I was still unable to contemplate life as a gay man. I lived in two separate and unequal worlds, terrified of the one meeting the other. I knew I wanted to pursue a career in psychology, an impossibility in Greece at the time, and I was obliged by law to start my 30-month military service in Greece or lose my passport. I decided to dodge the Greek draft and take refuge in the USA, where I was guaranteed an immigrant visa through my brother who had become an American citizen. Catalyst for that decision to immigrate to the USA were the news of a splashy new psychotherapy theory in Los Angeles, named primal scream therapy, which promised to cure homosexuals and (re)turn them to heterosexuality through a process that was regressive and cathartic.

Immigrating to the states represented a painful loss, a difficult life transition, and an amazing opportunity. The loss was deep, as I was abandoning for the second time in my life all the people I had become close to, up until then, as well as both the Greek and the European/Swiss cultures. My first few months in the USA were both full of excitement at the new culture and full of loneliness and heartbreak at cutting off my lifeline to all things Greek, European, and to all the people I loved and felt close to. My first year was also full of hope of "shedding" my faggot mantle through primal therapy, and the dreams of a new life, both personally and professionally. In the first six months, I came close to dropping everything and returning to Europe. Yet, toward the end of the first year, I had decided that the living environment in Los Angeles, where I settled, was a far better place for me, as a gay monster, than anything I had experienced in the old continent. Part of my need to immigrate was to lose myself in the anonymity of a huge city, and Los Angeles offered that.

The process of primal scream therapy was intense, and the results were deep and visible but certainly not in the desired switch of sexual orientation. Besides falling madly in love with one of the straight male therapists, I was able to cry and rage, both functions that had remained dormant, or rather undeveloped, in my life until then. During the first year I drew nonstop portraits of my mother, severe with non-seeing eyes and later innumerable portraits of myself, dishevelled, multi-coloured, and crazed out.

As primal therapy progressed, I began to feel more entitled to be who I was, which at the time, I had to concede and knew to be a gay man. Yet, because I had started the therapy with such vigor and determination to turn straight, I pursued straight relationships early on and before I knew it, I was dating, having sex with, and living with another immigrant woman, named Lena, from Sweden, who was also attending primal scream therapy for her own needs for personal growth. We started our relationship with the known fact that I was gay, but we were both determined to make it as a straight couple and to raise a family together. We were the same age. We lived together for four years, getting married after the first.

It is a measure of the variety of sexual experiences in people that from the get-go I was fully functional and remained happily functional sexually with Lena. Her deep love and desire for me were more than enough to allow me to enjoy myself sexually with her and perform with no trouble at all. As my relationship with my wife, Lena, progressed successfully, primal scream therapy was pushing me to be more myself, meaning queerer. Ironically, as I was establishing beyond any doubt my gay identity, I was in the process of committing myself to a heterosexual union. It was also during this time that I allowed myself for the first time since pre-school to engage in female related endeavours. I designed, cut, and sewed male and female clothing in the then popular unisex style, something that spoke to me intimately. I let my hair grow long, shaved my beard, and started wearing the unisex clothing I designed and made for myself and for sale.

Under the social cover of being in a heterosexual union, I felt safer and freer to allow the female identity impulses to come out. In all my adult life, those years with Lena were the only period I allowed myself to be free of facial hair. All the rest of my life, I have been obsessively hiding my subjective perception of my facial features as being too feminine, and therefore unacceptably risky to betray something deeper in me. The irony of this lifetime hiding behind my facial hair is that I look attractive in a masculine way with my full beard and get a lot of compliments about that. This otherwise trivial detail only follows and substantiates my life-long experience of living in two different worlds. The one I experience inside of me and the one that others around me experience and report back to me. If nothing else, this autobiographical narrative is a desperate, late life attempt on my part to officially bridge the chasm between these two worlds, an exercise that continues to fill me with anxiety and dread.

Gay Heaven, Rochlin Therapy

My marriage did not last because I could not give up on being with men in lust and in love. I was not happy missing men, and it affected my life and our relationship. It is a measure of the terror of being myself that it was Lena who gave up on us first and moved out. Once our relationship had ended, I decided that this was the end of my multi-decade effort to live a functionally straight life. I felt I had tried enough and had struggled a hell of a lot and had done everything that one could do to avoid slipping into the gay space. So, I started having a busy gay sexual life. I soon developed a wonderful tight group of gay male friends, most of whom were in actual relationships with each other, which was a wonderful eye opener to me, and a tangible reassurance that life in gaydom was not equivalent to hell.

At the same time, I finally dared to follow my plan of becoming a psychotherapist and completed a Masters in Counseling Psychology, which opened the door for me to later acquire the state license in this profession. I worked for several years in a psychiatric crisis intervention program, a wonderful initial clinical training experience, and then started working as a therapist at AIDS Project Los Angeles with mostly gay men who had HIV or AIDS and their partners. By then, several years after my divorce from Lena, my life had become 100% gay. I identified fully as a gay man, almost all my friends were gay men, I worked with gay men in a gay organization, and I fully participated in the gay ghetto community of West Hollywood, sexually, romantically, socially, politically, and culturally. I had come to believe that I had finally earned, particularly through my work at APLA, a place in the sun; that I deserved to be alive and be part of the human community, something I had never felt I deserved until then. The decade of my forties was probably the single most carefree and relaxed time of my life, notwithstanding the fact that this was the decade when the AIDS epidemic was ravaging our gay community, and that I was working in the middle of that tragic reality. The social and existential drama of the AIDS epidemic easily eclipsed any personal issues. I honored the fact that I was working for and with my "brothers" in the time of their most urgent need, and that made me feel really good about myself, for the first time in my life.

I went into psychotherapy for the third time, in the early stages of my full "gay recovery." The focus of my therapy was issues of intimacy, and I had chosen an excellent gay male psychotherapist. I stayed with him for a few years and worked well but superficially, in the manner of Rogerian client-centered modality. As client, I brought no questions about my gender identity, just issues of committing to a relationship with a gay man. Neither I nor my therapist detected any questions about my early childhood history of gender confusion. I interpreted that reality as a typical stage in many gay men's childhoods, which was the prevailing cultural understanding in the gay community at the time.

Between the sissy boy and the gender-confused child there are so many shades of gray, which I was unclear and unquestioning about, as was my therapist. Before long, that third time in psychotherapy turned into a review of weekly life problems and very little effort was made by either of us to go deeper into my life issues, beyond the basic area of intimacy. My gender identity seemed set and clear, as was my gay sexual orientation. The only question that we dealt with is how to get myself to marry one, as opposed to running away from them all.

In sex and romance, I was very active, even promiscuous, especially in the pre-AIDS period. I was especially attracted to men who did not want me, and that included straight men, of course. At the time, I thought that the main factor for my attraction to straight men was my fear of intimacy and committed relationships, a real life problem for me, but I wonder now to what extent the reason I turned down so many eligible, excellent, and very interested gay male partners was possibly the fact that underneath my consciousness only a straight man was acceptable for marriage. My sexual fantasies had always been about straight men, acting gay for pay or by seduction or coercion, beginning at age 19 when I started masturbating.

Female Ghosts—Pacifica—Walker—Homeless Guy—Cyber Sex—Mid Life Crisis

In my late forties things started changing, all at the same time and in several aspects of my life. I had grown stale and bored with my work as a psychotherapist and decided to enroll in a doctoral program in clinical psychology at Pacifica Graduate Institute. A little prior to that, I had entered psychotherapy again, for the fourth time, and significantly, I signed on with a gay male Jungian psychotherapist I had known in the community, and to whom I was sexually attracted but who also interested me because of his avant-garde theorizing about gay identity. Those two processes—the academic and the therapeutic—started my descent, if you will, into my long lost or ignored feminine side. In school, the archetypal, Jungian process, which was intellectually thrilling and intra-psychically dynamic, led me deeper into myself. What I encountered was the girl I used to be as a toddler and pre-schooler. My classmates were deeply encouraging and supportive. So was my therapist, who encouraged me in experimenting, ever so timidly, with cross dressing and with trying to date a homeless straight man who was willing to have sex of sorts with me, in exchange for a temporary reprieve from homelessness and pennilessness. These two parallel descending staircases into the female side of me brought out depression, which was aided and exacerbated by the timely fact that I turned 50 during that process. Depression was in the works for me for quite a few years during my late forties, also because my entire social network, which consisted almost exclusively of gay men, had died because of AIDS. Suddenly, yet not so unexpectedly, the day after my big

50th birthday party, I came to feel without a shadow of a doubt that my life in these first 50 years had been a complete personal failure and was doomed to remain that for the next 50, if I was unlucky enough to live that long.

I struggled through five years with that midlife crisis. In the early part of that, I became even more acquainted with the fact that hiding in me was a powerful need to be a woman, at least on a sexual level, by spending a year and a half busy in cybersex, at a time when computers did not have any video equipment. This allowed me to pretend I was a woman and engage in frenetic cybersex with straight men over the Internet. It was shocking to me both how powerful the sexual connections were over the web and even more important, how powerful my eroticism felt when I pretended I was a woman, connecting via cyberspace with a straight man. My personality changed when I pretended to be a woman. I became freer, more aggressive, and much more self-assured in my communications and interactions with my cybersex straight male partners than I had ever been in "real life" as a gay man with my gay male sexual partners.

The fourth aspect of my change was the hair on my head. I decided to let my hair grow to woman's length over a period of several years. It was a powerful experience that was not entirely positive. On the one hand, I was enjoying the fact of openly flirting with the female side of me, as my hair grew long, curly, and lush. On the other hand, I started gaining weight. I experienced a strange feeling of incompatibility between the femininity of my long hair, and my male, athletic body. I could not do sports with long hair, possibly because it reminded me of my masculine body. So, I stopped, little by little, my daily exercising, aided by my depression, and increased my food intake. In the past 19 years, since my 50th birthday, I must have accumulated about 70 pounds to my normal weight, even after I cut my hair short again. My romantic socializing ceased to exist, initially because of my depression, but also because of my desire for straight men had uncovered the senselessness of trying to date gay men.

The Sexual Dichotomy—"Gay-for-Pay" Straight Men versus Gay Men

In this last decade, the difference between my erotic desires toward gay and straight men has become increasingly clear. My real sexual passion was for straight men, even to the extent that I would gladly engage in specific sexual practices with them, which I found disgusting and avoided with gay men. Gay men's penises somehow were unappetizing, even disgusting, whereas the penises of straight men, I discovered to my surprise, were deeply attractive. On the other hand, my anxiety when being in bed with a straight man was so high that erections and orgasms became sometimes more difficult to reach, as I was, like any stereotypical cliché of a woman, more interested in, and more worried about, their pleasure than mine. At the same time, I began noticing more and more how exciting it was for me to experience the visible indifference, even disgust, that straight men felt and exhibited toward me and how non-exciting, even annoying, and practically a sexual turn-off, it was for me to experience the sexual interest that gay men showed toward me in bed.

Initially I explained this as a lack of love for myself, a reality that is hard to refute or ignore in my life, but eventually I started thinking that my excitement in the sexual disinterest that a straight man exhibited toward me might have more to do with validating my female side. Conversely, the annoyance and sexual deflation I experienced with gay men who were turned on to me had to do with my experience that my female was being trampled, so to speak, when my sexual partner related sexually to me as a man and became aroused by my maleness.

Superseding all considerations is the fact that a basic loving encounter between two people can produce sexual excitement and an orgasm for me. As in my sexual life at the time with my then-wife Lena, there are often times when an encounter with a tender, loving gay man provides me with an enriching sexual experience.

The Deeper Awakening Too Late

In the last decade, as issues of professional retirement and mortality have become important preoccupations in my life, a powerful nostalgia and homesickness for Greece developed in me, and I started spending all of my vacation time in my last job as a college professor, in Greece. I have grown close again with old classmates and friends from elementary school and their families. I retired from teaching psychotherapy and from mental health in general and have returned to live in Athens, for most of the year, in the same neighborhood where my family lived when I "deserted" Greece 50 years ago.

My passion for living in Greece, in Athens, of speaking Greek, or relating to Greeks in my daily life, is indescribable. English, which is my best language by far, is the language of my brain, whereas Greek comes from my gut, even though it is academically challenged in my case, because my education in Greek ended with high school. This is how language shows me the split in my life. I fled Greece at 19, because my gut could not stand the terror of being a gay monster in Greece, and my brain sought cultural shelter and the intellectual challenges that Greece did not offer. Switzerland and the States were good to my gut, by giving it a solid rest and allowing it to breathe, even if that meant that I did not proceed with the direction in self-actualization that other people have taken, the trans-way. I do not wish and do not dare to become a woman, more fervently so than in any other time in my life. I cannot imagine my life as an old woman, whereas it is not so bad, even pleasant, to be an old man. On the other hand, I am more sexual than ever.

I am obsessed with my sexuality, which still is dominated by masturbation, always involving fantasies of sex with straight men.

I am not a woman. I stopped fantasizing about being a woman by puberty, and I stopped dreaming of being rescued by a man by the age of 35, when I started having a career and a social identity that made me proud. But I have never stopped lusting for a straight man, and I cannot imagine that I ever will.

The subtlety, diversity, and intricacy of human experience is fathomless, I believe, and very difficult to decipher and understand. Being back in Greece, I am finding that unbeknownst to me, after 50 years away, I have been missing out on Greek men! It is funny, it is outrageous, for an old geezer like me to be still so sex and romance obsessed, exactly because I have not had my fill until now. It adds insult to the injury to have searched for lust and romance in the four corners of the world, in order to return and find out that nobody is as attractive to me as a Greek man. It is the culture, it is the language, and it is the personality of Greek men, including this everlasting macho veneer that is still so prevalent and bodes so problematic for nontraditional relationships.

There was another amazing closing of a circle in the last few years. Upon my retirement from teaching mental health, I started writing a column in a Greek financial newspaper on the politics and the economies of Greece and the Eurozone. I rediscovered my initial professional and intellectual passion, which is politics.

In conclusion, I would like to say this: This chapter has become a much more harrowing document and experience that I had anticipated when I started on the project. It has been extremely difficult for me to sustain more than a couple of hours of work in any single day on this paper. I feel it also provides a distorted view of my life, as a whole, by focusing on the single most difficult, problematic, and painful area. My life, as a whole, is much bigger than that, and it includes many areas of happiness, comfort, peace, privilege, good luck, love, human warmth, intellectual and professional success, and a hell of a lot of fun.

Spending all this time describing and lamenting how "life has done me wrong" has been a difficult task for me, which I undertook for a couple of reasons. One, foremost, is my personal narcissism. Who does not want to talk about him/herself? I got to talk about both himself and herself in one chapter. What privilege! The other reason is that the issues that find safe harbour in the acronym LGBTQ are multiple, diverse, and largely, I believe, still unexplored. Sharing my perspective and experience adds to this exploration.

And then, there is a third and last reason. This story is about silence, shame, subterfuge, secrecy, avoidance, camouflage, etc. I hope that this chapter serves as a kind of antidote to all these poisons, personally, but more importantly, also socially. As the amazingly successful AIDS activist movement proclaimed and proved: SILENCE EQUALS DEATH.

Part IV

Native Language, Foreign Tongue

Speaking Oneself as an Immigrant

Chapter 7

Living between Languages
A Bi-Focal Perspective

Jeanne Wolff Bernstein, PhD

The experience of returning to my homeland after 30 something years of living in the United States leaves me fairly certain that I will never feel at home in one country or the other. Having moved as a young woman from Germany to the US was one experience, but moving back to Austria, a German-speaking homeland of sorts, is another new experience altogether. While the first move was daring and adventurous, full of possibilities and new discoveries and the subsequent establishment of my familial and professional life, it is the second move, back "home" to Europe and my supposed maternal language that has had unforeseen effects and is the focus of this paper.

Arriving in the United States as a young woman in my twenties, I encountered all the usual surprises and common discoveries. Berkeley, in particular, was in the last phases of its hippy existence, and arriving at that time seemed to open up many new perspectives and possibilities of living, loving, and working. At that time, I could be clearly identified as a woman coming from a foreign country, a country with a dark past and a language with an intonation that was difficult to hide. I considered it to be a triumph each time I was not instantly identified as a native German speaker. When I was recognized as such, I felt defeated and considered it a source of embarrassment. More often than not, there was a sense of unease in the unasked questions about my past and, in particular, about my parents' past. Over time, even though my accent faded and my grammar improved, I remained a foreigner, a European, and many additional years of living in California could not change that fact. At the same time, I became a foreigner in my own home country; I had lost track of the political and social actualities. I never voted for any political figure in my homeland and had lost sight of the day-to-day political debates. At the same time, I grew apart from my family of origin, missing out on many family occasions and get-togethers. Since I had made the decision to leave, I was considered to be the one who had turned her back on her home country. Nobody had pressured me to leave; this was not a forced exile. Instead, I had followed a strong urge to move away from a country in which I had not felt at home and with which I was not internally identified. Retroactively speaking, with a sense of *Nachtraeglichkeit*, I think

I was so strongly unconsciously identified with the very people who had to flee Germany that I chose to take a similar path. Now I understand that once I had left and had taken all the steps to establish a life in another country, I would never be the same person again. What began as a perhaps light-hearted adventure turned into a life-changing experience. As the psyche is divided, now my life was to be divided forever between two cultures and two languages. You know you can never go back to one but always remain divided between two. As Beltsiou writes in her chapter, "In migrating we make ourselves at home in the foreign and at home with our foreignness."

My identification with this internal foreignness was probably one of the many reasons I was attracted to the work of Jacques Lacan in my psycho-analytic education. He emphasizes the subject's internal disharmony and de-centeredness, the I as Other, as the fundamental structure of each individual. His concept of the mirror stage represents this drama of a tension between an internally felt sense of insufficiency and an anticipation of a promised sense of unity and permanence. As Pagel writes, "What I long for is a me, but what mine is, reveals itself as otherness and this otherness reveals itself as alter ego. What seems to promise identity, proves itself to be unreachably foreign. Fas-cination and aggression form the circle of this unstable relationship" (1989, p. 28, translation mine). "I is Other," Pagel writes, which is, I think, the expe-rience of many immigrants who end up living double lives, caught between their internally held, possibly rejected early experience of their homeland and their later, wished-for, and often idealized life in a foreign country.

For years, I could not have imagined returning back "home" to Europe. I looked upon people who decided to return to their homeland as "losers," since they had failed to come to terms with their new lives in the United States. Ensconced in an endless series of comparisons between my two coun-tries and cultures, I had come to identify myself as an American with Euro-pean roots and a European sensibility, the latter being more plainly sensed by others than truly felt by me. What people see and make of you and what you internally feel becomes a sharply divided experience for any immigrant because, while you may have internally adjusted to your new life and new customs, the Other, the native, continues to see and hear you as a foreigner. In retrospect, I realize that I needed to come to a foreign country to re-live this double-edged experience of feeling at home while others continued to consider me a foreigner. I could not have lived this bi-focal experience had I decided to remain in my homeland. After a few years English had become my primary language; I spoke, wrote, and dreamt in it and made jokes in it and would only venture into German when I made telephone calls back to my family or read the occasional newspaper in German. I made no efforts to find fellow Germans in Berkeley because my wish to be separate from what I deemed to be a more conventional life was too strong. In contrast to younger German immigrants who may be less connected to and further removed from Germany's Nazi history, I also had no desire to be associated with fellow compatriots because of the shame I felt because of our common post-war history. I did not want to deny history, but I wanted to be removed from it, and through this removed stance, I began to look at German pre- and post-war history with a clearer mind. As I became increasingly absorbed in the English-speaking world, the boundaries between my two languages became well established. I lost my facility for speaking German and sounded awkward and strange when I returned to Germany for vacations. Did I forget German on purpose, I wondered, or did my capacity to speak German fluently vanish as a way of separating from home? Idioms were the first thing to go, and then entire words seemed to disappear. As I grew more proficient in English and felt more at home in it, I began to lose the ability to build bridges between the two languages and was often truly lost in translation, standing between two places.

Now that I have returned to a German-speaking world, a very peculiar and unexpected sensibility has unfolded inside of me. While I had disliked most everything connected to Germany and to being German by birth, I have slowly come to re-discover German as a language that speaks to me again but in ways that it had never spoken to me before. I now hear and read German through the lens of a foreigner and play with words as I hear them and as they come to me. I am intrigued by the word constructions, by the ease with which one letter can turn the whole sense of a word upside down, or take delight in realizing how one syllable like "ver" can dictate the structure of a whole language. Take the word *Verlust*, strictly translated as loss; however, what gets lost in this translation, is that *Verlust* literally means a loss of lust. I have known and spoken this word my entire life, but it was not until I came back into my maternal language that I could hear the playfulness in this word. In "Als Freud das Meer Sah" (when Freud saw the ocean) Goldschmidt, a writer and brilliant translator, argues that Freud could have never discovered the unconscious without the syllable "ver." Writing for a French audience, Goldschmidt says, "Language is the escape of another language; it embodies the longing (*Sehnsucht*) for what language cannot express in its own words. In his analysis of parapraxes, Freud discovers that an internal kinship exists between those incidents (*Zwischenfaelle*) that express themselves in the pre-syllable ver: *versprechen, verlegen, verhoeren, verlesen.* ...We also find in the word *Verdraengung* (repression) in German a gesture of its own: one which extinguishes itself" (p. 54). Unlike in French, and in English, I might add, this small, three-letter syllable takes up centre stage in the German language and performs magic all around itself. Take any of the words, Goldschmidt lists from Freud's 1901 text, *The Psychopathology of Everyday Life*, and you can see what I mean: *versprechen* or *Versprecher* means a "slip of the tongue," but it also means "a promise." Or *verlegen* means to misplace something, but it also can be heard at the same time as an adjective that means being "shy." It becomes even more powerful with the word *verhoeren*, which denotes "mishearing" but as a noun also means "interrogation." Goldschmidt concludes that Freud was just merely noticing how the inexpressible bubbled to the surface as he observed the movements of the German language and argues that "The German language always already knew everything about itself! Without ver, Freud would have never had the basic idea (*Einfall*), which led him to the discovery of psycho-analysis, what would have happened without ver, without un, without ueber, to Freud?" (p. 55).

Goldschmidt writes, that at every moment, language offers its own sur-prises, "that is why it is language, and what language cannot do on its own, shows up/is being demonstrated in another language" (p. 66).

At another point, Goldschmidt asserts, that "Freud had observed the German language through another language, a language which speaks through German and upon which his entire analysis was founded" (p. 73). It was Freud's remarkable gift to be so acutely and yet playfully atten-tive to what language could do, express, and perform. In other words, according to Goldschmidt, everything was already hidden in German, and it was simply the fact that Freud allowed himself to be seduced by this language that enabled him to discover the language's linguistic secrets that had already always been hidden in it. "Language," Goldschmidt writes, "is nothing else but to say the unsaid and to express the inexpressible" (p. 99). He argues that unlike French, for instance, where infancy is closely connected to "not-speaking," infants meaning without speech, German, speaks constantly of childhood, keeping words, like belonging, origin, and lineage in common usage. The child continues in the German language, whereas it is separated and distinct in French. My newly re-found pleasure in playing with words may speak of this intimate connection with the lost pleasure children typically experience as they learn their first words and begin to play naturally with them. Is "free association" not an invitation back to the childish pleasure of being guided by mere word connections (*Wort-verknüpfungen*) as they appear in one's mind without invoking the rational side that exerts critical judgments and screening out of irrelevant or morally offensive ideas?

With this new-found pleasure I had gained in the German language, I thought again of Freud's concept of "*Nachtraeglichkeit*," which has regained prominence in the recent psychoanalytic literature. What is rarely mentioned when people try to wrestle it away from Strachey's unfortunate translation of "deferred action" is that the word literally means "to carry something behind somebody," like a bellboy who carries your luggage behind you in a hotel, eventually catching up with you in your room after you have inspected it for yourself. Staying with this metaphor, I thought that English was perhaps standing in for the bellboy, relieving me of the heavy luggage of my German roots and allowing me for an extended period of time to enjoy and explore my new hotel room, California. However, eventually my luggage arrived and caught up with me, forcing me to deal with what I had initially hoped to leave behind. As I already remarked in my essay "The Photography of Shimon Attie," Freud's idea of "*Nachträglichkeit*" is epistemologically linked to the German word "*Nachtragbarkeit*" which means resentment. "This affinity," I wrote, "may not be entirely coincidental, as it is only through retrospection that one's [own] story can flow again—a story that had been sequestered in crevices of bitterness, shame and resentment. Through an imaginary break-in, memory can start rolling again, pursuing its diverse and unpredictable paths, which seemed to be blocked as long as the past was held in an anxious grip" (2000, pp. 368–369).

Something was catching up with me; I could no longer maintain the distance from my home country as I had wished and had succeeded in doing for several decades. A voice inside of me spoke to me and encouraged me to go back to this Europe I had left with some resentment and to give it another chance. The suitcases had to be packed again and returned to the continent I had left 37 years ago. There was no warm welcome back home again but instead a period of getting acquainted with a country and a language that I had left behind a long time ago. I discovered some old customs but was mostly interested in the new realties, rules, and words that had emerged during my long absence, many of which had been influenced by the US. Here I was, a European with an American passport, now standing in line at the Austrian immigration office, asking for permission to obtain a visa to work in a country that I had once considered my temporary home. The humour was not lost on me when the Austrian immigration officer commended me on my good German. To return as a stranger to my own country has been a doubly decentring experience. Nothing on the outside reveals me now as a foreigner, no strange accent betrays me, except for when I suddenly cannot think of a word in German or when I formulate a sentence according to an English syntax rather than a German one. At those moments, I feel like I am living in a hybrid space, no longer knowing which language to speak, feeling at a loss in this liminal, self-created world of confused tongues. The foreignness that I had worn so plainly—for others—on the outside in the US I have begun to carry now on the inside, living the *heimlich* in the *Heimisch*, the secret, the uncanny, as Freud wrote (1919) in my internal at-home-going-on being.

The desire to compare languages and cultures no longer has such a powerful hold upon me as it did during my first migration. Instead, I have grown more curious about bringing, as Goldschmidt writes, each language to speak (*Die Sprache zum Reden zu bringen*). I observe what I can do in each language and see what it allows me to do and what affect and effect it produces in me in turn. Goldschmidt writes, "The whole Freudian endeavor consists in bringing language to speak and to see what language has to say and to pay attention to it" (1998/2010, p. 24). As Beltsiou notices as well, languages can no longer be simply divided into more deeply emotionally resonant or performative ones. I do not feel more deeply touched in my maternal language than in my adopted one. My immediately lived experience is that I terribly miss certain expressions in English, which I simply cannot translate into German. I miss the ease with which I can say "one's mind" in English. I am about to voice it in German and then stumble over *Kopf* or *Geist*. The same goes for "mindful" or "thoughtful"; I simply land in a cul-de-sac, a dead-end, as I try to fabricate a word that pays some justice to the one I miss saying. Here Goldschmidt speaks to me again when he writes: "The silence of other languages with regard to certain words exposes the profound depth out of which language has emerged" (p. 28).

In *The Instance of the Letter in the Unconscious*, Lacan writes of the predominance of language,

> And the subject, while he may appear to be the slave of language, is still more the slave of a discourse in the universal movement of which his place is already inscribed at his birth, if only in the form of his proper name. Reference to the experience of the community as the substance of this discourse, resolves nothing. For this experience takes on its essential dimension in the tradition established by this discourse. This tradition, long before the drama of history is inscribed in it, grounds the elementary structures of culture. And these very structures reveal an ordering of possible exchanges, which—even if unconscious—is inconceivable apart from the permutations authorized by language. (1977/2002, p. 140)

Coming back to this maternal language and hearing and speaking it now through the mind of a stranger has convinced me once again of the structuring power language exerts upon our deepest emotions, longings, and desires. For instance, while I can say in English and German, "I miss you"/"*Ich vermisse Dich*," that direct expression of a loss is impossible in the French language; there it can only be constructed passively, and nothing in the language could make you express this feeling otherwise. "*Tu me manques*"/"You are being missed by me." In a recent seminar on Lacan, I noted this limitation and force of language and learned in this international group of students that the same sentiment in Spanish translates as "I make you smaller." Knowing different languages no longer constitutes merely a mastery of different vocabularies but affords the ability to play within one language and between languages. Do we not as analysts take the position of an outsider, of the third ear with and through which we can hear the foreignness in the patients' speech and their at-homeness in their foreignness as a means of touching upon the unconscious meanings, lurking behind their conscious statements? Is an analyst not, as Joyce McDougall (1978) wrote, "an immigrant with a temporary visa, drawing upon herself forbidden desires, idealized representations, threats, fear and anger belonging to the original objects?" (p. 292).

The analyst is also called upon to act as a witness to unbearable and unformulated experiences, especially when it concerns work with patients who have been severely traumatized. Both Boulanger (2005) and Peskin (2012) speak of the necessity of actively bearing witness to the patients' horrific, traumatic experiences as a means of allowing them to become witness to their own psychic survival. Were we at this moment to play with the English word "witness," which focuses on "wit," or the possibility of losing one's wits/losing one's mind—wit is the older word for mind—and look at the German word for witness, *Zeuge*, playing upon the expanded possibility of *zeugen/Zeuger*, "to sire," "to father," or "to beget" (which also means "to create/creator"), we can observe what is at stake in this active act of witnessing. In a way, what becomes repressed and slides under the bar in one language appears in another, providing the very function that was missing in the moment of trauma: a father who provides a structuring function, in which words are created and experiences are symbolized again.

Thus, returning to a homeland has unexpectedly given me a new alertness to the present, to things said and unsaid. I think I can now act as a more forceful and outspoken witness to the pieces of history that still risk being ignored, resurfacing in Austria over and over again in the guise of a strict and inhumane immigration policy, for instance, in which foreigners are treated with disdain and held in contemptuous disregard. They are forced into living situations that are cruel and degrading. It is possible that I had to leave my homeland in order to gather forces and become more courageous and outspoken about the injustices and cruelties I had observed and intuited at a young age but was not able to confront directly. Coming back to this estranged home helped me return and meet my past in a more differentiated way, a journey that is reminiscent of the process of psychoanalysis.

In my position as an analyst, I hope to have discovered a fresh ability to listen to my patients' words with a foreign ear, possibly standing between the two languages that Freud wrote about in *The Interpretation of Dreams*: "The dream-thoughts and the dream-content are presented to us like two versions of the same subject-matter in two different languages. Or more properly, the dream-content seems like a transcript of the dream-thoughts into another mode of expression, whose characters and syntactic laws is our business to discover by comparing the original and the translation" (1900, p. 277). I think I have made it my business as well to return to the early writings of Freud, such as *The Interpretation of Dreams* and *The Psychopathology of Everyday Life* to recapture one more time, this time in Freud's mother tongue, the fervent spirit of Freud's early works and of his radical discovery of a linguistic unconscious. Living now not far from Berggasse 19 and Liechtensteinstrasse 17, where Berta Pappenheim resided as a young girl, I cannot overlook the fact that so much of our present work of psychoanalysis began with this young woman, who not only taught Josef Breuer the "talking cure" but whose symptomatology also began with a confusion and repression of language. Breuer writes, "... she was at a loss to find words," Breuer writes, "and this difficulty gradually increased. Later she lost her command of grammar and syntax, she no longer conjugated verbs, and eventually she used only infinitives. ... In the process of time she became almost completely deprived of words" (1893, p. 25).

At a moment in history in which much of psychoanalysis is once again medicalized and domesticated with a strong current running toward greater coherence and more mutual relatedness, I believe it is a necessary step to go backwards and to remind ourselves of the beginnings of psychoanalysis as it was struggling against the mainstream, battling against a homogeneous medical establishment. It was then, through a radical exploration of the unconscious "as a mental life that belongs to someone else or ascribed to this other person" (1915, p. 169) that Freud was able to break through these conventional barriers and offer individuals the space within which they could re-appropriate their lost and forbidden desires.

In my desire to depart from home and to find myself at home in a foreign country where I was not considered to be at home by the outside, only to return to a home country where I now live this hidden estrangement inside of myself, I have at last discovered the uncanniness the *Unheimlichkeit* of the *"Heim*," the strangeness of being at-home-ness.

References

Beltsiou, J. (2010) *Home lost and found*, unpublished talk, IARPP, Madrid.

Boulanger, G. (2005) From Voyeur to witness: Recapturing symbolic function after massive psychic trauma. *Psychoanalytic Psychology*, 22: 21–31.

Breuer, J., & Freud. S. (1893). Studies on hysteria, Fraeulein Anna O. *The Standard Edition of the Complete Psychological Works of Sigmund Freud*. Trans. James Strachey. London: The Hogarth Press, Vol. II.

Freud, S. (1900). The interpretation of dreams. *The standard edition of the complete psychological works of Sigmund Freud*. Trans. James Strachey. London: The Hogarth Press, Vol. IV.

Freud, S. (1915) The Unconscious, *S.E.* Trans. James Strachey. London: The Hogarth Press, Vol. XIV.

Goldschmidt, G.A. (1988/2010) *Als Freud das Meer sah, Freud und die deutsche Sprache*. Frankfurt: Fischer Taschenbuchverlag.

Lacan, J. (1977). The instance of the letter in the unconscious or reason since Freud. *Ecrits*, Trans. Bruce Fink. New York, NY: Norton and Norton, pp. 138–168.

McDougall, J. 1978 (1992). *Plea for a measure of abnormality*. New York, NY: Brunner/Mazel Publishers.

Pagel, G. (1989). *Jacques Lacan, Zur Einfuehrung*. Hamburg: Junius Verlag.

Peskin, H. (2012) Man is a wolf to man: Disorders of dehumanization in psycho-analysis and psychotherapy. *Psychoanalytic Dialogues*, 22: 190–205

Wolff Bernstein, J. (2000). Making a memorial place: The photography of Shimon Attie. *Psychoanalytic Dialogues*, Volume 10, pp. 347–370.

Chapter 8

The Place across the Street

Some Thoughts on Language, Separateness, and Difference in the Psychoanalytic Setting

Irene Cairo, MD

Introduction

The poignancy of the experience of living in a foreign language is beautifully captured in Eva Hoffman's haunting memoir, "Lost in Translation." Polish born, brought first to Canada and then to the US, she writes, "When I fall in love with my first American, I also fall in love with otherness, with the far spaces between us and the distance we have to travel to meet at the source of our attraction."

This visually evocative imagery seems to me particularly expressive of the inevitable drama of the immigrant's experience, a drama that erupts most clearly when she later writes, "Should you marry him? The question echoes in English: Yes. Should you marry him? The question echoes in Polish: No."

Some Thoughts about Language

Two categories that constitute an invariable model in all languages regard person and time. Every individual thinks of "myself" in regard to "you" and to "he/they." Every time a statement uses "I" it evokes a you, an other. And every speech takes place in a particular moment.

Those qualities of human communication, universal, are special in the context of an exchange between a native speaker and a foreign speaker, the immigrant. Mistakes, misunderstandings, and distortions inevitable in any communication are more likely to occur, and are often more poignant, in an exchange where the language spoken is a foreign one for one participant, and even more when the language is foreign to both.

A message is sent. The source has an intention, the target who receives the message may or may not be open to maintaining a dialogue. In psychoanalysis, this "circuity" is essential. The information that each participant—analyst and analysand—sends to the other occurs in a very special context. There are specific codes that relate to the analytic situation. There is an implicit understanding that there is an unconscious intention behind the message and that such unconscious content will be discovered.

We know that speech is both a connection to the mother and also the means of separating from her. This drama is often disguised by the immigrant's family learning of the language of the adoptive country. When immigration has occurred in childhood, it is quite possible that the immigrant's new language does not even reveal an accent. If race and culture are not in themselves revealing of difference, the immigrant may appear to blend, and then that silent drama of alienness so beautifully and sadly revealed in Eva Hoffman's story cannot even be shared.

Along those lines, the acquisition of the new language by the immigrant—or the reacquaintance with the new language, if it had been learned before—is in many ways similar to the acquisition of language by the child. Some aspects are similar: Like the child with the parents, the immigrant often feels left out of the communications that are not understood. Also like the child, at first acquiring the new language can be contaminated by conflict not inherent to language difficulties, but rather an inevitable development as an expression of the emotional complications of the immigrant's experience. For the child, as Melanie Klein (1928) has shown, part of the Oedipal conflict is played out in being excluded from the adult communication that takes place before the child is capable of language. However, as for the child, the acquisition of the new language can be a joyous experience or be immersed in feelings of loss and mourning. If the process is one of growth, the result is manifested in the deepening of affective experience and enriching of the capacity for thought.

Framework

As I formulated in the abstract, this paper is centered on clinical observations made on patients whose analysis is conducted in a language different from their own mother tongue. These observations regard the emergence, within the analysis, of that mother tongue, not spoken by me. This development was not only inevitable but perhaps essential to an analytic process that exerts a pressure on the patient beyond the usual deprivations of the setting. Perhaps this idiosyncratic event could be matched to other clinical situations in which some other action by the patient is also inevitable and necessary and requires for the moment, the suspension of exploration and interpretation. In the clinical vignettes I present here, the complexity of those moments was only able to be revealed later, as the deepening understanding progressed. The meaning of my patient's act, the emergence of the mother tongue in the session, the affective development and integration, was only available later. There is, of course, always a tension between what can be represented and what was experienced. In Poland's (1998) words, sometimes we are necessarily, the "other" of a communication, a new object with whom a new transferential event acquires new meaning and permits a different integration to occur, but the patient's insight remains totally private.

Some aspects of what occurs in the session cannot be simply translated as the process of transference and countertransference. The logic of *association*, as Moreno (2014) describes, is at the center of our classical clinical understanding. But the logic of *connection* implies the creation of something new that cannot be explained—or understood—by our classical psychoanalytic methods. The world of representations does not fully account for what occurs in a link.

In psychoanalysis, one discovers new meanings through a long and effortful path of associations. Thus, the recommendation is to minimize the real presence of the analyst, to stimulate the unfolding of fantasies. But connection brings us into contact with that which was expelled from our world view by the power of language and reason, traits that do not represent but are. Moreno speaks of the effect of "presentations" (different from representations, then) as basic to the emergence of anything radically new.

It is common in my practice to work with patients who speak more than one language; it is also common for some of my patients to share more than one language with me. Often for those patients, the development and integration of multiple affective currents within the course of analysis is linked to the use of a different language from the one the analysis is normally conducted in, often some expressions have to occur in a language different from the usual. The subtleties of isolation, displacements, or splits, mediated through the use of each language, are observable, and the privileged access the patient has to these defensive uses can with relative ease be shared with me and confirmed further.

All of my patients know that English is to me a foreign language. However, the patients I refer to in this paper are limited with me to the language of the country that surrounds us both. Immigrants themselves, they know that like them, I am an immigrant. In the vignettes I bring here, the use of their mother tongue in the session, a language totally foreign to me, posed different problems from the ones I was familiar with, and also different from the issues of bilingualism or multilingualism most commonly written about, relating to the different affective use of one language versus another. These are often situations where the patients themselves are conscious of the difference. Eva Hoffman's story cited at the beginning is an instance of that kind of situation. At a certain time, these patients felt an intense need to express themselves in their mother tongue. These episodes represented a development of significance, an inevitable and necessary mark of their particular analytic process.

It is common for such a patient to occasionally fail to find the right word in English and struggle to find an approximation. Is the translation in the mind of the patient different from any other translation from the emotional experience into words? How does the patient recognize that I have truly understood, when he or she has used a word in a language he or she knows I do not speak? Does it matter whether or not I *exactly* understand?

In their seminal work, *The Babel of the Unconscious*, Amati-Mehler et al. (1993) have emphasized how correspondence between different languages exists only if correspondences are pursued deeply and extensively through the fabric of language. Referring to Hagege (1985) and Jakobson, (1962), they emphasize how a sign cannot occupy the same place in its own language as that occupied by the sign of another when we try to translate it. As the authors describe, it is possible for some patients to do a "commutation" from one language into another, rather than a translation, if they are truly polylingual, and "native speakers" in two languages. It is also true however, that the "non-spoken language" exerts pressure at different times, in different ways, sometimes through slips or through inhibitions. Also, languages are inevitably related to cultures, and polylingualism is not the same as poly-culturalism. It is generally only one culture that is forcefully transmitted by the parents, a fact that appears very evident in the case of the patients referred to in this paper. The pressure to speak the original language is, for all these patients, not only the result of a formal regression, but also a complex development within the analytic process, in which *the analyst* is perceived with some characteristic that "anchors" the transference and permits sometimes old feelings or a new set of feelings, to emerge: an "original creation" (Poland, 1992), that takes into account some trait of the analytic situation and yet is based on a template that the patient carries from his or her history, previous to the analysis.

The patients who are the subject of this paper give in to the pressure to speak the mother tongue, and thus, a new, and, to me, utterly incomprehensible language makes its appearance. The patients quote a colloquialism, repeat a sentence, or recite a poem, and thus display before me, *as an action*, a form of verbal expression that they know is not available to me. What is the meaning of this action? How do the patients create a bridge toward me through the language that actually is foreign and not available to me? It is this latter aspect that I have chosen to write about.

Initially my foreignness serves for these patients the function of an easy vehicle for identification. The immediate realization of my foreignness acts as an important affective link. As the work progresses, this admittedly superficial identification is subject to multiple vicissitudes. There remains sometimes explicit, sometimes unspoken, a notion that unlike other experiences, where they also struggle to make themselves understood, to translate visual images from dreams, or infantile experiences, or unbearable feelings, they will never be able to use their mother tongue to communicate with me, that language that was closest to the development of their thinking and the only one they shared with the primary object. As early emotions and archaic memories press for discharge it would seem inevitable that for these patients, the native language would be present in their minds with more intensity or peremptoriness. As the climate of the session becomes "heated" and more conflictive material appears, as defenses change, the requirement to speak a "later" language becomes more burdensome. I believe that this requirement is above and beyond that which *all* patients experience in any and every analysis, where pressure to act and enact are present simultaneously on both patient and analyst. If the relationship to the new language is relatively unconflicted, and obviously if the first language has not undergone repression, this specific burden may be minimal.

However, as will be seen, the patients I describe here clearly manifest a conflicted relationship to thinking and to words, and both presented with difficulties in tolerating the deprivation inherent in the analytic situation.

In the continuous delineation of closeness and difference between analyst and analysand, do these patients try to "touch me" with the foreign words, in parallel to what Rizutto (1995) describes in regard to the role of the voice of the analyst? In the particular cases I have chosen, a similar phrase was used by both patients, a description of a place "across the street," in regard to transference situations of separation and difference. The circumstances and the context of the emergence of the foreign language seemed connected with a moment when the patients were aware of my difference, this basic difference between us, with different and specific transferential meanings for each patient. Yet the mention of "a place across the street" seemed for both to be used as a metaphoric allusion to this difference and separateness as I will try to show later.

The two very different clinical vignettes, quite contrasting in outcome, that I have chosen to illustrate my ideas underscore the idiosyncratic developments in each analytic encounter, which, as usual, always have the potential to be quite creative.

First Clinical Case

Ms. A. was 20 years old when she first came to see me. A single college student, she noticeably stammered, yet she explained that whereas this symptom was very bothersome to her mother, she herself had little interest in correcting it. (This statement would later prove quite inaccurate.) Instead, she talked about her difficulties in relationships with men. She was a bright, engaging young woman. I saw her for two years in psychotherapy, interrupted by her very religious Jewish father when she started a relationship with a non-Jewish man, which the father attributed to my influence. He placed her in psychotherapy with a prominent (and prominently Jewish) psychiatrist, a treatment Ms. A. continued for several years. Eventually she married (a Jew) and had two children. After the birth of her second child she looked for me and came back to see me. I recommended analysis, and she accepted. Language was quite a dramatic issue. The parents belonged to a small Middle Eastern sect. Mother spoke Hebrew well, and father haltingly, since his only Hebrew before immigration had been religious. They did share the original dialect of their own parents, which mother spoke poorly and none of the children spoke. The three siblings had three different birth countries. Father traveled often because of business; mother was passive, depressed, and isolated, hospitalized for depression at least once during Ms. A.'s childhood. Ms. A. was left largely in the care of nannies, with whom she spoke French, the language of that first immigration. When she was 13 the family migrated to the States.

Her English was perfect, acquired when, as a child, she began attending an English school. It was the language of the treatment, yet she would often use a word in French, when she felt it would be the "right" word. She felt sure I understood, and when I questioned this, the questioning introduced some doubt in her, which she handled, subsequently, by adding an approximation in English, to whatever word or expression she had used in French, with resignation about the inadequacy of translation, which she also assumed we shared.

Analysis began when she was 33. Early on in the treatment, her relationship to the French language as the idealized language of the old country became obvious. In the city where she was born and grew up, there was a family who lived in the apartment across the street, whose family dinners around the table, visible through the window, were illuminated in winter evenings, sending a glow into her heart. That was a family, she was certain, where everybody spoke the same language, where everybody easily shared their feelings and thoughts with one another. The French language, like the "family across the street," was the ideal place of beauty, harmony, and unity, in contrast to her fragmented, and at times chaotic, experience with her own family. In her unconscious mind, clearly, I belonged to that family across the street.

The material I report is from the fifth year of a four session a week analysis. The sequence occurred when my February vacation was approaching, a vacation I had taken regularly each year.

An analytic development at this time was her increased freedom in regard to her work and also in the relationship with her husband, which allowed her to take a vacation for the first time since they married. She went to Central America. At her return she felt excited, having had a good time, and experimented with the Spanish language. One Spanish word that she had found beautiful, which she reported that she repeated to herself a lot (as she did in the session when she told me about it), was: *Escucha! Escucha! Escucha ...*" ("Listen", in Spanish). "Doesn't it sound beautiful?" she added, radiantly smiling.

Ms. A.'s mother was visiting, and she admonished Ms. A. about things her children should and should not say. In that context, Ms. A. began to talk about her incredulousness that in analysis I seemed to expect her to talk about EVERYTHING. Ms. A. described how she had made a point of letting her children be quite free about expressing whatever they wanted, but she did not feel truly free herself. How can she talk about everything?

She added that her mother expressly forbade it. She repeated the words in Hebrew, translating later into English, "This cannot be said" and also, again in Hebrew: "This must not be said." "Even worse," she added, "It is forbidden to say this" (again first in Hebrew then in English).

Two weeks after the irruption of Hebrew into the session, she commented that her husband had remarked that her stammering had markedly worsened; did I notice? I suggested it had been since the time of her recollection of her mother's injunction. I further said she was trapped between her own internal prohibition to tell me everything and her intense desire that I could *escuchar* her. She cried, explicitly acknowledging the intensity with which that Spanish word had connected her to me.

On a Monday session she talked again about her feelings about my approaching February vacation and also related how she had been asked to hold the baby boy of some friends for a circumcision ceremony. She commented she had never seen an uncircumcised penis, which looked scary to her. Her non-Jewish boyfriend years ago, being an American, was also circumcised. She canceled the Tuesday session calling me in the middle of the hour and on the phone told me she had had a dream the night before but lamented she would have to wait to tell it to me until the next day.

This material, then, is from the Wednesday session,

I have been waiting to tell you this dream! It is so beautiful, so very, very beautiful ... It was about a journey... a journey by boat, it was a very lush place. But also full of loneliness, scary. It was a place I have never been to. ... M. (husband) was there. He was being chased by sharks. ... However, they turned out to be fins, you know, scuba fins. ...When I first remembered the dream I thought it was scary, but it was not. ...Well, it was beautiful but also a bit scary. ... Now it reminds me of what we talked about on Monday, the uncircumcised penis ...I am also reminded of "Swept Away"... I realize why I may not have wanted to tell you the dream right away, it was scary. ...I think I also realize why you go away at this time of the year. ...You are going away for Valentine's Day. ... We had a conversation with B. (brother) about our parents' sex-life. We cannot imagine it. ...He thinks my father was having an affair with N. ... N. is the one who toilet trained me. ... You know there is something about the dream like the house across the street. ...
Never again that kind of life. ..."

She associated to Central America, then to the analysis as a journey, to her fantasies that my husband is probably Spanish (the uncircumcised penis). The dream showed us the condensation of various themes: the passionate, romanticized, idealized union, always takes place in a foreign land, "across the street." I have the ideal family, the ideal husband, and the romantic marriage. I have also been the ideal mother, but I am also now, on another level, seen as N. the woman in the sexually illicit relationship with father, now also a castrating figure who, through toilet training, forces her to hold inside what she wants to discharge, including her baby parts when I am away. Mother and father are never in her mind sexually united. The session sequence is also no accident: On Monday she begins to tell me about her feelings about my coming vacation, interrupts the flow of her feelings with the missed Tuesday session and then brings me the dream on Wednesday. I reminded her how she so dearly valued my being able to listen, and she had made sure I did, through the effort to speak my language. Yet she thinks it is scary to tell me her longings, her sexual feelings, most particularly her angry feelings, her sexual fantasies alluded to in "Swept Away," her dangerous shark-like feelings under the surface.

Second Clinical Case

Mrs. D. is a 51-year-old female working in the health field, the first child of poor, uneducated Holocaust survivors. Both parents lost their first families (spouses and children) during WWII. Mrs. D. has been haunted by these events all her life. She was born in a displaced persons camp and came to the US before age two. Until that time Yiddish was the only language she had heard or spoken. Her English is perfect, and there was never any reference to other languages. Mrs. D. has been in some form of psychotherapy for most of her life. The main focus of her mental pain concerned her tortured relationship with her mother, who in order to escape the Nazis abandoned a daughter who was subsequently murdered. The mother, probably severely borderline, abused Mrs. D. physically and made her the depositary of her own undigested guilt from the death of her first child, corresponding to the projection of the psychotic part of the personality (Bleger, 1967). This was the nucleus of the relationship and the focus of all treatments before she came to see me. After a prolonged consultation period, Mrs. D. started psychotherapy and eventually analysis. Mrs. D. was extremely agitated and depressed in the course of the first year of four-times-a-week-analysis. She had extraordinary trouble holding on to any gains made in treatment, mistrusting the analysis and me. The work of each session was destroyed time after time, her thoughts fragmented and discarded. She literally would bang her head with her fist, sobbing: "I hate my mind," whenever she had uttered a new thought. However, in the next two years Mrs. D.'s relationship with her children, her husband, and her work improved, while she focused more and more resentment on me and the analysis. The material I am going to report is from the fourth year of analysis.

A frequent subject in the last year had been the burden of having to constantly run to the mother, to respond to her various paranoid and hypochondriacal complaints, and her own ensuing anger, a subject repeated with multiple variations.

Suddenly, she undertook looking for a person who could visit the mother every day and monitor her ailments. This was a subject she had never spoken about in the sessions before. In narrating the way she had arrived at this decision, with a rather pleased, albeit somewhat incredulous tone, she said: "You know, there is an expression in Yiddish—she says it—it means ... the closest would be 'unexpectedly, in the middle,' 'in the midst of this,' but, literally, 'unexpectedly,' SO! Look what happened. I asked the cashier in the supermarket, and she turned out to know this Catholic Italian nurse, who lives across the street from my mother, and I've already talked to her, and she already met my mother, and they like each other, and she is going to do it."

I mentally took note that she had found—across the street—a Catholic Italian woman, and that it was the first time she had used a word in Yiddish. A marked change began to take place in the analysis. For weeks, Yiddish now was often brought in, mostly in colloquialisms. When a few weeks later I inquired if mother had sung to her in Yiddish, she then—in tears— proceeded to sing a song that she believed her mother may have sung, also remembering her father's singing, Yiddish now clearly emerged as the language of tenderness.

Discussion

In the communication that takes place in analysis, language of course is privileged. In the development that goes from the infant's intrauterine listening to sounds, including the voice of the mother, to the possibility of sophisticated multilingual adult expression, the vicissitudes of speech and of disturbances in the area of verbal expression are infinite.

The mother tongue remains irrevocably tied to the mother: It is the system closest to the primary objects, and closest to the nonverbal communication of infancy. A language learned later, or sometimes simultaneously, but from a different object, offers in certain circumstances the possibility of creating a *transitional* space, an area of separation and difference.

Any language mediates the expression of affect, but during development, the language of the adult facilitates or inhibits. Verbal language can communicate or miscommunicate. In the course of development in bilingual and multilingual patients, the adult's words, integrated in age-specific mental structures, serve as elicitors or inhibitors of actions. Languages do differ according to what they compel or do not compel one to say, or in some instances, to do. Hector Bianchotti said: "Bilingualism compels us to lie." In contrast, as Amati-Mehler, Argentieri and Canestri (1993) suggest, "Multilingual exposure enhances the possibilities of expression, not only allowing us to hide and to lie, but also allowing for different truths to emerge." The process observable in the analytic situation permits something to be constructed anew. In the end, the patient must feel an internal coherence and authenticity, shifting from primarily defensive to primarily creative uses of language, from lies to truth.

But the focus on language proves incomplete. If the relationships within the family as well as the adaptation to the new culture are relatively unconflicted, a playful alternation of languages takes place in immigrant families where the acquisition of the new language and the encouragement to keep alive the original language manifest themselves in many ways.

Within the experience of a psychoanalytic encounter for these patients the knowledge of the impossibility of translation is a preformed, specific limitation of that encounter. Yet, for truth to emerge, at times the patient may need to bring the exiled language into the treatment.

In the processes of analysis I described here, we can see both a very conflicted relationship to language in general and specifically a dramatic emergence of ambivalence in regard to the maternal figure. The process of analysis I describe here is unusual in the intensity of the conflict embedded in the use of language. Few other instances in my practice have been as revealing of ambivalence in regard to the primary objects as these. In the context of having identified with me from the beginning in our foreignness, I believe these patients probably used the language that was foreign to me as a vehicle of declaring difference and separation from me, with contrasting aims. For Ms. A. there was from the beginning a nostalgia for the idealized lost country as the monolingual paradise, and she also idealized, together with the language, the relationship with N., who toilet trained her. Her mother spoke an inhibiting language, appearing in her mind as severe, forbidding. The stammering remained tied to this highly ambivalent relationship. For a long time, she behaved toward me as she had toward the young maid of her childhood, learning the language of the foreign caretaker, who was willing to receive her words and movingly connecting anew to this beginning language. To this purpose, she first used the language of her adopted country (French) as she casually shared, then she played with learning "my" language. My native Spanish, which she loved to learn, was the equivalent of N.'s native French. Her longings, related to the French figure and the French language, shaped her initially idealized attachment to me. Yet the repetition of Hebrew in the session actualized the potentially aggressive feelings emerging now in the transference, connected with the aggression mobilized by my leaving, and made the transference split impossible to maintain. In the dream the danger appears as the sharks, and in the associations to the sadomasochism of "Swept Away." Now N., the French maid from her childhood, was revealed casually as the castrating toilet trainer and the "romance" of the father. Yet, Ms. A. could only briefly escape the Oedipal reality of the couple formed by her parents, since my imminent vacation made all aspects of the old Oedipal rivalry reemerge, shark-like, under the beautiful landscape of water. Only after she spoke Hebrew, remembering the mother's prohibitions, was she forced to acknowledge our difference and then my frustrating limitation.

I am now different from her; I am leaving her with my Spanish husband; I am now *both* a repressing and a sexual figure. The continued exploration of her relationship to language, including the stammering, was only possible now. Poignantly, she now acknowledged many instances of self-consciousness and embarrassment in regard to the stammering.

For Mrs. D., the never before used language ushered warmer, more tender feelings that only rarely had been expressed within the analysis in any form. The new helper for the mother, was as "unexpected" (the closest meaning of the Yiddish expression) as the new development in the analysis. It was when I finally made the explicit comment that she had now begun to use Yiddish quite often, in her sessions, though clearly realizing that I did not understand it, and always making the effort to translate, that it gradually unfolded how in the transference now I was the lost older sister. As I was helping her with the burden of mother, the sister would have shared this burden and would also have shared, with her and mother, a native language. Gradually, she appeared less agitated and more hopeful.

In each case, the irruption of a language never used before, permitted, or ushered, a new perception of me. It further served as a vehicle for a transferential change. For Ms. A., the initial idealization collapsed, and the irruption of the split-off, primitive, angry, forbidding language brought up an exaggeration of her symptom. Now impossible to ignore, the split belonged in the treatment.

For Mrs. D. the perception of me as different, which had been always a focus of hostility generally expressed as mistrust that I could understand the tragedy of her background, now ushered a change. The Italian Catholic helper (almost un-disguisedly a new transferential figure) was the companion, the provider of support, the sister re-found. The use of the language of her early childhood with me signaled a more intimate, tender relationship, a segment of her infantile experience that most likely was connected to a maternal role of the father's, a role that we may infer had *saved* her, protecting her from the chaotic environment her mother created.

In each of these instances then, the use of a language foreign to the analyst reflected a more integrated affective development, a more authentic and truthful connection, and an act of trust in the analyst's ability to comprehend.

Whereas for Ms. A. I had been an ideal figure, visible only through the window, "across the street," an inaccessibility that prevented true contact (and protected me from her aggression); for Mrs. D. the same phrase meant the surprising awareness of my availability and closeness despite my difference.

The emergence of the old language seemed, for these patients, inevitable. The subject of further exploration was the observation of the way I became entangled into the phenomenon. Technically, I believe a premature focus on this pressure of articulation in the native (to the analyst, foreign) language would certainly distort the process. In turn, the analysis at certain points therefore may seem grossly distorted by this phenomenon, but its tolerance by the analyst can only be beneficial.

With my patients, I knew I had to tolerate the increased and at times prolonged incursion into the old language, because nothing would better serve as a vehicle for the reintegration of affect in regard to the primary object.

In the process of thinking about these clinical developments, I remembered being greatly affected by Balint's (1979) moving account of the patient who did a somersault in the session. His discussion of that patient disputed traditional concepts of regression, acting out, and transference. In connecting to Winnicott's ideas about the capacity to be alone in the presence of another, Balint believed that the seeming self-absorption of his patient was the impression given by her being "entirely absorbed in the area of creation." My patients did something (speak a foreign language to a person who would not comprehend) that they never did in outside circumstances, where indeed it would have been either exhibitionistic, or bizarre, or both. I believe that these episodes represented here a development of significance. Nothing served better at the moment to my patients than to express, both the lived memory of the event, the native language present in their body so to speak— the link with a particular facet of their relationship to the mother and the need to communicate something in regard to me, their foreign analyst.

I can only hypothesize on the vicissitudes of language development for my patients. For Mrs. D., clearly a mark of disturbance and inhibition concerned her thinking, not just her words; for Ms. A., a disturbance of great visibility was present in her stammering. Both patients had probably benefited from the learning of a second language, which was tied to a clear improvement in the objects for an audience and the desire to communicate states of mind. This desire was reawakened and intensified in the context of the analytic experience with a new "foreign" object.

For these patients, the mental capacity for symbolic expression and communication functions, certainly connected but not identical, remained compromised in the course of development. The analysis provided for the creation of some new pathways of articulations for these various functions.

Some Further Reflections

In thinking about what French psychoanalytic authors call "the actual" I became acutely aware of some very specific aspects of these two clinical reports. Both these patients have traumatic histories, both have a background of a greatly disturbed relationship with the maternal object. The fact that the language that erupted into the treatment is precisely the language tied to the maternal object strongly suggests that elements of that relationship could not be transformed in the course of the analysis as far as I report here.

Somatic decompensation and suicide are reported frequently as derivatives of early trauma. Were these episodes much milder expressions of that early trauma? Were these elements of early identification, which could not—certainly at that point in the analysis—be accessible to symbolization, mediated by memory, language, and self-observation? These are further questions to examine.

When working with multilingual patients, we perhaps should dismiss technical notions that define certain actions as "acting in," notions that constrain our field of observation. Furthermore, it may be possible to design research where multilingual patients are instructed to use any of their languages in response to certain emotional stimuli (TAT-like cards, short stories). Obviously, self-reported observations of multilingual analysts could also further illuminate these phenomena.

Conclusions

My task as the analyst went beyond interpretation in the moments described here. The foreign language was an unarticulated message, a measure of our difference, a music (harmonious or dissonant?) of the analytic moment. I believed at the time that I should not try to put the affective moment into any words, not only because I did not yet understand its meaning, but also because inevitably it would be understood as a prohibition, not just a boundary. It seemed the prosody may have been important, the pragmatics of the moment, the reaching out through the evocation of another voice, the voice connected to the early objects. It is likely that some important work of the moment took place at a preconscious and unconscious level. The words of Canestri (1994) seem appropriate: "The reality of the analytic experience is a new class of reality in which the psychoanalyst, like the artist, tries in formulations to create interpenetrations between different codes and languages, as he searches for an integration of that which mental suffering has dissociated." I would only add that at times, like the artist also, the analyst is silent, creating a musical pause, or leaving the canvas blank, for a new space to be created, in which affect will erupt.

References

Amati-Mehler, J., Argentieri, S., & Canestri, J. (1993). *The Babel of the unconscious: Mother tongue and foreign languages in the psychoanalytic dimension.* Translated from the Italian by Jill Whitelaw-Cucco. Madison, CT: International Universities Press, Inc.

Balint, M. (1979). *The basic fault: Therapeutic aspects of regression,* Ch. 20. New York, NY: Brunner/Mazel.

Bleger, J. (1967). *Simbiosis y Ambiguidad*. Buenos Aires: Editorial Paidos.

Canestri, J. (1994). Transformations. *International Journal of Psychoanalysis*, 75: 1079–1092.

Hagege, C. (1985). *L'homme de paroles. Contribution linguistique aux sciences humaines*. Paris: Fayard.

Jakobson, R. (1962). *Selected writings*. The Hague: Mouton.

Klein, M. (1928) Early stages of the Oedipus Complex. *International Journal of Psychoanalysis*, 9: 167–180.

Moreno, J. (2014). *How we became human: A challenge to psychoanalysis*. New York, NY: Rowman and Littlefield.

Poland, W. (1992). Transference: "An original creation." *The Psychoanalytic Quarterly*, 61(2): 185–205.

Poland, W. (1998). The analyst's witnessing and otherness. *Plenary Address, American Psychoanalytic Association, Toronto, May, 29, 1998*.

Rizzuto, A. (1995). Sound and sense: Words in psychoanalysis and the paradox of the suffering person. *Canadian Journal of Psychoanalysis/Revue Canadienne de Psychanalyse*, 3(1): 1–15.

Part V

Name Changes

Names, Name Changes, and Identity in the Context of Migration

Pratyusha Tummala-Narra, PhD

In the past century in the United States, an increasing number of parents have been found to be less likely to use common, Euro-American names and instead name their children in ways that indicate distinctions along cultural, ethnic, and social class lines (Twenge, Abebe, & Campbell, 2010). A name often signifies fantasies, wishes, and fears rooted in family and social histories. In the context of migration, names and changes in names across time and generations implicate cultural adjustment, ethnic identity, transition from "foreigner" or "other" to "American," loss of heritage culture, and the hope of re-making identity. This chapter addresses the intrapsychic, interpersonal, and social implications of parents' choices of names for their children and the renaming process among immigrant-origin individuals. I explore the social context of naming children in the United States, the process of naming in pre- and post-migration contexts, and the effects of naming on intrapsychic life. Additionally, I describe the complexity of identity that can be discovered through the naming and re-naming process with special attention to both normative process of migration (e.g., acculturation) and stressful aspects of migrant family and social life (e.g., traumatic stress), through a discussion of a clinical case vignette. This vignette describes components of a psychoanalytic psychotherapy with a client who migrated to the United States to flee persecution in his country of origin, from my perspective as an immigrant, Indian American, female psychologist.

Social Context of Naming

Recently, on the first day of a class that I teach, I asked a group of graduate students to introduce themselves and to share what they knew about how they were named. Specifically, I asked them about who named them and whether they knew what meaning their name carried. I was struck by the responses of many students who connected their names to a parent who had chosen the name based on a person, often a relative, who was deeply admired in the family. I was equally struck by the responses of several other students who stated that they didn't know where their names came from and those who compared the relative lack of personal meaning attached to their names to that of the names given to their siblings. Still other students provided a translation of their names from their parents' native languages to English (e.g., Spanish to English) or stated that they had an "American" name and a name rooted in their heritage language or that of their parents. The responses from these students underscored, at the very least, the importance of names as indicators of internal, affective experiences, interpersonal relationships, acculturation, and identity.

The students' responses point to a broad range of experiences within American society that influence the process of naming and renaming. While there are numerous contextual influences in the choice of names, there are several salient issues relevant to immigrant communities: acculturation, experiences of discrimination, and traumatic stress (American Psychological Association, 2012). Psychological models of acculturation (Berry & Sam, 1997) have described the process of acculturation as one that involves the utilization of different strategies (e.g., assimilation, separation, marginalization, integration) in response to adjusting to a new cultural context, with integration being the most desirable strategy. Integration, according to this perspective, involves the individual's ability to preserve the native or heritage culture and become an active part of mainstream American society. While recognizing that acculturation entails varied experiences among immigrants and refugees, this approach assumes that every migrant group experiences similar psychological processes (Bhatia & Ram, 2009). Specifically, this view does not consider the influence of social, political, and economic issues that shape the migrant's intrapsychic and interpersonal adjustment. Alternatively, the notion of diaspora has been used to more aptly describe the experience of immigrant communities who become a collective as a way of maintaining connections to their cultural heritage and/or country of origin. Although the term diaspora has been traditionally thought to reflect either a group with common origins in scattered geographic regions or individuals' idealized fantasies of the country of origin, recent definitions of diaspora further encompass a sense of collective history (Daniel & Johnson, 2010; Tummala-Narra, 2014). Diasporas are also thought to form under conditions in which communities are not recognized and/or silenced in the mainstream society (Bhatia & Ram, 2009). Over the past decade, acculturation has been conceptualized as a non-linear process that is complex and reiterative, especially in light of an increase in globalization, transnationalism, and access to information and connection to loved ones via the Internet.

Cultural identity has been viewed as a type of "positioning" (Hall, 1990) rather than a static aspect of the self. Specifically, acculturation and identity can be understood through an examination of the effects of colonization, war, and immigration policy. For example, an individual who leaves his/her country of origin, that was colonized by a European country, to escape poverty and then emigrates to the United States experiences oppression both in the pre- and post-migration contexts. How then does this person develop identity in a Western, White-dominated country where he/she finds opportunities and at the same time faces discrimination? In which pre- and post-migration contexts is he/she privileged, and in which context does he/she lose privilege? How does he/she make decisions about friendships and romantic relationships and raising children in the new country? These questions are at the foreground of the naming experience among immigrants and refugees. As such, the issue of identity must be addressed with the recognition that the unique trajectories of immigrants and refugees are defined through social, cultural, political, and economic histories and circumstances and reflect complex and often contradictory identifications with the culture of origin and the new culture.

Acculturation further involves the immigrant's internal experience of the values inherent to the new cultural context. For example, American society values a sense of personal freedom and autonomy in ways that may be experienced positively and negatively by immigrants and refugees whose cultures of origin may have emphasized more collectivistic ideals. The ideals of self-reliance and meritocracy are especially salient in the immigrant experience as the hope for better educational and economic opportunities are often a driving force for many immigrants. A sense of optimism concerning the possibility of securing a better economic future for oneself and one's family, however, lies against a backdrop of discrimination for many racial minority immigrants and refugees and their children.

Racism and other forms of discrimination (e.g., sexism, homophobia, classism) pose challenges to a sense of safety in the mainstream culture. While immigrants and refugees throughout the history of the United States have experienced discrimination, racial minority immigrants and refugees who are perceived as non-White are especially targeted as the potentially dangerous "other." This is evident in the profiling of immigrants as people who take jobs away from "real Americans" or as terrorists and criminals (American Psychological Association, 2012). Negative stereotypes that portray immigrants and refugees as "primitive" or less developed than Euro-Americans or positive stereotypes of "model minorities," serve to diminish the full range of internal and external experiences of immigrants and refugees. Recently, racial trauma has been thought to have profound consequences in intrapsychic and interpersonal aspects of immigrant's lives (Bryant-Davis, 2005; Tummala-Narra, 2011). Specifically, racial discrimination has been found to contribute to mental health problems, such as depression, anxiety, and suicidal ideation (Takeuchi et al. 2007; Tummala-Narra, Alegria, & Chen, 2012). Even when immigrant-origin individuals experience a positive ethnic identity, it does not necessarily protect against the negative effects of discrimination (Smith & Silva, 2011). In fact, both overt and aversive racism contribute to a sense that one does not belong in mainstream context and to mental health distress, such as self-esteem, depressive and anxiety symptoms, and suicidal ideation (Sirin, Ryce, Gupta, & Rogers-Sirin, 2012; Smith & Silva, 2011; Tummala-Narra, Alegria, & Chen, 2012).

Consequently, immigrants both work toward and away from "Americanization" of the self and family, often with deep ambivalence concerning the choice to migrate. The optimism underlying the immigrant experience and the disillusionment shaped by experiences of discrimination and separation from loved ones coexist, contributing to divergent approaches to the transmission of culture to subsequent generations. This can be apparent in the choice of names either for oneself or one's children. Specifically, immigrants often contend with choosing a name that is "American" or more likely to be accepted by White Americans. In some cases, an immigrant or a refugee may attempt to protect his/her children by disconnecting from the heritage language and culture and more or less exclusively identifying and interacting within mainstream culture. On the other hand, immigrants and refugees may cope with discrimination by making active efforts to secure identifications with the heritage language and culture and protect their children from becoming too "Americanized." In this latter case, they may be more likely to choose names for themselves and their children that indicate a sense of ethnic identity.

Additionally, tensions between parents and children and those between the first and second generations may reflect acculturative stress rooted in problems such as discrimination and language and communication barriers. For example, a first-generation parent (born outside the US) who migrates to the US with the hope of maintaining a strong connection to her cultural heritage may be deeply distressed by her daughter's growing interest in identifying with mainstream American popular culture. At the same time, her daughter may fear that she may not live up to her mother's expectations, while struggling to fit in with her peers at school. In this case, it is likely that the parent feels limited in her ability to help her daughter navigate divergent expectations and values within the home and outside the home (Mann, 2004).

Cultural identity and the naming process may also be influenced by histories of political and intergenerational trauma. Atrocities such as the forced separations of Native American children from their parents and communities, the forced migration of Africans to the United States and slavery, colonization, and the Nazi Holocaust are all experiences through which names and identities were transformed, either through force or choice. For many refugees and displaced individuals, experiences of torture and betrayal by governing groups in the country of origin may contribute to a desire to create a new identity that is associated with safety and survival (Foster, 2005). In some cases, traumatic stress experienced by one generation is carried forth to subsequent generations, and one indicator of this transmission is one's name (Danieli, 2010). In the case of Jewish immigrants in the United States, name changes occurred not only in the context of escaping and/or surviving the Nazi Holocaust, but continue to occur in present day. Efforts to ward off anti-Semitism and obstacles to survival and success are often the reasons many Jewish Americans choose to change their birth names to Anglicized names. We have seen these name changes, for example, among famous actors and comedians, such as Cary Grant, Kirk Douglas, Judy Garland, Jon Stewart, and Joan Rivers, from their Jewish birth names. For many Jewish Americans, name changes may indicate a pragmatic assimilation in which they maintain a close connection to a Jewish identity and heritage and at the same time be perceived as White Americans. On the other hand, for immigrants who are seen as racial minorities, such as those from Africa, Asia, Latin America, and the Caribbean, visible features, such as skin colour, hair texture, and eyelid shape, impede the ability to pass as White despite having an Anglicized name.

Names and name changes must further be understood in the context of interpersonal violence. For example, an individual with a history of childhood abuse by parents and lack of protection by extended family and ethnic and/or religious community may decide to change his/her name to a more Anglicized name in adulthood as a way to create safe distance from the perpetrators. At the same time, he/she may struggle with ongoing racism or discrimination based on skin colour from those outside the ethnic community, contributing to profound identity conflicts. Interpersonal violence experienced by immigrants can evoke dilemmas concerning loyalty to one's ethnic community and one's sense of belonging in mainstream society and a disavowal of particular aspects of identity (Tummala-Narra, 2011). The ability to shift either consciously or unconsciously across multiple cultural and linguistic contexts, which is typical of migrant experiences, may be constrained for survivors of trauma who may find it harmful to identify with a particular cultural context. Further, identity in the face of traumatic stress, as in non-traumatic circumstances, is negotiated across the lifespan in both pre- and post-migration contexts.

Choosing Names Pre- and Post-Migration

Immigrants' and refugees' choices of names are thought to at times produce social capital in "mainstream society." In other words, a name can afford an individual greater access to social networks that facilitate social and economic opportunities and privilege within mainstream culture. There is evidence, in fact, that immigrants who take on mainstream names earn more income compared with immigrants who retain their birth names, which sound foreign to majority or dominant groups (Bursell, 2012). In other instances, the choice of names is thought to maintain connection to and continuity with heritage culture and loved ones. Yet, in both cases, immigrant-origin individuals contend with names while negotiating multiple cultural contexts. For racial minority immigrant-origin individuals, names can either contribute to or protect against discrimination and stereotyping. In many cases, when children are given a heritage name and an "American" name, names of the heritage culture are kept private at home, while "American" or White, European American names are made public. A parallel experience occurs when an individual's name is pronounced incorrectly by individuals outside of his/her ethnic group and correctly by individuals within his/her ethnic group. The experience of dual names and pronunciations can pose challenges to positive ethnic identity and to a sense of belonging in mainstream society, especially when the separation of the private and public is reinforced through increased access to resources, such as the opportunity to obtain an interview for employment.

Undoubtedly, immigrants, refugees, and their children, in their choice of names, embark on a negotiation of acculturation often in a mainstream context that seems to simultaneously encourage individual choice and freedom and an adherence to White, Euro-American norms. There are many variations in how names are negotiated. Immigrants who arrive at the United States as adults or as children may or may not choose to maintain their birth names. Children of immigrants with a heritage birth name may choose to keep their birth name or change it and later in life to change it back to the birth name. It is important that the naming and renaming process be understood in terms of developing and shifting identity and that critical transitions and circumstances fuel decisions about the progression of naming across the lifespan. This is evident in Jumpa Lahiri's novel, *The Namesake*, where an Indian immigrant father, Ashoke, names his son, Gogol, after the Russian author Nikolai Gogol. Ashoke's choice of his son's name is related to his survival of a train accident. Immediately prior to the train accident, Ashoke had been reading Nikolai Gogol's novel, *The Overcoat*, and associated the name, Gogol, with survival. His son, Gogol, is born and raised in the United States and grows up unaware of the reason for his unusual name as a person of Indian heritage. When Gogol turns 18, he decides to change his name to Nikhil, a name that he associates with an Indian heritage, rather than the Russian birth name given by his Indian father. Gogol's decision to change his name to Nikhil perhaps represents his claim to a sense of belonging within Indian culture, but also more broadly belonging *somewhere*. Gogol is a name that is not typically given to Indians and therefore leaves this son of Indian immigrants without a sense of home. While his parents are unhappy with this decision, his father states, "In America anything is possible. Do as you wish." To Gogol's surprise, at the court, the process of changing his name legally seems anticlimactic. It is possible that Gogol may have hoped that this name change would provide more clarity concerning his identity, instead of remaining on the border between India and the United States.

The Namesake depicts the shifting of names and identities throughout the lifespan across generations and the question of who defines the significance of the name itself. Names in the pre-migration context bear different meanings than in the post-migration context, as circumstances, cultural values, and relationships transform. It is likely that Ashoke's intended meaning of choosing Gogol's name from the viewpoint of an Indian who grew up in India is disconnected from his son's experience of carrying this name as an Indian in the United States. The name, Gogol, holds different meanings in these two different cultural contexts and generations. For Ashoke, the name Gogol may have represented a connection to survival and a sense of connection to his family and home in India, whereas for Gogol, his name may have represented a sense of disconnection and alienation from his Indian ancestral home and his American home. Ashoke, upon Gogol's announcement that he will change his name, comes to accept that the meaning of the name had transformed for his son who viewed himself as an American. Gogol, a few years after changing his name, meets a Bengali, Indian woman whom he imagines has a shared identity. However, he comes to realize that he shares only part of his new wife's identity and that she too is haunted by her own identity conflicts. Both Ashoke's and Gogol's experiences demonstrate the fluid nature of identity and the naming process and how name change at one point in one's development does not necessarily mark the dissolution of one's identification with heritage culture or with mainstream culture.

Many immigrants and refugees negotiate the place of heritage language in their own lives and those of their children. It is often the case that the mother tongue or heritage language is considered an indicator of identity. Language is an organizer of cognitive and affective experiences (Akhtar, 2011), and as such the experience of naming rests heavily on primary heritage language for first-generation migrants. For the second generation whose primary language is not English, naming can serve as a connection to parents, grandparents, and heritage culture. Sometimes, the level of proficiency in a heritage language or in English is associated with authenticity and belonging in a particular ethnic group. Having a heritage name or an Anglicized name can have implications for ascriptions to group membership. Specifically, someone who chooses an Anglicized name for himself/herself or for his/her child may be assumed to identify more closely with mainstream culture, whereas someone who chooses a heritage name may be assumed to identify with his/her heritage culture. In choosing a name, parents further contend with an imagined identity for their children. Some parents imagine that their children will successfully integrate into mainstream society to a greater degree than was possible for them, if they give their children Anglicized names. Other parents deliberately stay away from choosing Anglicized names for their children, after leaving their countries of origin that were occupied or colonized by European countries and where members of their communities may have been forced to change their names. The issue of choice in naming becomes especially contentious in the latter case.

The dilemma inherent to naming is illustrated in the experiences of migrants who adopt Anglicized names to be used in public and retain heritage names to be used at home and within their respective ethnic communities.

The reasons for this binomial identity are varied, reflecting a wish to make it easier for others to pronounce names and be accepted by others while maintaining cultural identity (Thompson, 2006). Yet, for many immigrants and refugees, binomial experiences continue to indicate a broader social expectation of the need to accommodate the mainstream at the cost of a more integrated experience driven by real choice. Increasingly, first- and second-generation individuals seem to choose names that reflect a hybrid identity, where chosen names are either translatable from heritage language to English (e.g., Pedro to Peter), or pre-migration linguistic traits are blended with Anglicized names (e.g., Lily which can be Anglicized or Indian) (Sue & Telles, 2007).

Names and name changes can further hold different meanings across gender. Acculturation seems to have distinct features for men and women. For example, it has been noted that women are less likely than men to want to return to their countries of origin, possibly because of new opportunities and more egalitarian gender norms in the United States (Morawska, 2011; Tummala-Narra, 2013). There may also be generational differences that intersect with gender in the naming process among immigrants. In a study of assimilation, gender, and naming, Sue and Telles (2007) found that US-born Hispanics were more likely than immigrant Hispanics to give sons translatable English names, perhaps as a way to bridge heritage culture and mainstream American culture. These researchers also found that English names were given to daughters more than to sons, possibly in an attempt to protect daughters from discrimination and to ensure that sons carry family heritage names. This does not mean, however, that daughters carrying Anglicized names are without a conflicted position on the issue of naming.

For example, my Mexican American client, Mary, who married an African American man, decided to keep her Mexican last name, as she saw this to be a symbol of her connection to her heritage language and culture. In Mary's view, having an Anglicized first name and "giving up" the Mexican part of her name would leave no visible trace of her ancestry. The study of acculturation and names is still in its infancy. However, the complexity of individual, interpersonal, and social factors that influence naming is clear with important implications for individual's psychological life, which will be elaborated in the following section and in the case illustration.

Names and Intrapsychic Life

Psychoanalytic perspectives are well positioned to address the complexity of the intrapsychic and interpersonal aspects of names. In particular, relational psychoanalytic perspectives emphasize the place of intersubjectivity and mutual influence in relationships and in the construction of the identity (Mitchell, 1988; Benjamin, 2011). As such, the processes of giving, acquiring, adopting, and changing names can be conceptualized as a product of unconscious and conscious interplay among the individual, family, community, and broader society. Inherent to naming in the immigrant and refugee contexts is the experience of ambivalence. Eng and Han (2000) have eloquently described the phenomenon of racial melancholia among Asian Americans, which refers to an unresolved or "suspended assimilation" (p. 670) whereby an ideal of Whiteness is unattainable. In this perspective, the notion of "model minority" serves to pathologize and "other" Asian Americans, as they are seen as perpetual foreigners despite the fact that they, their parents, and grandparents may have all been born and raised in the US. The stereotype becomes fixed in mainstream perceptions, regardless of the immigrant's or the refugee's internal life (Bhabha, 1994). Eng and Han noted that the ideal of Whiteness is rooted in social context of a racialized society rather than individual desire for Whiteness. This position suggests that the social is internalized, with ambivalent identifications with mainstream and heritage cultures. Further, there are implications for what is required to achieve survival and success, as Asian Americans may be required to adopt and mimic the model minority stereotype in order to be visible to mainstream society (Eng & Han, 2000).

Carrying an Anglicized name in this context of model minority can have different implications than carrying a heritage name. Recently in American society, we have witnessed an overt embracing of racial and cultural difference, as evidenced in the adoption of food, music, and fashion in mainstream culture. At the same time, it is clear that implicit and at times explicit messages that each different ethnic or racial group carries specific characteristics and skills, such as athleticism or intelligence, are pervasive in our society, underscoring politics of power and privilege. As such, having a name that is Anglicized can both contribute to one's ambivalence about cultural identity and challenge "us" versus "them" distinctions both within one's ethnic community and in mainstream culture (Bursell, 2012). Having both a heritage name and an Anglicized name can also contribute to ambivalence about cultural identity and to the experience of privatization of the heritage name, making some aspects of identity more acceptable than other aspects of identity. Having only a heritage name can be experienced as reflecting a sense of connection to heritage culture but a sense of otherness outside of one's ethnic and/or religious community.

Each of these variations implicates the multiplicity of identity and shifting self-states created in relational contexts. Bromberg's (2006) description of self-states is relevant to the significance of names among immigrants. In his view, self-states, in the face of dissociation, are necessary to maintain connections to aspects of one's relational experiences. In a social context in which heritage, Anglicized, or hybrid names are met with ambivalence, an individual may develop split-off aspects of the self and split-off identifications with cultural aspects of identity. While many migrants may have access to different versions of the self, both real and imagined, across different cultural contexts (e.g., country of origin, adopted country) through their interactions with family and similar ethnic friends either in person or via the Internet, some migrants, such as refugees and those experiencing traumatic stress, may leave parts of the self behind (Harlem, 2010). This experience of missing or losing aspects of the self may also be pronounced in the case of international adoptees in the United States, who typically have no choice in names or in access to their cultural heritage. It is important then, that psychotherapy involves the client's examination of multiple and sometimes forgotten and/or repressed experiences of the self. The significance of names, along with experiences steeped in specific sociocultural contexts, can be remembered, forgotten, and remembered again. Names and name changes can reorganize cultural experience and identity. From a relational psycho-analytic perspective, such shifts can occur for the client and for the therapist. As such, the therapist must be prepared to examine his/her own cultural history and assumptions about the client's cultural history and the meanings accompanying these histories (Tummala-Narra, 2015). In the following section, I discuss a clinical vignette to describe the fluid nature of naming and its implications for cultural identity and relationships in the lives of clients who migrate to the United States under traumatic circumstances.

Case Illustration

Alex is a Hmong American man in his mid-30s with whom I worked in weekly individual psychotherapy for almost four years. He is married to a White woman from French and Scottish ancestries, and the couple has two young daughters. He sought help to relieve symptoms of anxiety that increasingly made it difficult for him to concentrate on tasks at home and work. When I first met Alex, he expressed that he worried that the anxiety would over-whelm him and his ability to be a good father, husband, and son. He had never worked with a therapist and came referred to me by his family physician.

Alex arrived in the United States from a refugee camp in Thailand in the 1990s when he was 20 years old, with his mother and younger brother. Soon after witnessing his father's death as a child during the civil war in Laos, he fled with his mother and brother to Thailand. The family had not since been able to trace extended family, including Alex's grandparents who had lived in another part of Laos. In addition to the unpredictable nature of the escape and resettlement process, Alex and his brother endured repeated physical violence by authorities en route from Laos to Thailand and while living in three different camps in Thailand. While Alex described feeling somewhat safer in the third camp, he recalled that the feeling of hunger was persistent, sometimes for days at a time. There was no time to prepare for leaving Laos and little time to prepare to leave Thailand and relocate to the United States. There was no funeral for his father and no way of knowing who in his extended family may have survived.

Before Alex arrived on the West Coast of the United States, he had no available images of his next destination but only a hope of survival. When his father died, Alex became the "man of the family," always vigilant about the safety of his younger brother and his mother. Throughout the first year of living in the US, he and his family were provided some basic needs such as housing and food. They struggled with a new cultural environment and felt most challenged by learning a new language, which was necessary to secure employment. Their mother worked as a seamstress and a cook and when at home tended to withdraw from others and cried frequently. Alex lost his birth name, Vag, when his English language instructor suggested that he change his name legally to an "American" name like "Alex" so that he could find a job more easily. After several years of struggling to meet basic needs and working on obtaining English proficiency and a GED certificate, Alex was able to find employment as a clerk in a small business. Alex believed that he could not have accomplished this with a Hmong name. In fact, he recalled numerous incidents when he, his mother, and his brother were called racial slurs, and an incident in his early twenties when he and his brother were physically assaulted by three White men after being called "foreigners."

Alex and his brother worked together in a small business, and eventually both brothers attended and graduated from a local college. A few years after he established a business with his brother, he met his wife through a mutual friend. He recalled falling in love with her immediately, although at times later he wondered if she could truly understand his life history, especially the series of traumatic experiences prior to relocating to the US. Although his mother and his wife maintained a cordial relationship, Alex felt that his wife was not always empathic with his mother's depression.

When I initially met Alex, he described himself as "lost" and unsure about whether or not he wanted to remain married. He loved his wife and yet felt deeply alone in his marriage. He hoped to "save" his marriage so that his daughters would not be hurt in the process of a separation or a divorce. In his sessions, he repeatedly talked about his wife not fully appreciating his cultural heritage. Alex reported feeling as though he had been cheated of his influence on his daughters. He stated, "I feel like there is nothing Hmong about the girls. They are totally American and don't know anything about their father. They act like full Americans. They have American names, eat American food, and have American friends." When I asked Alex to discuss in more detail what interested him about his wife when they first met, he stated, "I liked her sense of independence. She never seemed too bogged down with anything. She always made her own decisions." Alex continued to talk about how he wished sometimes that he could have had the freedom to make choices without carrying the responsibility of caring for his mother and brother. He later connected this with the weight of his responsibility as a father, as his daughters were growing older. In our sixth month of working together, he expressed, "I'm not sure if she (wife) knows how to pronounce my name." This was the first time that he referred to his name as something other than Alex and revealed that his name was actually Vag and later changed to Alex. I responded, "How do you pronounce your name?" He proceeded to teach me how to pronounce his name, and later in the session we talked about what it felt like for him to explain his name to someone. He stated, "Well, you probably know what it's like for people to have a hard time pronouncing your name," to which I replied, "Yes." In fact, in our first session, I had helped Alex learn how to pronounce my Indian name. It is interesting to note that his real name emerged well into the course of our work together, only after he had experienced our relationship as safe enough to talk more openly about his identity.

Our conversation about the absence of his name in his present-day life led to further exploration of his identity as a Hmong man, which remained largely invisible to some of the most important people in his life, including his wife and daughters. While he had hoped that marrying his "American" wife would draw him further away from a traumatic past and integrate into mainstream society, he became increasingly anxious about losing a connection to his father, extended family, language, and cultural heritage. He was named by his father, and he referred to his name as his "inheritance" from his father. His mother continued to call him Vag, but his brother over the years shifted to calling him Alex. In psychotherapy, he wanted to be referred to as Alex through the first two years of our work. In the second year of psychotherapy, he began to talk more explicitly with his wife about his loss of connection with his Hmong heritage. He was surprised to learn that his wife had been quietly and eagerly waiting for him to reveal more about his cultural heritage and his traumatic past but that she had worried about disrupting his sense of privacy. Gradually, he was able to find new, more direct ways of communicating his sense of loss and anxiety to her. He eventually asked her if she would call him Vag, to which she agreed immediately. In our third year of working together, he asked me to call him Vag, which was of great relief to me. I realized that I too had been waiting for him to feel safe enough for this to be possible. I came to recognize that Vag's decision to rediscover his name paralleled his discovery of a safe interpersonal space in which he could feel more fully like himself. Later in our work, as he discussed his experiences of loss and trauma in Laos in more detail, he revealed that he was never actually called by any name, except by his mother and brother, in the refugee camps where he had spent extended time. His mother and brother were his source of continuity, and he was gradually able to find a sense of continuity with his wife and children.

The case of Alex/Vag illustrates the importance of exploring conscious and unconscious processes for a more complex understanding of the ways in which identity is negotiated in the context of migration. Identity conflicts are lived through naming and renaming. In the backdrop of pre- and post-migration traumatic stress, naming can be experienced as involving choice at times and necessity at others. Choosing Alex felt imperative to survival and success, rather than a true choice that occurs against a range of viable options. The birth name, Vag, given by his father, was both sacred and marred with loss and victimization. Rediscovering Vag perhaps involved an exploration and acceptance of all of these life experiences. Names further hold meaning for the therapist. I was struck by how much I attended to the meanings attached to my own name and the various permutations my name has taken in my own immigration history. I both related to Vag's experience of being told what my name should be in order to make it easier for other people to bear the complexity it held for them. I could also relate to the wish to make it easier for myself by not having to pronounce my name or spell my name out on an almost daily basis. The experience of having to explain one's identity through one's name repeatedly takes its toll. This is in sharp contrast with the pre-migration context, where the pronunciation of a name does not signify otherness. While identifying with Vag's experience of otherness, I was relieved to know that Alex had a birth name that he was able to redis-cover, as I wished for him to feel more fully engaged in his own experiences, both in the past and in the present. Our ability to talk about these dilem-mas of names and identity made it possible for movement in this direction. Eventually, Vag contemplated more deeply about what type of "inheritance" to pass on to his daughters, as they had "American" names. He and his wife decided to legally add Hmong middle names for their daughters.

Concluding Comments

Vag's case underscores the fluidity of names in the lives of immigrants and refugees. His journey through the naming and renaming process reflects experiences of pride and belonging with a heritage culture and a fear of being associated with the heritage culture and wish to belong in the new, mainstream culture as a way to achieve a sense of safety in the face of trau-matic stress. Even under non-traumatic circumstances, immigrants face dilemmas about their own names and those of their children and how names can potentially help to ensure a better future. As such, akin to the process of acculturation, naming is thought to be a reiterative process deeply embed-ded in sociopolitical circumstances and occurring throughout the lifespan.

In psychotherapy, names are important indicators of transference and counter-transference that inform the therapist about the client's subjective life. In fact, clients and therapists form associations to each other's names from the onset of psychotherapy, perhaps as soon as an initial telephone con-tact. Well into our work, Vag, in one session asked me, "Did you ever wish that you had a different name, you know one that was easier for people to say?" I responded, "Yes, and then I thought about what I wanted." Toward the end of our work together, Vag thanked me for directly responding to this question several months earlier. He said, "It helped make it ok that I wanted my name back." Vag and I had distinct experiences as refugee and immigrant, respectively, but our experiences with names carry a significance that shapes our internal lives and how we are perceived by others. Names further indicate a sense of pride, desire for belonging, and new possibilities of hybrid identities.

The attention to the subjectivity of the client and of the therapist is a critical part of a psychoanalytic approach. The experiences of naming among immigrants and refugees raises questions about the influence of acculturation and acculturative stress (e.g., racism, language barriers) on intrapsychic life and relational experiences within and outside of one's ethnic communities. As such, the client's experiences of the therapist and of the therapeutic relationship are important to consider in potential impasses and enactments that reflect broader social dynamics and interactions concerning issues of immigration, language, ethnicity, and race (Ainslie, Tummala-Narra, Harlem, Barbanel, & Ruth, 2013).

References

Ainslie, R.C., Tummala-Narra, P., Harlem, A., Barbanel, L., & Ruth, R. (2013). Contemporary psychoanalytic views on the experience of immigration. *Psychoanalytic Psychology, 30(4):* 663–679.

Akhtar, S. (2011). *Immigration and acculturation: Mourning, adaptation, and the next generation.* New York, NY: Jason Aronson.

American Psychological Association (2012). *Crossroads: The psychology of immigration in the new century, Report of the APA Presidential Task Force on Immigration.* Washington, DC: Author.

Bhabha, H.K. (1994). *The location of culture.* New York, NY: Routledge.

Bhatia, S., & Ram, A. (2009). Theorizing identity in transnational and diasporic cultures: A critical approach to acculturation. *International Journal of Intercultural Relations, 33:* 140–149.

Benjamin, J. (2011). Facing reality together discussion: With culture in mind: The social third. *Studies in Gender and Sexuality, 12(1):* 27–36.

Berry, J.W., & Sam, D. (1997). Acculturation and adaptation. In J.W. Berry, M.H. Seagull, & C. Kagitcibasi (Eds.), *Handbook of cross-cultural psychology: Social behavior and applications, Vol. 3* (pp. 291–326). Needham Heights, MA: Allyn & Bacon.

Bromberg, P.M. (2006). *Awakening the dreamer: Clinical journeys.* Hillsdale, NJ: Analytic Press.

Bryant-Davis, T. (2005). African American women in search of scripts. In E. Cole & J.H. Daniel (Eds.), *Featuring females: Feminist analyses of media* (pp. 169–183). Washington, DC: American Psychological Association.

Bursell, M. (2012). Name change and destigmatization among Middle Eastern immigrants in Sweden. *Ethnic and Racial Studies, 35(3):* 471–487.

Daniel, B., & Johnson, L. (2010). Conversations on the African diaspora(s) and leadership: Introduction to the Special Issue. *Urban Education, 45(6),* 767–776.

Danieli, Y. (Ed.) (2010). *International handbook of multigenerational legacies of trauma.* New York, NY: Springer.

Eng, D.L., & Han, S. (2000). A dialogue on racial melancholia. *Psychoanalytic Dialogues, 10(4):* 667–700.

Foster, R.P. (2005). The new faces of childhood perimigration trauma in the United States. *Journal of Infant, Child, and Adolescent Psychotherapy, 4:* 21–41.

Hall, S. (1990). Cultural identity and diaspora. In J. Rutherford (Ed.), *Identity: Community, culture, difference* (pp. 222–237). London, UK: Lawrence and Wishart.

Harlem, A. (2010). Exile as a dissociative state: When a self is "lost in transit." *Psychoanalytic Psychology, 27(4):* 460–474.

Mann, M.A. (2004). Immigrant parents and their emigrant adolescents: The tension of inner and outer worlds. *The American Journal of Psychoanalysis, 64:* 143–153.

Mitchell, S.A. (1988). *Relational concepts in psychoanalysis: An integration.* Cambridge, MA: Harvard University Press.

Morawska, E. (2011). 'Diaspora' diasporas' representations of their homelands: Exploring the polymorphs. *Ethnic and Racial Studies, 34(6):* 1029–1048.

Sirin, S.R., Ryce, P., Gupta, T., & Rogers-Sirin, L. (2012). The role of acculturative stress on mental health symptoms for immigrant adolescents: A longitudinal investigation. *Developmental Psychology,* 1–13. DOI: 10.1037/a0028398.

Smith, T. B., & Silva, L. (2011). Ethnic identity and personal well-being of people of color: A meta-analysis. *Journal of Counseling Psychology, 58(1):* 42–60.

Sue, C.A., & Telles, E.E. (2007). Assimilation and gender in naming. *American Journal of Sociology, 112(5):* 1383–1415.

Takeuchi, D.T., Zane, N., Hong, S., Chae, D.H., Gong, F., Gee, G.C., Walton, E., Sue, S., & Alegria, M. (2007). Immigration-related factors and mental disorders among Asian Americans. *American Journal of Public Health, 97(1):* 84–90.

Thompson, R. (2006). Bilingual, bicultural, and binomial identities: Personal name investment and the imagination in the lives of Korean Americans. *Journal of Language, Identity, and Education, 5(3):* 179–208.

Tummala-Narra, P. (2011). A psychodynamic approach to recovery from sexual assault. In T. Bryant-Davis (Ed.), *Surviving sexual violence: A guide to recovery and empowerment* (pp. 236–255). Lanham, MD: Rowman & Littlefield Publishers, Inc.

Tummala-Narra, P. (2013). Women immigrants: Developmental shifts in the new culture. In L. Comas-Diaz & B. Greene (Eds.), *Psychological health of women of color: Intersections, challenges, and opportunities* (pp. 257–274). Westport, CT: Praeger.

Tummala-Narra, P. (2014). Diaspora. In S. Thompson (Ed.), *Encyclopedia of diversity and social justice* (pp. 299–231). Lanham, MD: Rowman & Littlefield.

Tummala-Narra, P. (2015). Cultural competence as a core emphasis of psychoanalyticpsychotherapy. *Psychoanalytic Psychology, 32(2),* 275–292.

Tummala-Narra, P., Alegria, M., Chen, C. (2012). Perceived discrimination, acculturative stress, and depression among South Asians: Mixed findings. *Asian American Journal of Psychology, Special Issue: Secondary Analysis of the National Latino and Asian American Study (NLAAS) Dataset-Part I, 3(1):* 3–16.

Twenge, J.M., Abebe, E.M., & Campbell, W.K. (2010). Fitting in or standing out: Trends in American parents' choices for children's names, 1880–2007. *Social Psychological and Personality Science, 1(1):* 19–25.

Part VI

Trauma and the Immigration Process

Chapter 10

On Leaving Home and the Flight from Trauma

Dori Laub, MD

(This paper was previously published in *Psychoanalytic Dialogues*, 2013, Volume 23, Issue 5, pp. 568–580.)

When asked to write an essay on my experience as an immigrant, my first response was that—despite my multiple changes of countries and cultures—I have never actually had the experience of being an immigrant. When I paused to think, I realized that my answer was both true and untrue. My experience as a newcomer, although it contained all the elements of an immigrant's life, was tainted by something different—more powerful, almost negating what is usually considered to be a normative immigrant experience.

I felt like the perpetual refugee from an overwhelming, life-threatening situation that was constantly pursuing me, even though the places I left were, by and large, safe havens that had generously offered me refuge and security. I realized that what coloured my new arrivals was their being embedded in a childhood, two years of which had been spent in a Nazi concentration camp. This inevitably informs my work as an analyst when treating patients who were affected by trauma. The clinical vignette I shall present in this paper will illustrate this point.

Autobiographical Notes

As a child of five, I was deported with my parents to Transnistria, the Romanian version of camps to which Jews were sent during WWII. Romania was a military ally of Nazi Germany, and Transnistria was in the territories it had occupied in the Ukraine. The River Bug was the demarcation line between German and Romanian occupied territories, and the Einsatzgruppe "D," which operated there, often transferred Jews from the Romanian to the German side for execution.

The Red Army liberated us about two years later, in the spring of 1944. It is then that my next migration took place. The home I came back to no longer felt like home. The toys I had left in a certain closet were gone. Although we had returned with and were protected by the victorious Soviet Army, and Romania itself soon became a Socialist People's Republic (i.e., a satellite of the Soviet Union), the horrors of the past were tangible in the air, and anti-Semitism, although officially forbidden, was present everywhere. I excelled at everything, became the best pupil in my school for two years in a row, and became a dedicated member of the Communist Youth Movement, the Pioneers. I wrote up my memoirs of the camp and posted them in weekly instalments on the school billboard, but I do not remember if anyone ever spoke to me about these memoirs.

It was a great relief when we received the permit to leave Romania for Israel in 1950, shortly after my Bar Mitzvah. Those were extraordinarily moving times, to be part of the hundreds of thousands of "exiled" Jews who were coming back to their homeland. No hardship mattered—living in a tent or tent hut for years, spending three hours a day on a bus to go to and come back from school, living in poverty, etc. One memory stood out that made up for all the deprivations. After our arrival, we spent about a week in quarantine for new immigrants—a camp surrounded by a barbed-wire fence. One afternoon, my mother and I sneaked out through a hole in the fence to visit relatives in a refugee camp near Haifa. A Jewish uniformed policeman, who stood nearby, turned his head the other way and did not stop us from leaving!

An aunt who had arrived in Israel several years before took me out from the refugee camp to live in her apartment in a suburb of Haifa so that I could resume my education as a pupil in the eighth grade of a local elementary school in an established, well-to-do community. I joined my class at the beginning of the second trimester and within three months was caught up in all subject matters. Again, I excelled in everything. Hebrew was a relatively new language for me, but I mastered it well enough to finish my first school year in Israel ranking third in my class.

The transition, however, was quite momentous. There was only one other refugee child from Nazi occupied Europe in my class, although his family had not been deported from Romania during the War. The other children came from non-survivor parents who had immigrated to Israel at various points in time. They all belonged to the Vatikim—the "old timers." All of my classmates were or wanted to be "Sabras"—the cactus fruit that designated those born in Israel—tough and prickly on the outside, yet sweet and soft on the inside. The image of the Sabra was very different from that of the refugees who were nicknamed "soap"—an allusion to the erroneous belief that the bodies of the gassed victims were used by the Nazis for the production of soap. I wanted to be a "Sabra" too, not only because the alternative was to remain a socially tainted refugee, but also because it meant preventing the return of the inner horrors I had successfully been able to suppress. My mother had torn up my camp memoirs years before, for fear that the border inspection on leaving Romania would regard them as "suspicious documents."

There was an incredible sense of coming home, during those early years in the State of Israel. Families that had recently been reunited settled in close proximity. Friendships and social ties were the fabric of everyday life. In tents and later in tent huts, evenings were spent singing the songs of the old country and those of the new. Sharing and mutual assistance were the self-understood principles by which everyone lived, even if one was not a member of a commune—a kibbutz. There were no social classes or differentials in incomes. The construction worker and clerk earned the same (or even more) as the physician or banker. Lawyers, by and large, found no work in their profession. Bus drivers belonged to an elite because they formed a cooperative that owned the buses. No one drove a car. Everything—food, clothing, even copybooks—was rationed; "essential" food staples like bread and milk were heavily subsidized. Every product was of the same brand "LAKOL" (Hebrew for everyone) that guaranteed an acceptable quality and an affordable price. It was socialism in full bloom that made few exceptions. Apples, cherries, and walnuts were non-existent because they had to be imported from abroad, and that required foreign currency, which was sparse. Television did not exist in Israel because the ruling labour party, and in particular its leader Ben Gurion, opposed it in principle. It had to wait till the seventies for its entry to be granted.

In this environment, being an immigrant was the norm, while the elite class of the "old timers" was increasingly marginalized. Compulsory military service practically without pay—but with free rides on government-owned trains and countrywide hitchhiking—was the biggest melting pot. Soldiers in uniform could advance to the head of any queue (whether to buy movie tickets or board busses), as a sign of how much Israeli society valued their service. Belonging was never in question, nor was identity, in spite of the huge variety of ethnic backgrounds of the immigrants. We were all Jews in the process of becoming Israelis. The rather frequent wars solidified this experience. That held true for all my formative years in high school, medical school, and military service as a combat battalion physician. Yet, in spite of all this, unbeknownst to myself, I maintained a sense of inner exile. I never became a Sabra; I never became "one of the boys." I remained suspended in an in-between. I never spoke of my camp experiences, nor did anyone else.

When the Eichmann trial was held in Jerusalem in 1961, I remember listening with awe to the opening words of the public prosecutor, Gideon Hauser. His words sounded extraordinarily familiar, and in some way they belonged to me. I was riveted, hearing on the radio excerpts from the testimonies of the 111 witnesses. I felt very much a part of their world. Yet it was a world set apart, unreal, and located on that other planet, which I could freely enter but did not want to stay in for any length of time. I remember repeatedly passing the courthouse on my way to classes in medical school, seeing the long queues of people waiting for the doors to open. I felt drawn to join those queues, but in the end never set foot in the courtroom and never attended a hearing of the Eichmann trial.

Even more compelling was an incident involving one of my classmates, Levi Neufeld, who had been my roommate during medical school. His parents placed him with a Polish couple before they were deported and murdered during the Holocaust: This is how he survived. He was an eccentric young man, sociable but difficult to get along with. He was financially better off than most of the other medical students (because of restitution monies obtained from Germany), yet he wouldn't share things he owned or food he bought. Such sharing was commonplace among medical students living in the same apartment. One was not supposed to touch what was "his" in the refrigerator. As we approached final exams, Levi Neufeld felt increasingly terrified. I spent one day reviewing with him material for his first exam, Dermatology. That was the only exam he took and passed with a good grade. He showed up at some of the other exams but left in terror before they began. Eventually he gave up trying.

There were rumours that he was roaming the streets of Jerusalem by motorcycle; then he just disappeared. Months later a series of murders occurred in various parts of the country. A man with an Uzi gun was shooting from behind bushes, killing people at random. The police suspected Neufeld as being the serial killer. I was warned that my life was in danger because he had made threatening remarks about me. The biggest manhunt in the history of Israel took place in 1963, involving more than 4,000 policemen who searched for Levi Neufeld and combed the country, to no avail.

What was most striking about Neufeld's situation were the simultaneous generosity and short-sightedness of the medical school. It was willing to allow this student many opportunities to take his exams, but to my knowledge never considered him to be in need of psychiatric help. No one made the connection between his history as a child survivor and his present difficulties in facing life and taking his final exams. This simply was not an item on anybody's agenda at that time. Nor was it on my own. I knew the history of his survival but gave little thought to it. Paradoxically, he was seen not as a victim, but as the attacker from the dark of the night.

Levi Neufeld's body was found more than a year later. He had hung himself in the attic of an abandoned house, months before the first Uzi murder occurred. There was a letter near his body in which he apologized to his friends. The Uzi murderer has not been found to this day.

The Cultural Blind Spot

My avoidance of the Eichmann trial and of the psychic reality of Levi Neufeld are just two examples of a widely shared cultural blind spot. While the Holocaust was regularly memorialized, tangibly present in everyday life, and the subject of widely read fictionalized books by Yechiel Dinoor (under the pen name Katzetnik, signifying a concentration camp inmate), it was not a topic of inquiry for those studying human behaviour. It was also never mentioned in my psychiatric rotations during medical school. Working as a psychiatrist in a state hospital in 1965 to 1966, we knew that there was an Auschwitz patient who was regularly admitted every year during the same month. We administered our usual protocol of 12 electro-convulsive treatments, and he felt better and was discharged. Everybody knew he was a survivor. Nobody asked why he returned at the same time on a yearly basis. Decades later, I found out that there had been thousands of Holocaust survivors hospitalized in Israeli institutions for decades, some since the end of the war. In their charts there was very little information about their Holocaust experience. They were largely diagnosed schizophrenic or bi-polar and given conventional treatment, which was of limited help. As late as the 1990s, repeated surveys showed that there were close to 1,000 Holocaust survivors among the 5,000 chronically hospitalized psychiatric patients in Israel at that time, constituting nearly 20% of this population. Many had never left their institutions. Contemporary psychiatric literature had very little to say about these patients. Psychiatrists saw the Holocaust experience as strengthening those who had survived it, as demonstrating their resilience and their psychological fibre.

That blind spot was not limited to Israel. Sigmund Freud himself had very little to say about his own experience of the Nazi persecution. Anna Freud also practiced restraint throughout her life in addressing the topic, in spite of her work with Dorothea Burlingham in treating child survivors from Terezin after the war. The same applied to the many hundreds, if not thousands, of psychoanalysts who immigrated shortly before and after World War II, to the American continent: both the United States and Latin America. There is relative silence in their writings about the experience of Nazi persecution, the escape from it, their refugee and immigrant status in the new country, and the cultural dislocation they all went through. The exceptions are analysts like Bruno Bettelheim (1941), Edith Jacobson (1959), and Heinz Kohut (1985) who wrote about it early on. The analysts who had themselves been survivors, like Anna Orenstein (1985) and Henry Krystal (1988), ultimately addressed the experience. Only in recent years is this psychoanalytic blind spot being investigated by writers like Emily Kuriloff (2013) and Ghislaine Boulanger (2004). One can only wonder about the proximity of terror and the ubiquity of loss and cultural exile such a massive blind spot covers. I mentioned earlier my own sense of inner exile of being suspended in an in between.

Through my departure for the United States in 1966, I made my self-exile in a sense, more real. I consciously planned to come solely for the purposes of training, as most of my classmates from medical school also did. The difference was that the vast majority of them, perhaps over 90%, returned to Israel after the completion of their training.

On the other hand, I kept discovering new opportunities and forms of being creative, which I would probably not have found in Israel. Psychoanalytic training was probably the most profound such engagement. My best clinical training, however, preceded it. It occurred during my two-year fellowship at the Austen Riggs Center in Stockbridge, MA. My best analytic experience was with my first analyst, himself an immigrant from Europe, who was quite familiar with what happened in World War II. When I kept telling him of my camp experience as a sunbathed vacation in a meadow, on the bank of a river, arguing with a girl my age about whether one can or cannot eat grass, he stopped me in my tracks and told me of what he knew from the depositions given by women liberated by the Swedish Red Cross in Theresienstadt: "Some of them insisted that the conditions there were so good that women were served breakfast in bed by SS officers" (a particular way in German culture whereby love is demonstrated to a woman). This interpretation of my denial was quite effective. I started talking of my real experiences in the camp. Unfortunately, my analyst departed for the West Coast, and I continued for five years with an American-born, ex-Jewish analyst, who in my experience heard absolutely nothing of what I had to say. It was my third analyst who grasped my wish to leave the psychoanalytic "concentration camp" and helped me do so. It was he who finally emotionally tuned in to the world I lived in. Now I could go forward in my life. He was American born but open to my refugee experience.

On "Coming Home"

In what follows, I shall address a series of events that constituted for me homecomings from exile. In 1973 as the Yom Kippur War started, I was able to be on a plane back to Israel on the fourth day of the war. At JFK, a small group of Hasidic Jews asked me to lay tefillin so that I would be protected during my trip. I agreed—we didn't need to talk—we shared the same experience. What faced me upon arriving in Israel was utter desolation. The streets were empty and people were listening disheartedly to the news on the radio. With each setback it felt like this was really the end. The next morning, I found myself in a military base near the Golan Heights, ready to receive psychiatric casualties from the Syrian front line. They poured in by the hundreds, having decompensated because of the brutality of the war and because they served in makeshift units, not the reserve units with whom they had been called up for active duty and training for a full month each year. In order to man a tank, whoever came was taken to form a crew that had to fight together, even though the soldiers had not known each other before. What increasingly impressed me was that the most severe psychiatric casualties, suffering either from a depressive coma or from a psychotic agitation, were soldiers who were children of Holocaust survivors. A radio operator heard the last utterances of a tank commander who had passed his station to refuel and get ammunition a few hours before. "I've knocked out nine Syrian tanks; if I had more shells I could continue." Then the voice went silent. In the soldier's family there was an abundance of shadows of people that had been murdered in the Holocaust, but they were hardly mentioned. The frontline experience resonated with the familiar sense he had grown up with, of having such knowledge of close people who had died, yet not having been able to directly experience such knowledge.

Another soldier suffered from a psychotic agitation after he had booted a Syrian POW officer in his chin. He grew up in a family with a father who talked of the brutalities in the ghetto where German soldiers smashed babies against the wall. He had been a military policeman trying to prevent civilians from approaching the front line—but he couldn't stop a car with two civilian passengers who wanted to join the fighting. Hours later, he saw that car destroyed with mangled bodies in it. I listened to the stories of the soldiers and pieced the fragments together and attempted to uncover with them the resonances between their recent battle experiences and what they grew up with, the often-untold stories of their parents. For many, this helped.

After terrifying weeks, which felt like the end of the State of Israel was unavoidable, the tide turned. The Israeli forces pushed back the attack and started advancing into Egypt and into Syria. The American airborne weapons supply started, and then there were no more shortages. Casualties were heavy, but Israel was saved. For me, this was a homecoming experience, perhaps my first. I made a decision that I would dedicate my professional life to the study of and work with the effects of the Holocaust on survivors and their children, as an example of many different traumatic experiences and their effects on one's psychological well-being.

After the Yom Kippur War, while continuing with my regular work, my psychoanalytic training and my private practice, my central endeavour became the research on the effect of traumatization in Holocaust survivors. Listening for and listening to trauma added a new perspective to my thinking and to my work. I patiently waited for those muted echoes from the remote past or from the previous generation. Very little, however, in my psychoanalytic training had endorsed that sort of listening. I felt I had to professionally move to a different yet parallel track in order to pursue my psychoanalytic training. I had placed myself within the narrow confines of what I considered to be the "correct" theory of psychoanalytic practice, deliberately excluding anything I had learned before, either through my life experiences or in training at the Austen Riggs Center. I wanted to keep my psychoanalytic framework "pure" and uncontaminated. This was all before the Yom Kippur War, and looking backward I can now better understand what motivated my puritanical "zeal."

Having the "Wrong" Papers

It was 1969. I had finished my first year of my own training analysis, started my classes, and was ready for my first control case. I dutifully informed the education committee that because of my exchange visitor status, I could not guarantee my stay in the US beyond the next three to four years. I was stunned at the response I received, which I now consider to be quite realistic. If I could not guarantee my stay, I could not start a control case, and if I did not start a control case, I could not continue with my next year of classes. De facto I had to stop my training and abandon my cherished goal of becoming a psychoanalyst.

While I intellectually understood the Institute's policy, emotionally I felt "found out," caught by my persecutors while not being in the possession of the "right papers." I experienced them as totally unempathic to my plight, cold hearted, almost inhuman.

Months of uncertainty and panic followed. In desperation I turned to Jay Katz, a senior institute faculty member who also held an appointment at the Yale Law School and through his thick German accent openly professed his refugee status. He referred me to an immigration lawyer who discovered a very recent change in the immigration law, which allowed for a visa change specifically for physicians, who were considered in short supply in the US at that time. I could guarantee my stay and start my first control case.

In retrospect, I have little doubt that these events had a profound impact on the quality of my work as a psychoanalyst and were at the root of my aforementioned psychoanalytic "zeal." All my life experience, and my clinical experience not withstanding as a regular candidate in training, I indeed missed hearing the footsteps of trauma. This was the case with my first control patient whose father disappeared during World War II while serving in the Pacific Theater. He was considered dead until he returned toward the end of the war and received a high congressional medal. The two most likely explanations for father's mysterious absence for years was that he was in a POW camp or hiding out in the jungle. It is possible that he had stories to tell when he returned home after the war or that he suffered from symptoms of PTSD. Not once during the training did I ask her what she knew about her father's experiences during that period. Neither did the supervisor of the case, who himself had been a refugee from Europe, suggest that I ask such a question. The analysis focused entirely on the patient's early years with a bereaved, depressed, and emotionally absent mother and with her intense sibling rivalry with her brother who was born within a year of her parents' reunion. It was as though a three-way pact of silence operated, involving patient, analyst and supervisor, regarding the possible traumatic experiences her father may have had during the war, whose shadow may have continued hovering over the family long after his return. All three unconsciously disavowed those traumatic resonances and kept their distance from them. The analyst and the supervisor may have done so for fear of stirring up memories from their own traumatic past. Not surprisingly, this analysis was interrupted in its fourth year, because it was going nowhere. In my thinking, I felt to some degree alienated from my profession.

The Advent of Testimony

A totally new opportunity opened for me when a local television producer—Laurel Vlock—asked me to give my testimony for a Yom Hashoah program. I declined and suggested that instead we take a number of testimonies from survivors and attempt to produce a film like "The Pity and the Sorrow" by Marcel Orphul, which I had recently seen. A few weeks later, she called to tell me that she had a camera crew available and if I could invite survivors for that evening we could start. My office was promptly rearranged to serve as a studio, and four survivors were going to come. Neither of us knew what to expect. We assumed that all four testimonies would be finished within two or three hours. To our great surprise, the recording continued until the early hours of the morning. Survivors came out with fully formed testimonies, not prepared ahead of time, but emerging during the interview. I was smitten by the intense immediacy of the experience, the intimacy in which it took place, and by the level of reflectiveness survivors displayed. One woman spoke about the fantasy she had of being in a train that passed by the concentration camp, looking in from the outside. She was, so to speak, on a fence from which she could imagine both the inside and the outside of the camp. Another survivor spoke about the two parallel worlds she inhabited and did not want to connect; she wanted to keep them separate. Another witness spoke about the hunger endured for four years in the ghetto and what this hunger led him to do. In the middle of the night he would come down to the kitchen and cut off a thin slice from his sister's bread ration. He would never have imagined himself doing such a thing and felt embarrassed about it to this very day.

After that long evening of testimonies, both the television producer and I knew that we had to continue. We were able to receive the support of the "Farband," the local survivors' organization who helped us raise the initial funding. The project spread like wildfire into other communities and other states, eventually reaching Europe, Latin America, and Israel. There was a tremendous commonality for those participating in the Holocaust Film Project, which is the name we gave it, before it became part of Yale University in 1982. Later it was renamed the Fortunoff Video Archives at Yale. To become part of Yale felt like an official public confirmation of our communal experience. In a sense, I was no longer an immigrant or in exile while doing this particular work. Beyond that, most of the patients who were in analysis with me were children of Holocaust survivors, like me. Our communal hiding of a traumatic past came to be its shared home, the acknowledgement and pursuit of an innermost truth. My work with other patients had also shifted; I now listened for trauma cues or rather waited for them to come, for the traces of a threatening life-changing event. I had returned to myself, to my people, Jews and non-Jews alike, those who had endured intense traumatic experiences, and I have become, I think, a more authentic therapist through this return.

Remaining an Immigrant in an Emotional Home

In re-reading the preceding pages, which are mostly autobiographical, what conclusions do I reach? For an analyst to do his work, he must reside in his own emotional home. Stolorow, from his inter-subjective perspective, would call it a relational home, a space where an inner truth can be safeguarded and protected, as well as shared with others who are receptive to it (2007). Only in such privileged space can processes of association, symbolization, and creative insight flourish.

Forced assimilation is inimitable to the preservation of such internal protected space to the safeguarding of personal truth. Whether it is self-imposed or an outcome of societal pressure, vast portions of the self are disavowed and thus are lost to introspection and associative work. Memories, feelings, traditions, a sense of belonging and identity; all these riches may be relinquished and what remains can be a constricted, shallow self, plagued by an inner sense of brokenness, alienation, and detachment. Boulanger rightfully emphasized the sense of inner contextual discontinuity and uprootedness assimilation entails (Boulanger, 2004). Assimilation weakens the integrity of the psychoanalytic identity, rendering it more vulnerable to societal pressures, more prey to the temptation of salesmanship, and more ready to accept societal scotomata.

It is therefore preferable for the psychoanalyst to remain an immigrant who keeps both cultural perspectives: the one stemming from his tradition and background and the other acquired in his new home side by side and in dialogue with each other. A scotoma from one cultural perspective can be best viewed from the other, thus allowing for a fuller appreciation of both internal and external reality. This may entail additional psychic work, additional vigilance, and an inevitable degree of nostalgia for the culture left behind. This is necessary and worthwhile, however, because the price paid for the denial of one's past far exceeds the price of mourning it.

When I speak of an emotional truth and an emotional home, I do not restrict myself to the geographic locality or to ethnicity—the above-mentioned homesickness notwithstanding. People who lived through a common or similar emotional experience could share an emotional home. This can be true for exiles, for immigrants, perhaps for all new arrivals. There is an emotional truth in the language that is shared that is not necessarily known to others who have not gone through this experience. I find this in particular true for survivors of genocide, be it the Holocaust, Rwanda, Cambodia, Armenia, or Bosnia. There is a mutual understanding, and to a certain degree there is a sense of homecoming involved in it. I found this to be true when working with Bosnian refugees in the Yale Video Testimony Project conducted in the early 1990s and listening to testimonies and also Tutsi Rwanda survivors given to Taylor Krauss in a project modelled after the Fortunoff Video Archive (http://voicesofrwanda.org/home/) (Laub & Weine, 1994).

I referred to homecoming in my preceding autobiographical notes. What does home mean to me, and what homesickness do I feel? I visited Romania in 1978 with my family and went to the border village where we lived between 1946 and 1950. I reconnected with memories from that time, but essentially my memories were much more beautiful than the village I now found. Everything was so much larger and so much more colourful in my memory as seen through the eyes of a child of 10. I have no wish to return there nor do I particularly want to go to the city I was born in, which is now in the Ukraine, because I know that nothing I will find there will remind me of my earliest memories. I experienced Eastern Europe to some degree as a Jewish graveyard, which doesn't even have gravestones that I could honour through my visit. I could imagine what it was once like there, but really going there would be for me like visiting an in-between world of spirits waiting in abeyance, but also being kept captive in that abeyance.

The first language I spoke was German, and my family in Israel still speaks it with me. I also speak it on a daily basis with friends and close relatives, yet there is no sense of home coming for me in the German language; I find myself curiously split when I speak it with a gentile German. It is as though we speak across an unbridgeable abyss.

Being in Israel is always a homecoming experience for me, even though I am quite cognizant of the new perspectives I have gained since I left and am now quite reluctant to give them up. I still hope to find my way back to Israel without relinquishing too much of the new that I have gained.

What I find most of all as homecoming, however, is sharing and reflecting about a horrendous past and uncovering the ways in which it continues to reverberate in the present. This is for me very passionate, emotional, and intellectual work in which I feel very much at home.

On How Being a Trauma Survivor Fashions the Therapeutic Action

I would like at this point to present a clinical vignette that illustrates, I believe, the role my own trauma experience played in forming my therapeutic intervention. The patient, a professionally highly accomplished middle-aged woman, had undergone extreme traumatization during her childhood and early adolescence and grew up in a cult-like environment in which her abuse had consistently and explicitly been denied. She herself had totally repressed it. In her 30s, after having been administered an injection of a surgical anaesthetic, she recovered the memories of her abuse. Confronting her childhood caregivers with the abuse led to its steadfast denial, until she herself started doubting it. She became severely depressed, tried to take her life, and developed severe PTSD symptomatology, which was only minimally responsive to pharmacotherapy. The patient was referred to me by a colleague, who knew of my work. She had been in intensive psychotherapy for over 20 years, which had a life-saving quality. She knew that I was a Holocaust survivor, but on the rare occasions she alluded to it, it was with a somewhat dismissive undertone. How could I even begin to know what she had gone through—the bitter abandonment and betrayal she had experienced! I felt at such moments that she was "turning the tables" in denying my experience, doing to me what the grandiose clan leader had done to her when confronted with the abuse. In this way she was protecting herself from the dangerous intimacy of shared knowledge with me, which allowed her to keep me transferentially at bay, as her "real" persecutor. Interpretation of such defences were not effective and hardly made a dent in them.

There was a point, however, in which certain reality factors literally ripped away this defensive pattern. I had been the first therapist who succeeded in billing and collecting from her health insurance company the full cost of her treatment. After about three years, the insurance company requested a medical review. The patient refused any disclosure of her abuse history. Having dealt with such situations before and having experienced the wanton ruthlessness with which insurance companies sometimes denied payment for treatment, I felt completely at a loss. Once again I found myself at the mercy of a whimsical totalitarian power. I was petrified, and the patient knew it. I acknowledged to her that the present impasse stirred in me memories of my own childhood terrors. The situation had dramatically shifted, and we were on the same side now; I could no longer be her persecutor only. I came to be an insider who knew what she had experienced!

As the patient's professional work was closely related to the challenge I was facing, she could carefully instruct me how to effectively respond to the insurance company. Moreover, she gave me permission to disclose her clinical history and reassured me that if the insurance company stopped payments, she could cover the cost of the treatment herself. The omnipotent totalitarian power had become a mere reality challenge for which an appropriate strategy could be devised.

As illustrated in this vignette, when I could authentically experience (and express) in countertransference the feelings of dread and utter helplessness inherent in the patient's traumatic experience, she no longer needed to hold on to the victim's position. I believe that in the treatment of this particular patient, my own direct historical knowledge of a resonant traumatic experience was useful in changing the treatment course for the better. I did recognize the patient's transferential contribution to the therapeutic impasse we almost reached but chose not to make it the focus of my interpretation at this point in order to protect the emerging work alliance.

Encountering Cultural Differences

How does my encounter with cultural differences impact my psychological listening? The answer depends on my relationship to my counterparts' cultural home. Roughly I can define four categories for the above.

> When the cultural home is very different from mine and I can, to begin with, maintain my neutral curiosity.
> When the cultural home has a certain affinity to mine but at the same time is very conflicted.
> When my counterpart belongs to the mainstream American culture.
> When it is one of my own that I encounter.

Encountering an immigrant from a culture very different from mine, whether in a social or clinical setting, I am immediately both aware and curious of the contours of her differentness, of the cultural home the immigrant comes from, inhabits, and projects. This resonates with a heightened awareness of my own differentness, both from her and from the mainstream cultural world we both live in. As memories of my own are stirred, I ponder and imagine her memories. Thus the process is set in motion in me, of coming to better know her, forming a mental gestalt of a culture, permeated by the excitement about the new shores I land on, about the discoveries to be made. This process benefits the therapeutic work when it occurs in a clinical sitting.

When the encounter is with someone from Germany, Austria, or Central and Eastern Europe, history begins to speak up in me. I think I know enough to imagine my counterparts' cultural landscape, but my interest in it and in her is not neutral. Centuries of animosity awaken in me. The persecution and murder of the Jews is in the centre of that animosity. I have the sense of an instant familiarity, of a counterfeit belonging. I have roots there but I refuse to belong, to be part of it. I cannot be one of them no matter how much familiarity I experience. When work as a therapist is involved, I must clearly go beyond such resentment to allow my curiosity and interest to come into play. If I am convinced that my counterpart has an authentic Nazi past, I doubt that I can, or even want to, take the aforementioned step.

When my counterpart is mainstream American, I know that I have to hold my impatience with what is stereotypical commonplace, rote repetitious phraseology and salesmanship, in abeyance. Weather conditions, sporting events, the dance of political correctness are of no interest to me. This is a social discourse that can completely colonize life and deaden every authentic spark. It is like a soap opera with a predictable happy ending: an exhibitionistic pseudo intimacy, which is an empty ritual at best. Emotional involvement, passionate debate, and aggression are kept at a safe distance, covered by polite chatter that can also be thinly veiled salesmanship. My response is often boredom, and I tune out. I do so because I sense that this is a highly defensive and ambivalent discourse in which I do not wish to engage. I miss the immigrant and the exciting journey of discovery into her cultural home at such moments.

If I can wait long enough and keep my impatience in abeyance, the clouds eventually part and a more personal, more conflicted and nuanced voice begins to emerge. Beyond the personal, I begin to hear the diversity of cultural homes in America itself. People who originate from the southern states, from Texas, the Midwest or California have their own specific style of thinking and of speaking. The linguistic idioms differ from each other. I empathically try to enter those landscapes and explore them, so that I can better hear what is being said. When the threshold from the amorphous is crossed into the more specific, Americans too become immigrants in whom the voices of other cultures from previous generations that immigrated from Europe or the Far East begin to be heard.

Upon encountering one of my own cultural homes, be it Jewish or Israeli, the experience and familiarity of the homecoming that I feel takes the form of a feeling of being overwhelmed by a rush of warmth and pleasure. It feels like meeting a relative or friend, someone I had always known. I do not need to ask much because I already know. And I do not need to explain much because I am already known. However, I have to keep in mind that in spite of the welcoming familiarity, we are at the same time also different. It is a journey by itself to come to know the members of my own cultural home, and although we have very much in common, I have to be careful not to project my experience on them because ultimately, we are not the same.

I want to emphasize that the experience of being in America differs very much for American born Jews from that of Israelis. I keep noticing this again and again with the fourth group.

The Advantages and Disadvantages of Being an Immigrant

When I ask myself what are the professional disadvantages of being an immigrant, my first impulse is to say "none." I realize why I have this response: I never cease to be amazed and moved by the American openness and hospitality to newcomers. No other society in the world is as inviting, welcoming, and tolerant. No professional society in other countries extends such opportunities to those who are not home bred. Talent, initiative, and performance do not matter anywhere as much as they do in America. In no other culture is ethnic diversity the norm to such an extent. The melting pot does not require melting or relinquishing the core, relinquishing one's ethnic or religious identity. One is equal without having to become the same. One blends but can preserve one's separateness.

Yet this string of virtues and accolades, this positivity, reaches its limits and the questions about the disadvantages of being an immigrant remain.

Perhaps one should look for an answer inside oneself, in which case the relevance of discrimination against immigrants in the American society becomes secondary. Viewed from the inside, even the welcome to the melting pot levels differences. Superficially, assimilating to it seems easy. One just has to give up some personal eccentricities and yield to the temptations of the consumer-driven society and thereby begin to belong. Such belonging is, however, more like falling in step with the mass media, the mass production, and the undifferentiated mass experience. If everything is to become the same, one ends up marching to the rhythm of a drummer that is not one's own.

For me, when there is no differentness, there is less of a possibility of engagement. Polarities can interact, both negatively and positively. Sameness, on the other hand, extinguishes the spark in human interactions; societal intercourse remains superficial and flat. From my emotional perspective as a trauma survivor, my perception is that commitments to causes in the US change with the latest fashion, and they do not run deep, even if such commitment is made at the cost of one's life, as is the case with immigrant soldiers dying in American wars. Friendships are seldom struck for life and neighbourhoods are on a constant move. Ideologies of individuality and privacy provide an alluring but misleading refuge from both the loss of one's identity and the loss of a sense of belonging.

I carry the depth of engagement, the loyalty, and the level of commitment I grew up with into my work with patients, and they have a therapeutic effect, but I find little nurturance for these qualities in my own surroundings. Although this is a society that has shown extraordinary strength and resilience in times of crisis, ultimately everyone is on his own.

As an immigrant I cannot fully enter such a covenant. I can therefore never be called "one of the boys," if being one requires embracing the aforementioned mentality. I cherish my authenticity and my differentness, even though they come at a price, which is that often I find myself alone.

On balance, being an immigrant changes the way one experiences life in the US. One's life trajectory can indeed materialize outside the cultural mainstream. Preferences, appetites, and habitual ways of thinking and feeling do not really have to change. When noticing the multitude of other foreigners pursuing their own different subjective pathways, this is rather commonplace. In the end, diversity prevails. At the same time, a certain longing for one's culture, a certain homesickness, a wish to return for the purer form of what was left behind continues to be there, dimming the brightness of the present. No self-consciousness is required for having those feelings. They are simply the norm.

How does this affect the analyst working with his patients? It is crucial that he be aware of the multiplicity of perspectives he brings with himself, to what he hears and sees in his patients. His own inner diversity can enhance his tolerance for the many othernesses he encounters. Perhaps it is only through resisting the temptation and the pressures of becoming the same that he can listen to the patients as they really are, without succumbing to the generalizing effects of theory and the homogenizing produced by fashion and political correctness.

References

Bettelheim. B. (1943). Individual and mass behavior in extreme situations. *The Journal of Abnormal and Social Psychology*, 38: 417–452.

Boulanger, G. (2004). Lot's wife, Cary Grant and the American dream. Psychoanalysis with immigrants. *Contemporary Psychoanalysis*, 40: 353–372.

Jacobson, E. (1959). Depersonalization. *Journal of the American Psychoanalytic Association*, 7: 581–610.

Kohut. H. (1985). On courage. In C. B. Strozier (Ed.), *Self psychology and the humanities: Reflections on a new psychoanalytic approach* (pp. 5–50). New York, NY: W. W. Norton.

Krystal, H., & Krystal, J. H. (1988). *Integration and self-healing: Affect, trauma, alexithymia*. New York, NY: The Analytic Press.

Laub, D., & Weine, S. M. (1994). Psychotherapeutische Arbeit mit bosnischen Flüchtlingen [Therapeutic work with Bosnian refugees]. *Psyche*, 48(12): 1101–1122.

Ornstein, A. (1985). Survival and recovery. *Psychoanalytic Inquiry*, 5: 99–130.

Stolorow, R. D. (2007). *Trauma and human existence: Autobiographical, psychoanalytic, and philosphical reflections*. New York, NY: The Analytic Press.

Mourning and Melancholia in Immigrants

Chapter 11

The Immigrant's Neverland
Commuting from Amman to Brooklyn

Lama Zuhair Khouri, MS, LMSW

(This paper was previously published in *Contemporary Psychoanalysis*, 2012, Volume 48, Issue 2, pp. 213–237.)

Introduction

James Barrie's *Peter Pan* (1911) captures aspects of immigrants' emotional lives that I came to see while working with adolescent boys who were Arab immigrants like me. I chose the story because it sums up the emotional experience that led me to write this article. My concern is with an internal space where the immigrant feels as if he[1] is attending a never-ending funeral of land, culture, language, relationships, and life (Lijtmaer, 2001).

How does it feel to go back home and not find the one you left? What is the impact of realizing that the relationships the immigrant held in his mind, and for which he longed, are no longer there? How does the loss of the old country affect the immigrant's sense of himself in the new land? To limn this experience, I examine three narratives: The experience of the boys, my own experiences, and the story of Peter Pan. I include excerpts from the diary notes and treatment records I kept while working with the group.[2]

The Beginning

Every Wednesday morning, for almost three academic years (2004–2007), I would take the southbound F-train to Brooklyn. My destination was a multiuse room at a public school, where four sixth and seventh grade immigrant boys and I would weave the fabric of our Arab/American experience and learn to hold its multitude of colors and threads. My tools were a backpack loaded with art supplies and snacks, a head filled with memories of many years ago, and a heart overflowing with nostalgia.

My father's image accompanied me: his round face, white hair, a warm glow in his eyes, the smell of his cigar, and the comfort of his presence reciting lines written by an Arab American poet. Neither of us could remember the name of the poet, but supposedly he had lived in Brooklyn. My father would recite these lines whenever he recalled that I was leaving for the United States—most likely for good. In the following lines the poet describes his feelings when he saw fruits from his homeland at a farmers' market:

> … And when it saw me awestruck,
> It knew I was an immigrant,
> It greeted me silently,
> And my heart welled with longing for my homeland[3]

The goal of the group was to ease the boys' transition and integration into school and US society: Arab immigrant middle-school boys were at risk for poor academic performance, were isolated socially, and had frequent clashes with other minority students.

At the time, I did not realize that as I accompanied the boys on their journey of settling in and adjusting to life in the United States, they would bring me back to where I came from and force me to contend with losses that I had tucked away for 23 years. I thought I would be the bridge that symbolized the integration of the East and the West. Instead, I was another pedestrian on the bridge between the two, and it was they who helped me embrace various aspects of my immigration experience. The three years left me more aware than ever of the pain of mourning a time and space lost forever, yet undying in my mind.

The group was composed of four boys,[4] three of whom had arrived in the United States just a few months before the start of the group and barely spoke English. Two of the boys, Ayman and Zaid, were in sixth grade when the group started. The other two, Basem and Tamer, were in seventh grade. Ayman and Basem had moved to the United States with their fathers, leaving the rest of their families behind. The work began as an art therapy group, but as the boys got older and more self-conscious about their artistic skills, it moved to talk therapy.

Peter Pan: The Immigrant

Peter Pan was an immigrant. Like the boys and me, he left home in pursuit of a better life. He told Wendy that one night when he was still in the crib, his parents were talking about what he was to be when he became "man." He rejected their plans and left the crib and ran to Kensington Gardens, where he lived for a "long, long time among the fairies" (Barrie, 1911, p. 28).

But one day Peter Pan dreamt that his mother was crying, and he knew exactly what she was missing—a hug from her "splendid Peter would quickly make her smile." He felt sure of it, and so eager was he to be "nestling in her arms that this time he flew straight to the window, which was always open for him." But the window was closed, and "there were iron bars," and there was another baby in his bed. He had to fly back, sobbing, to the Gardens, and "he never saw his dear mother again" (Kelley-Laine, 2004, p. 92).

Peter lives on the Island of Neverland, which is make believe, and everything that happens there is also make believe—time moves in circles, no one ages, and most of the events are pretend. He comes across as a superhero, an invincible boy who does not want to grow up. Peter likes to portray himself as independent and self-sufficient. He claims he "had not the slightest desire" to have a mother, because he thought mothers "over-rated." The lost boys are only allowed to talk about mothers in his absence, because the subject had been forbidden by Peter as silly. When he is away, the boys express their love—and longing—for their mothers: "[All] I remember about my mother," Nibs, one of the lost boys, says, "is that she often said to father, 'Oh, how I wish I had a cheque-book of my own!' I don't know what a 'cheque-book' is, but I should just love to give my mother one" (Barrie, 1911, p. 54).

Despite his claims of self-sufficiency, however, Peter longs for a mother. Every night, he sneaks into Wendy's house to listen to her mother's bedtime stories, which he relays to the lost boys in Neverland.

The Immigrant's Neverland

Part of the immigrant's psyche, like Peter Pan, lives in a "Neverland," a make-believe imaginary space. There, relatives do not age, his mother still expects him for Sunday lunch, the dog waits for him at the door, and his friends look for him on the weekend. It is where he is understood without explanations, where he does not need to spell out his name or pronounce it, where his actions and reactions are just the way they should be, where everyone looks familiar, and where he safely blends into the background. Like Peter, the immigrant does not want to grow out of his Neverland or accept that his country, as he knew it, is no longer there. He does not want to mourn, for doing so means losing home forever.

The immigrant is not consciously aware that the interpersonal scene back in his home country is not the same. Time did not stand still: his friends aged and their roles changed; parents, siblings, and cousins moved on, and the space that he once occupied is now filled with someone or something else (there is already "another little boy sleeping in [the] bed," to use Peter's metaphor) (Barrie, 1911, p. 101). The immigrant is left suspended, never landing—a spectator to the events behind barred windows and painfully aware that even if he wanted to go back, he cannot.

For the immigrant, visits to his home of origin become a harsh reminder of his mortality and insignificance in the schema of life. The memories he has of himself back then, of the person he developed into—the one who "came from nothing, progressed from a primitive and physical state of being to a symbolic one" (Becker, 1973)—do not exist and there is no proof that he ever existed. He left no traces behind. The memories and emotional experiences he holds are nowhere to be found.

In my experience, the immigrant's trajectory entails an effort to assuage the pain of leaving no traces behind by creating something that can be productive in the new land and applauded in the old one. It has to be successful enough to make an impact back home so he won't be forgotten, valuable enough to mend the rupture (real or perceived) created by his departure, and desired by others enough to give him a sense of still being needed. Just as Nibs wanted to get his mother a "cheque book" (Barrie, 1911, p. 54), the immigrant wants to bring back proof that the losses were worthwhile and his love for his homeland is unrelenting. Thus, to view the pain and longing as pathological and to attempt to heal it before the immigrant is ready, feels to him like murder—as if separation will kill the person he once was. It is to deny that he ever belonged to a group. To move quickly past the wound robs the immigrant of the energy that propels him to harvest the fruits of severing his ties.

Just as Peter and the lost boys left their mothers behind, the immigrant leaves his mother figure—his motherland and all its symbols—behind. In the New World, he struggles with his loss of psychological existence as a member of the larger group, with whom he shares a permanent sense of continuity in terms of the past, the present, and the future (Volkan, 2006). Accepted ways of self-expression and old adaptation mechanisms must be shed: They are, at worst, dangerous and threatening; at best, they are unique or exotic.

The immigrant's "bit by bit" mourning of his homeland is seemingly perpetual (Freud, 1917). For all intents and purposes, his love object is not dead: The country is still there, his parents call regularly, his friends stay in touch, and he can reach his siblings anytime. But, he mourns his loss of his country on every significant occasion that takes place there. He might rejoice in a sibling's wedding, but he will not know the little stories and many encounters that kindled the couple's love; he might be sad that an uncle died, but he cannot and will not miss the uncle the same way others will. His presence at the funeral or his letter of condolence is that of an outsider; he is the undesignated mourner, unable to soothe or be soothed.

Straight on Till Morning: Arrival

When the immigrant first arrives in the new world, he spends much of his psychic energy adjusting and adapting. Unconsciously, he survives on the mistaken belief that his "secure base" is stable and he can "refuel" anytime (Akhtar, 1995).

When I first met Ayman, he was about 10 years old. His longing for home felt vivid, almost physically tangible. The first thing he said was: "Can I draw my house?" He grabbed a blue marker and showed me where each window was, where his room was, and how the garden looked. "You miss them," I said.

"So much, Miss Lama. I call them every other day and count the minutes in between." I felt a strong bond to him. Perhaps it was the intensity of his love for his country, which, at the time, I was not aware I shared; perhaps it was his age and the maternal feelings he evoked in me. Seven years later, I still have his drawing on my desk.

How does the arrival in a strange land feel? It is like birth, and, like birth, it is anxiety ridden and traumatic (Rank, 1952). It is like being pushed from the warmth, comfort, and familiarity of the womb into a strange world. It creates a "startle reflex," and the newly arrived immigrant feels himself floating in space with no links to the mother ship. He feels lost, confused, anxious, and disoriented, as if the person he was has been severed from everything familiar. Everything physical or metaphysical around him is alien; he has been abandoned in a strange world, with different sounds, smells, and sensations.

In the new land, he is misunderstood, and his methods of self-expression are meaningless. How can he communicate with a Westerner with respect when the word "please" does not even exist in Arabic vocabulary? How can he explain to someone that he dropped by his home unannounced because he genuinely cared, not because he wanted to intrude? How does he tolerate the attack his daughter receives just because she lovingly placed her hand on a boy's shoulder?

Each member in the group was to share his "departure story." Ayman began, and his was quite shocking: It had little to do with departure. It was about anguish, trauma, and violence. He spoke, like all of the kids, in Arabic: "I have a cousin, Mohamed. He was deaf and dumb. The kids in the neighborhood teased him constantly, but he retaliated viciously. He used to scare them. No one understood him, but I did. I was his friend, and we liked each other." One day a dog bit him. "He killed her and all her puppies."

"Couldn't anyone stop him?" I asked.

"No. He was like a mad man."

He proceeded to describe the most atrocious of rampages that no adult could contain. Mohamed planned to kill the dog and her family one by one, which took him a couple of days. He was unstoppable. The puppies were stepped on, swung to death, or thrown out of a high floor. The last dog, which Ayman's family thought had escaped Mohamed's wrath, was found in an alleyway with a knife in his throat.

The group was stunned. So was I. I still wonder what the meaning of this story might have been. Was this about feeling that part of his identity has been slashed, stabbed, and stepped upon? Was he telling himself: "I achieved the impossible by befriending Mohamed; I can do anything, including survive in New York?" Did he feel murdered, having left his home country when he was eight without his mother and siblings? Or did he desire to have someone scary around to ward off school bullies? Perhaps he was proud that he could understand and befriend Mohamed, when no one else could. Perhaps his anger at his parents felt just as murderous as Mohamed's attitude toward the dog's family. He could kill his parents and their puppies for sending him away like that. After all, if he was an only child, his parents wouldn't let him leave for New York, would they? One thing was certain: It was a story of trauma, anxiety, and distress.

The group continued and it was Zaid's turn to share:

> In the morning my mother, my older brother, my one-year-old sister, and I left for the airport. But at the airport they told us that my sister couldn't come, because she was not on my mother's passport. We had to leave her. I didn't want to have her left behind. I wanted to stay with her. But I had to leave. I left with my mother. My older brother stayed behind with my sister. The flight was long, and I hated the food.

"What did you do on the plane?" I asked.

Zaid replied, "My mother and I were scared of flying over water."

"So what did you do?"

"My mother is religious; she prayed all the way to New York."

When I imagined the anxiety he and his mother must have felt that day, the blood in my veins turned to ice: The grown-up who is supposed to protect him is just as scared as he is. And, she feels powerless and at a loss as to how to protect her son, let alone to soothe her own anxiety. I remembered how I felt every time I came into Kennedy Airport with my Jordanian passport: it was anyone's guess whether I would be stopped or interrogated for something I had missed on the passport or immigration forms or for some crime I did not commit.

As I was writing this article, I recalled a recurrent nightmare I had had during three difficult periods in my life (prior to leaving Jordan for London, leaving Jordan for New York, and during my divorce). I am at an airport and have just missed my flight. I am given an alternative arrangement and must catch another plane but, to do so, I need to take my luggage to the tarmac. There are just a handful of passengers, and none of them speaks a language I understand. When I board the plane, I realize that it is actually a space shuttle. The shuttle will take us to a strange planet that has no life whatsoever, is surrounded by darkness, and looks very odd—jagged, with twists, turns, and impassable mountains.

On January 29, 1985, I left Jordan for London. It was my brother's 16th birthday and I was two months shy of 21. Like most siblings, my brother, my sister, and I fought endlessly. But, on that day there was nothing between us except love, loyalty, and affection. My sister had left early that day for her classes at the university. My brother, the one who used to taunt and tease me nonstop, was silent. He stood at the gate watching me load my suitcases into the trunk of the car I was taking to the airport. When it was time to say goodbye, neither of us uttered a word. We knew an overt expression of affection would have left us both crying. But, when I left, he stood in the middle of our quiet neighborhood street watching me drive off until I disappeared into the horizon.

This was to be a scene I would experience over and over again. Every time I visited Jordan, the goodbye would feel like the first time. Except, that now my brother refuses to see me off. He usually passes by a night or two prior to my departure and his goodbye is a nonchalant, "See ya!"

In 1985, I was thrilled to be leaving for London. Paradoxically, I wanted to leave so that I could return and finally fit in: Living abroad felt both like a rite of passage and a status symbol. I had just finished my bachelor's degree from the University of Jordan, an inferior education compared to that in the West, when most of my classmates had studied abroad. I felt limited and challenged. Having a Western education, especially a British education, would immediately lift me to a higher plane, regardless of whether or not I gained something of value.

I did not realize, however, that living in the West might be a status symbol in Jordan, but that in the West being a Jordanian was a liability. I might have moved out of Jordan a middle-class girl, smart enough to finish college, competent enough to move to a foreign land, and loved enough that someone cried when I left. But I arrived in London an alien, inept, and frightened, gingerly approaching every corner of my life in case some social encounter would turn out to be a social minefield, tearing me apart.

The Island Come True: Life in the New World

Through interpersonal interactions and relationships with objects and object representations, the immigrant begins to develop new "me-you patterns" (Lionells, 1995). Such patterns become his new "personality coordinates," points of reference that outline his immigrant persona. But for the Arab immigrant, life in the new land can at times feel traumatic. The cultural shock one experiences and the resulting anxiety carries a palpable regression. The immigrant feels powerless and defenseless (Akhtar, 1999; Grinberg & Grinberg, 1984a, 1984b). His standard coping mechanisms are irrelevant in the new world.

When the group first started, anxiety and regression overtook us all. Sessions were tumultuous, chaotic, and, at times, violent. The boys seemed confused and frightened. It was hard for them to stay in the room, let alone gather around the table. This is no surprise when one considers that they had to function in an environment that was so alien to them that they might as well have landed on Mars. They had to attend classes in a language they did not understand; eat unfamiliar food; and live among students who mistrusted and disdained them—students who looked strange, dressed strangely, and had a strange code of conduct. Once, one of the boys told the group that he saw signs of the imminence of Doomsday: "People walk half naked; children are born out of wedlock; same sexes are getting married."

In the beginning of the work, I often found myself, along with the boys, in a whirlwind of anxiety and confusion. I struggled to reach a "participant-observer" stance (Wolstein, 1954; Sullivan, 1954) and was tangled in their drama. Holding the sessions in Arabic (which was not the language I used in my analysis) was especially difficult because it brought me to an unprocessed part of my "self." I felt powerless, resentful, and angry. Even to this day, I can vividly recall the heavy anxiety I carried every Wednesday. As a result, my romantic idea of a "holding environment" (Winnicott, 1965) and safe space was quickly thrown out. Instead, apprehension prevailed.

Tamer would throw around remarks about pickles, which was his nickname for penis; he and the other boys would build clay structures resembling an erect penis with testicles and would hold baby carrots between their teeth pretending they were the same. Of course, cucumbers and bananas never made the menu. At some point, however, while the boys were engaged in this bravado, I said in English (a language that brought me a sense of strength, substance, and balance): "Perhaps, some are acting silly because they are feeling uncomfortable." They did not respond, so I added: "Sexual talk is allowed in this room. I know you can't talk like this in your classroom or the school, but feel free to talk about sex here. But, if things get out of hand, I will have to ask you to stop." At which point, they all stared at me, jaws dropped. Initially, I thought they didn't understand. But, upon further consideration, I realized that they probably thought: "She actually dared to say this, and in public." Following that intervention, the boys' mockeries ceased.

Arab identity, like any group identity, does not exist in a vacuum. It is affected by interaction with the larger group. Externalized negative images of the latter eventually become an integral part of the minorities' identity (Volkan, 2004). To defend against such externalized negative images, I carried the shield of Christianity. Although I am far from a practicing Christian, I thought claiming such a strong Western symbol would protect me from the negative judgment and alienation I would feel as an Arab immigrant. It was, however, that very defense that alienated me from the boys, who were all Muslim.

The question I had been dreading finally came. Zaid asked if I were a Muslim. I dreaded it because I was concerned that the truth might create a rift between us and assign me a role or an image I did not want. I was shamefully aware of my desire, when I met Westerners, to disavow aspects of my Arab identity by always qualifying myself as a Christian Arab—as if to say: "Don't brand me with the rest of them." By "them," of course, I meant all Arabs, including the boys. In response to Zaid, I blurted out without thinking, "Christian," as if I wanted to get rid of this hot potato as fast as I could. As if I just could not tolerate holding it in my mind any longer, I wanted to throw it at the boys for them to toss around and make sense of it for me. Just as I feared, one of the group members sighed in disbelief, while the others were uncomfortably silent.

I asked Zaid, who had posed the question: "So, what does it mean to you that I'm a Christian?"

Zaid, who was stacking small pieces of wood together said: "We like everyone. I will make this figure Pope John Paul's tomb."[5]

The following session, Zaid assured me that I could convert anytime I wanted: "the mosque is always open." All I needed to do was see the Sheikh and not drink alcohol. I was flattered by his desire to save my soul. But, I also knew that it was too confusing for him to think that someone could represent the "enemy" and still be benevolent. Indeed, his art teacher informed me that he told her once: "It is said that only Muslims go to heaven and the rest go to hell. You are nice, you must go to heaven too, but you're not a Muslim."

My Christian shield was finally shattered following a visit from the principal. The visit made me aware that the details of my identity or life do not mean anything to many. An Arab is an Arab is an Arab. The principal came unannounced. He seemed just to chat and helped himself to the snacks. He acknowledged the boys' social and academic achievements but singled out Basem. As mentioned earlier, Basem was a seventh grader who arrived in the States without his mother. He came from a rural society and was often ostracized and made the scapegoat in the group. The principal said that although Basem was working hard and progressing academically, he was still acting immaturely. He added: "Basem is not behaving like a man. Manhood is important in your culture. Isn't that so? In fact, I think men are given special privileges over women just because they are born male." That comment was piercing and hurtful to Basem, the boys, and me.

The session took a different turn once the principal left. The boys went on to instruct Basem on how to behave appropriately. Basem, who was clearly hurt, withdrew to the back of the room and lay down on the floor, covered his face, and pretended to sleep. The boys were talking to Basem with such intensity that it felt as if they wanted to beat into him traits they seemed to believe an Arab American should have. I, in response, underlined the need to respect Basem and his way of being and pointed out the inappropriateness of the principal's comments. Tamer, who had been standing at the time, leaned over the table, faced me, and said in a tone he hadn't used before and with the passion and fear of a besieged, "We are Arab adolescent boys. We need to be careful."

In that moment, I got it. I know what it means to be a minority and to feel like a suspect all the time. It's like playing Russian roulette: You don't know whether the next time you go out of the apartment will be your last. All you know is that you are seen as the enemy and will not be trusted. You are guilty, even if no crime had been committed.

There was a sense of urgency in the room. The boys stood around the table and Tamer said: "A poor man in our neighborhood was sentenced to

15 years in prison because he sent money to help some poor people from our country to come to America."

Zaid added, "And another Sheikh went to jail because a terrorist was praying at his mosque."

I was a full participant in this process—I could sense everything they said, but I could not add to the dialogue and felt whatever I said could be the wrong thing.

When the session ended, I packed the boys' anxieties, along with their supplies. On my way to my next appointment, I found myself having the oddest thoughts: I wondered if I might be on some FBI list somewhere. I expanded my conspiracy theory and wondered what the boys and their families would think if they knew I had more Jewish and Israeli friends than Arab or Jordanian friends.

The boys externalized disavowed aspects of their Arab identity and projected them onto Basem: They criticized him for dressing the wrong way, using the wrong slang, eating different food. They saw him as smelly, pushy, and so on. Their reaction to him reminded me of how I felt about the group when I first started working with them. Seeing how the group was reacting to Basem, I realized that my negative reaction to the group was my way of disavowing aspects of my own identity: I did not want to look Arab or be Arab. I wanted to belong to the majority, the "White" majority—I did not want to share the boys' history, beliefs, or values.

An important shift in the group's dynamic occurred following an incident that exposed their and my vulnerabilities. It also created a bond among us that held throughout the remainder of our work together. The session started with Basem and Tamer having a fistfight over who was going to sit at the head of the table. They were deaf to my urging them to stop, so I pressed in between the two well-built angry boys only to be accidentally pushed, and I fell to the ground with a thump. The fall was the best thing that could have happened. One of the boys pulled me up (I do not recall who it was). The other boys were taken aback and stood still. I did not retaliate or disappear; in fact, I completely overlooked the accident. I drew their attention to the well-being of the group and reminded them of the goal of our work together. For the first time, they stood around the table working and talking calmly. For the first time, also, they all spoke in Arabic, and, yet again for the first time, no one stood or sat at the head of the table.

For the immigrant, the frequent day-to-day encounters and misunderstandings feel like an endless barrage of psychic assaults that are hard to tolerate. They force him to remain separate, in a "not-me" space where he can hide and go on with his life, as if these experiences do not belong to him (Bromberg, 1996; Sullivan, 1953).

The boys were sharing stories about their mischief and how they managed to break the rules, sneaking to the cinema without the knowledge of their parents or watching R-rated movies. Gradually, the discussion turned toward incidents of betrayal. They relayed stories of occasions when a relative or a friend told on them, causing them to be punished, at times severely.

I commented, "This sounds tough. Whom can you trust, after all? You're not sure if friends from your community might betray you, and who among the Americans you can be close to?"

I was perplexed when Tamer, the strongest in the group, said, "But I don't feel different from the Americans. I don't think they would misunderstand me." He continued, however, and seemingly contradicted himself: "I was going on the subway the other day and had a large camera with me that I carried in a black case. The police stopped me and searched me. They were extremely apologetic when they saw that I only had a camera." Ayman stood up and said with pride, "You should have told them: 'I'm an American citizen from the land of the free.'" He did so in a firm and loud voice with not a hint of fear or doubt. Incidentally, in Amman, Jordan, or other Middle Eastern countries, a statement of this nature would land him in a police station or a prison. If the police let you go, as they did with Tamer, you would count your blessings and hurry home.

Tamer continued that as he entered the train, the speaker announced, "If you see something say something. If you see any suspicious activity on the train or bus, do not keep it to yourself. ..." He didn't need to finish his sentence, we could all see him plastered to the door avoiding the piercing gaze of petrified subway riders, and we burst out laughing. We did not laugh just because the situation was comical, but also because it was tragic.

Like Peter, the immigrant is the hero of his Neverland. He is the director, producer, actor, and audience of the memories and stories he narrates to himself. At any point in time, and depending on his circumstances, the old country is idealized or denigrated—he recalls it as a perfect paradise, sheer hell, or anywhere in between. He molds the memory of his previous life and relationships as if to satisfy or protect himself from the pain of "no second chances" (Lijtmaer, 2001). The immigrant finds himself oscillating in his feelings for the homeland.

A few minutes into one of the next sessions, Tamer came in flaunting a letter of acceptance into a good technology high school. He was bursting with pride, and he and Ayman were flexing their academic muscles, with Ayman saying that he, too, could get into the best school. The group went on listing the fate of previous Arab middle-school students and giving various theories regarding the reasons for their success or failure.

Ayman said, "I want to be a businessman."

"Doing what?" I asked.

"What do you mean?"

Tamer interjected, "You donkey, what kind of business, she means!"

"Oh, I don't care, as long as I sit in an office with my legs up ordering people around," Ayman said, half joking.

Tamer said that his father never finished school, but he made a good life for himself. Basem added that his father barely could read or write, but he too made a good life for himself.

Tamer said, "My dad developed a successful trading company, buying and selling things to and from our country."

In the following session, however, Tamer came in disgruntled and in a bad mood. As soon as he arrived, he verbally attacked Basem, accusing him of being smelly. Tamer asked me if I would still be at the school next year and if the group would continue. I said yes to both questions.

"I will stay too," he said.

So, he indirectly told us that his grand plans for high school were off. I asked about his earlier plans and what had changed during the week. He shrugged his shoulders and waved his hand as if telling me, "It is hopeless and I don't want to talk about it."

I said, "If you don't feel like sharing with us, that's fine too."

Tamer said, "There are no Arabs from my country at the school, only a few from other countries. It will be very boring."

"What do you mean by 'boring?'"

"There won't be anyone to kid around with."

I turned to the rest of the group and asked how they felt about it. Basem and Ayman said they wouldn't mind being in a place with few Arabs. But, they invariably shared that, in the future, they would prefer to return home or work within their communities. They had no ambition or desire to move out of the confines of their neighborhoods.

Tamer, as if reconsidering his idealization of his people and his country, said, "I don't think people from my country are so nice. They only care about how much money you make."

Ayman said, "It is a lawless country. Even if you kill someone, all you need to do is bribe the judge and you'd be exonerated."

Tamer said, "When we visit back home and the people know you're American, they suddenly think you're fabulous because they assume you're rich."

"It sounds like there is no value for human life," I said.

Tamer said, "You know, Miss, I heard on the radio this morning that White people do not hit their children, but everyone else does."

Zaid interrupted, "Hitting children is necessary."

I felt that Tamer's comment was not only about child-rearing practices, but related to his struggle to reach a balance between his loyalty to his parents, on the one hand, and to his own future, on the other. I had a strong sense that he must have been either hit by his father or asked to forsake the technology high school out of allegiance to his society or his parents' fear that he would become too Americanized.

The group went on to describe a recent ceremony at the mosque when, although the Sheikh sounded as if he was advocating corporal punishment, he was, in fact, saying the opposite—or at least this is what the boys believed. Basem said that his father misunderstood the speech and pointed out to him how hitting was necessary.

Ayman said, "Our parents have no clue. They don't think. They would just hit you no matter what."

Wendy's Story: Islam, the Transitional Object

In Peter Pan's story, Wendy might be called the transitional object (Winnicott, 1971) for the lost boys. In their pretend play, Wendy was the mother, Peter the father, and the boys the children. Wendy would pretend to cook, mend clothes, and tell stories. Her favorite story was about her real family back in London: "three children [who] had a faithful nurse called Nana" (Barrie, 1911, p. 72). Such play was Wendy's way of making sure her brothers did not forget their home. In fact, she tried to imprint the old life in their minds by preparing examinations: "What was the [color] of Mother's eyes? Which was taller, Father or Mother? Was Mother blonde or brunette?" (p. 72).

To survive psychologically, the immigrant creates connections to resuscitate pathways that link him to the larger group. Such pathways take the form of music, poetry, smells, tastes, and, more often than not, at least in those from Arab countries, religion. Religion creates the illusion that reality has not changed. It gently allows the immigrant to move from what is subjectively conceived to what is objectively perceived (Sengun, 2001). Religion becomes the security blanket and, like a security blanket, at times it is chewed up, bitten, and reconfigured with the aim of making it personal (Winnicott, 1971).

For the boys in the group, because Islam addresses many day-to-day issues (in addition to being a powerful illusion and bond), it also became the blueprint for navigating the new world—the guide to making the right—or perceived as right—life choices. The boys leaned on religion to give them direction.

The boys often spent the session reciting verses from the *Quran* or repeating lovely hymns. Religion was the one thing they could hold in their hearts, the one thing that kept them connected to themselves and the group. This was not, however, easy or clear-cut. Often, it seemed they misunderstood the teachings and misinterpreted the text.

One session, Tamer brought an iPod to the room. It was a new version that played videos as well. I asked if I could look at it. Ayman, who was using it at the time, was about to give to me but pulled back and said, "No, I don't think you should see it."

I assumed that whatever he was watching was sexually tinged. Feeling somewhat self-conscious and uncomfortable with sexuality around the boys, I reacted as I would have if I were in the Arab world. I agreed and went right back to my seat, as a good Arab girl would do. But I did ask him to put it away and join the group. I understood later that the iPod contained verses from the *Quran,* and Ayman thought it might not be condoned for me, a woman, to touch it.

Tamer asked, "Is it *haram* [not condoned by Islam] to save a song on an iPod where you also have audio text from the *Quran?*"

"Good question. I'm not sure," I said.

Ayman said, "No, it's not."

Zaid offered, "It's not *haram* if you save it in a different directory or under a different file name."

"Ah ha. What do the others think?" I asked.

Ayman said, "You are not supposed to listen to *Quran* except when you're worshiping. You can't listen to it with music going on."

When the boys misunderstood the text, the sessions became chaotic and tense, as if their transitional object did not maintain its integrity and they could not claim ownership of it or interpret it in a way that continued to soothe.

In another session, after the boys settled down, I began by saying, "In the past couple of weeks, several of you have mentioned how difficult it was to be a Muslim in this country."

Zaid, who was the old soul and most conservative in the group, said, "Yes, it is very hard to have to see women dressed in miniskirts and so provocative but still act as a Muslim."

"What does acting like a Muslim mean?" I asked.

An intense, and largely incoherent, discussion ensued. The boys raised important questions: Who is a Muslim? Is it a sin to desire a woman? Is it a sin to have sexual relations with a Western woman as opposed to an Arab woman? How many wives did the Prophet have? Is polygamy truly sanctioned by Islam? They spouted answers back and forth, most of which were contradictory and confusing. (Imagine the chaos and anxiety on a trading floor during a market crash, but make the dealers preteens with carrots and grapes for ammunition.)

One such discussion went as follows: In response to the question of who is a Muslim, Basem said, "Everyone who believes in God is a Muslim."

Zaid countered, "This doesn't make sense. A true Muslim has other duties."

Basem interrupted, "Yeah, yeah, I know the duties." He proceeded to enumerate them.

Zaid jumped in to continue his argument, "The Jews believe in Jesus and God, but they are not Muslims?"

Tamer barked, "What did you say? The Jews believe in Jesus. Idiot! The Christians believe in Jesus."

Zaid responded, "Whatever."

Basem, who believed that the *Quran* disapproved of television and cinema, became especially agitated and grabbed a bunch of grapes from Ayman's plate. At that point, the tension escalated, ending with Ayman and

Basem engaging in a fistfight. I intervened firmly, and the group quieted down, but the air was heavy, as if the climax left them flat and empty but still perplexed and anxious.

I said, "You're not upset with Basem, or that anyone was saying something you didn't believe in. Do you realize that this was the most agitated you have been in quite a long time?" I continued, "I think you're agitated because things are confusing. You are Muslims in a Western country. You would like to do the right thing, but you don't know what that might be. At the same time, what you know to be true about Islamic teachings seems hard to abide by."

The Barred Windows: The Immigrant's Trauma

It was a Wednesday like any other. The sun was barely out, the apartment was quiet, and everyone sound asleep. I peeled myself off the bed and tiptoed to the kitchen to drink a good dose of caffeine before being bombarded with the demands of the busiest day of the week.

Drinking my coffee with eyes half shut, I noticed the cell phone blinking— a text message from my sister that read, "Baba got poem. Call him." No sooner had I finished reading it than the landline rang. "Twenty years later and they still don't get the time difference," I thought to myself. I picked up the receiver ever so slowly, emphasizing the grogginess of the morning.

With the deepest and most hoarse tone I could muster, I said, "Alloo."

A reprimanding voice on the other end said, "What's this poem you sent?!"

"Hi, Mama."

She softened a little and answered, "We got the poem."

"What did you think? Did you like it?"

"Sad. It made your father cry."

"I'm sorry to hear that," I answered, feeling content that I touched him so deeply but sorry to have caused him pain.

My mother, feeling powerless to kiss the pain of the separation away, retorted, "You made your choices. No one asked you to leave."

Ignoring her attack, I asked, "Which part did he find upsetting?"

"Something to do with being in New York but missing home."

My mother's words faded as I charged into New York's streets. Darting from one appointment to another, loaded down with what I liked to call "my mobile office"—laptop, snacks, drinks, card games, notebook—I was oblivious to the heaviness the conversation had left in my heart.

The school in Brooklyn looked exactly the same, the boys seemed the same, and nothing about the day was different except for the activity room. It had just been used to celebrate a group of grandparent/guardians. The table we usually used was covered with a delicate lace white cloth. Candles were lit and the aroma of home-cooked food filled the air. The participants seemed to get along and their presence left a comfortable and warm energy behind.

At the boys' request, I had brought my laptop to the session. They wanted to listen to Arabic music. Ayman and Tamer were not there. Zaid and Basem were thrilled to see the laptop and quickly began to hover over it asking to play a specific song.

Wanting to make the experience valuable from my own perspective, I said, "Let's take a few moments to talk about the song before we start." Then, continuing, I asked, "Okay, so what is this song?"

"It's a song we play at weddings," said Zaid.

Basem, bursting with excitement, said, "When someone is getting married, everyone in the town knows. The music is blasting till late into the night. No one comes and knocks at your door to turn it down as they do here."

Zaid said, "You don't need to get an invitation. Everyone knows there's a wedding and they all come."

Basem, unable to wait any longer, said, "Miss Lama, please, let's play the song."

As the song was playing, the two boys were transported to Neverland. They began to sway and hum tunes of a song, the words of which they didn't seem to understand. Basem asked Zaid to dance the traditional *debkeh* (line dancing). They stood side by side and struggled with the steps but were elated nonetheless. They were swaying and twirling as if nothing else mattered. No longer were we in Brooklyn. The three of us were transported thousands of miles away, and Tinker Bell's dust was the melody floating around us.

I wish I could tell you that I capitalized on this moment and helped the boys establish a connection with that part of their culture. Unfortunately, I didn't. After too brief a reflection, I asked if they wanted me to teach them the steps. A few moments into my demonstration, I realized that my intervention was unhelpful. The boys came crashing down from wherever Tinker Bell had transported them. The atmosphere in the room changed. They stopped dancing, they returned to the table, and their humming and swaying stopped. Their heads hung over their chests, and the energy remained low to the end of the session. It was as if the crash reminded them of the reality of their existence: They couldn't have the song blast all night, and the big wedding with everyone in the neighborhood invited is not going to take place in Carroll Gardens or New York. It will be in Amman or Cairo or Sana'a and—like Peter—they will not be invited.

When the session ended, I was overcome by a wave of sadness and longing for my country, as if all the mourning and losses of the past 23 years came gushing over me without warning. The warmth of the room put in stark relief the loneliness and coldness of life in the United States. Something about the deep love for the land I felt the boys were expressing, as well as my father's feelings around the poem, opened my eyes to a deep wound.

The poem I had sent to my father was written by one of his and my favorite Arab American poets, Illya Abu Madhi. The poem is entitled "The

Immigrant." Abu Madhi beautifully portrays the sense of dislocation, loneliness, and longing an immigrant can feel.

At the last session with the boys, I brought bandanas in addition to the usual snacks. I thought they were a somewhat masculine item the boys could keep as a memento of the group.

When Tamer saw them, he said, "This could kill you."

"What do you mean?" I asked.

"Gang members might suspect you belong to a gang that is competing with them."

"I didn't realize that. Please don't wear them publicly," I urged anxiously.

"Don't worry, Miss Lama, this will be our sign as a family and not a gang," Zaid said.

"Let's call it the Tamer's gang," said Tamer.

They signed each other's bandanas, and when it was time to say goodbye, their farewell, just like my brother's, was a nonchalant "See ya!"

In June 2007, the group ended. This time around, the F train was northbound to Manhattan, reminding me that when I said goodbye to my world in Jordan and headed north, it was a point of no return that ushered in a new era in my life, an era simultaneously beautiful and ugly, painful and pleasurable, death-defying and life-giving. That summer, I returned home to spend it with my father, who had lost his speech and memory to Alzheimer's. The only way to entertain him was to go through family albums. While reviewing these photos, it dawned on me that despite the phone calls, messages, letters, and visits, I had missed 23 birthdays, 23 Easters, and 23 summers. I missed weddings, funerals, illnesses, births, graduations, and promotions. Among my family, understandably, there was no need for me to take any significant role or to be part of day-to-day decisions. I was not a sister or a daughter; I was part of the diaspora: I was the one who lived in the United States. My sister did not need words or family albums to communicate with my father: their communication was silent. When they looked in each other's eyes, they said thousands of words no one else, and certainly not I, could hear.

The homeland I hold in my heart is not the Amman, Jordan, of 2012. It is the country and city I left in 1985, when my brother was turning 16, my sister was still in college, my friends were all single, my father was just a few years older than I am now, when a career in a helping profession was the farthest thought from my mind and when I was almost 21.

Tinker Bell: Standing in the Spaces

I started writing this article as a personal quest to understand a broken heart that did not seem to mend. I wanted to bring light into the void and pain I had felt for a long time. Is it nostalgia or mourning? Is it universal or specific? Is it trauma or just a part of life? I am not sure, nor am I sure whether it really matters one way or another. Nonetheless, to explore the questions,

I decided one morning to take a different route to the office and to play Arabic music on my iPod. As I pounded New York's streets, I kept my gaze on the asphalt. I did so to avoid the sight of non-Arab faces, glimpses of which felt jarring—a rude awakening to my sense of alienation. I wanted to cuddle the warm sensation the songs brought. As the music played, the image in my mind was that of my then 47-year-old mother swaying and dancing with me—her sparkling eyes, admiring looks, and loving touch promised a life-long connection.

Moving from one US city to another, or even from one Arab city to another, does not require the reinvention of one's self that goes hand in hand with moving from one culture to another. As the immigrant reinvents himself, his old self remains: Immigration leaves the individual's home-based objects, object representations, interpersonal relationships, and personifications frozen in time. They are, however, brought back to life when he visits the old land, only to find that he has no place there either, that no one understands or relates to his experience.

According to Freud (1917), individuals detach from the loved object "bit by bit." Each memory and expectation in which "the libido is bound to the object is brought up and hyper-cathected, and detachment of the libido is accomplished in respect of it" (p. 244). But, how can an Arab mourn openly the loss of his culture in post-9/11 America without appearing threatening or feeling threatened? Arab immigration is complicated by many things, but especially by the World Trade Center tragedy and its aftermath. A scene from the movie "My Name is Khan" comes to mind: The protagonist, who is a Muslim and suffers from Asperger's syndrome, is standing in line at the airport and praying from the *Quran* in a low but audible voice. The woman behind him reports him to the police. He is brought to an interrogation room and strip-searched. When I think of myself during those times, the word that comes promptly to me is SILENCE, a deafening silence. I see a Magritte painting, the sky clear blue, as it was on that wretched day, and I see myself without a mouth. I am frozen in my kitchen, while my Italian husband's culture floods the space around me, drowning me and my voice. He does so with my full, albeit grudging, consent. He can guarantee that my children will have a lifeboat to sail the waters of the West without the storms of misunderstanding, misperception, and prejudice that haunt Arabs like me.

My father passed away early this year. As I was waiting to board the plane that would take me back to Jordan to attend his funeral, I realized that there was no one in New York I could call who would truly understand the level of attachment a father and a child in my culture have.

In Jordan, I felt comforted by the flow of mourners, which lasted for days. Yet, I could not explain to anyone that the father I lost was not only over 80 years old. Mine was also 58 years old. He was not the grandfather of my American children. He was the father of my 20-year-old self, the man who unfailingly picked me up and brought me back to the airport on each and every visit; the one who promised to keep the window open.

Following his funeral on my way back to New York, I wondered why, in the last few trips, I had not been as emotional as I usually was. Why, following such a sad event, was I not torn, and why was the goodbye not as painful? Then, I realized I was "standing in the spaces" (Bromberg, 1996): My Neverland was my hybrid life and emotional reality (Akhtar, 1999). I was no longer dwelling in one world or the other but aware and accepting of both. I was not operating from an Arab-immigrant self-state (frightened, feeling "less than," and acting like an unprotected orphan), nor was I residing in a Jordanian-diaspora self-state (a stranger who did not belong and was forever homeless).

Standing in the spaces between my different self-states, however, does not mean freedom from pain. Dancing in the spaces does not mean happiness, nor does it mean sadness. Being in the spaces only means acceptance. It means that I am both Peter and Wendy. It also means that a bandana can be an all-American item as well as a token of a bond among Arab immigrant boys and their therapist. Standing in the spaces means that Tinker Bell can sprinkle her dust of Arabic melody, the smell of fried onion, and the taste of spiced food to revive the feelings of home; she can take me where she transported the boys while dancing. It also means that her dust cloaks my abundant Western life, my sense of freedom, my individuality, and my uncharacteristic Arab self-determination. It is on the faces of my American children, who, like Ayman, have civil rights and liberties and can always say, "I am American, from the land of the free."

> ... she had to tell him.
> "I am old, Peter. I am ever so much more than twenty. I grew up long ago."
> "You promised not to!"
> "I couldn't help it. ..."
> (Barrie, 1911, p. 156)

Acknowledgments

The work was funded by the FAR Fund and the Elsie Lee Garthwait Memorial Foundation and implemented under the Project for Refugee and Immigrant families of the William Alanson White Institute, directed by Ms. Elsa First. Dr. Seth Aronson provided clinical supervision. I wrote the article with the indispensable feedback, input, support, and encouragement of a writing group led by Dr. Muriel Dimen, whose members are William Ansorge, William Auerbach, Bill Lubart, Lisa Lyons, Susan Parlow, and Mary Sonntag. I am especially grateful to Dr. Dimen, who generously offered her time, feedback, knowledge, and editorial skills. I am also most grateful to Dr. Robert Berson for his gentle support, insight, sincerity, and inspiration, and for providing the space and safety to explore the metaphor of Peter Pan in my life.

Notes

1. I use the masculine noun when referring to immigrants, in order not to disrupt the flow of the text.
2. I emphasize that the ideas expressed below are by no means intended to apply to the experience of immigration as a whole, nor are they meant to apply to immigrants from other minority groups, or even all Arabs. This article is solely based on my own experiences working with Arab immigrant adolescents.
3. Author's translation.
4. The identity of the boys has been concealed to protect our confidentiality.
5. Pope John Paul II had died that week.

References

Akhtar, S. (1995). A third individuation: Immigration, identity, and the psychoanalytic process. *Journal of the American Psychoanalytic Association, 43*: 1051–1084.

Akhtar, S. (1999). *Immigration and identity: Turmoil, treatment and transformation.* Northvale, NJ: Jason Aronson.

Barrie, J. (1911). *Peter Pan.* New York, NY: Barnes & Noble Classics.

Becker, E. (1973). *The denial of death.* New York, NY: Free Press.

Bromberg, P. M. (1996). Standing in the spaces: The multiplicity of self and the psychoanalytic relationship. *Contemporary Psychoanalysis, 32*: 509–535.

Freud, S. (1917). Mourning and melancholia. In L. Strachey (Ed.), *The standard edition* (Vol. 14) (pp. 237–258). London: Hogarth Press.

Grinberg, L., & Grinberg, R. (1984a). A psychoanalytic study of migration: Its normal or pathological aspects. *Journal of the American Psychoanalytic Association, 31*: 13–38.

Grinberg, L., & Grinberg, R. (1984b), *Psychoanalytic perspective on migration and exile.* New Haven, CT: Yale University Press.

Kelley-Laine, K. (2004). The metaphors we live by. In J. Szekacs-Weisz & I. Ward (Eds.), *Lost childhood and the language of exile* (pp. 89–103). London: Karnac Books.

Lijtmaer, R. M. (2001). Splitting and nostalgia in recent immigrants: Psychodynamic consideration. *Journal of the American Academy of Psychoanalysis, 29*: 427–438.

Lionells, M. (1995). The interpersonal self, uniqueness, will and intentionality. In M. Lionells, J. Fiscalini, C. Mann, & D. Stern (Eds.), *Handbook of interpersonal psychoanalysis* (pp. 31–63). Hillsdale, NJ: Analytic Press.

Rank, O. (1952). *The trauma of birth.* New York, NY: Robert Brunner.

Sengun, S. (2001). Migration as a transitional space and group analysis. *Group Analysis, 34(1)*: 65–78.

Sullivan, H. S. (1953). *The interpersonal theory of psychiatry.* New York, NY: Norton.

Sullivan, H. S. (1954). *The psychiatric interview.* New York, NY: Norton.

Volkan, V. D. (2004). *Blind trust: Large groups and their leaders in times of crisis and terror.* Charlottesville, VA: Pitchstone.

Volkan, V. D. (2006). *Killing in the name of identity: A study of bloody conflicts.* Charlottesville, VA: Pitchstone.

Winnicott, D. W. (1965). *Maturational processes and the facilitating environment: Studies in the theory of the emotional development.* London: Hogarth Press.

Winnicott, D. W. (1971). *Playing and reality.* London: Tavistock.

Wolstein, B. (1954). *Transference.* New York, NY: Grune & Stratton.

Forever an Immigrant?
The Immigrant in Older Age

Chapter 12

Out of Exile

Some Thoughts on Exile as a Dynamic Condition

Eva Hoffman, PhD

(Previously published in *European Judaism*, 2013, Vol. 46, Issue 2, pp. 55–60. Copyrighted by author. Edited and reprinted with her permission.)

Several decades after you have left your country of origin—or have been thrown out of it—can you still consider yourself to be "in exile"? Can you continue to think of yourself as an immigrant? And if not, who are you, and where have you found yourself? What is your identity, and, so to speak, existential location?

These were some of the questions that kept coming to mind as I listened to the lively and interesting discussions at this year's Writing Worlds symposium on "Exile and the Imagination."

Exile is often seen as a permanent condition. "An exiled writer" tends to be always and forever identified as an exiled writer. An immigrant remains an immigrant. Sometimes, the writer too gives in to this conception. "Exiled" is a strong marker of identity, a handy and rather sexy sobriquet. But to keep it forever *as part of one's self-image* surely involves a kind of mis-description or at least over-simplification. The upheaval of exile is undoubtedly dramatic, and often traumatic, but one's relationship to it does not remain static, any more than any other aspects of identity or existential condition are static in the *longue duree*.

My own immigrant trajectory has, by now, encompassed several chapters. When I was not quite 14, my family emigrated from Poland to Canada; a few years later, I left for the US to study and stayed in that country for much of my adult life. Then, about 14 years ago, I came from New York to London, in what I thought of as a kind of halfway return to Europe.

There is no doubt that that my first emigration was a deeply formative experience, on the order of other fundamental and primary events—first love, first witnessing of death, first sensations of childhood itself. I feel myself to be shaped by the rupture of that uprooting as deeply as I do by my parents, say, or my historical background. There were lessons that followed from it that, in their wider implications, have affected much that I think and write. Basically, these have to do with the extent to which language and culture construct us; the degree to which they are not only supra-personal entities, but are encoded in ourselves and psychic cells. For a while, I was in effect without language, as Polish went underground and English remained a terra incognita, and what that brief but radical interval brought home to me was how much our perceptions and understanding, as well as our sense of presence and even life—aliveness—depend on having a living speech within us. When we don't have words with which to name our inner experiences, those experiences recede from us into an inner darkness; without words with which to name the world, that world becomes less vivid, less lucid. On the other hand, the ability to name things precisely, to bring experience to the point of conscious articulation, gives nuance and colour to our perceptions, our sense of others, and of ourselves. In a very real sense, language constitutes our psychic home. As with language, so with culture: What that first period of radical dislocation brought home to me was how much we are creatures of culture (or at least have been so through much of history) and how much incoherence we risk if we fall out of its matrix. By "culture," of course, I do not mean only the shaped artefacts of literature or art, but the entire web-work of visible and invisible habits, of psychological codes and conceptual assumptions—a kind of symbolic system of shared meanings that structures our perceptions from early on and that, within each culture, shapes the personality and sensibility.

For a long time, I was simply, and above all, an immigrant. This was how I was perceived by others, and this was how I perceived myself. I may have been progressing through the paces of the American educational system quite smartly, but although I was truly grateful for the opportunities that offered, my subjectivity stubbornly resisted being moulded into new shapes. And, as long as I did not fully inhabit the new language in which I was destined to live, I was indeed in a state of psychic exile.

And yet: Translation is possible, and so is self-translation. Eventually, through some gradual and elusive alchemy, the new language begins to drop into the subjectivity and inhabit the psyche. Aspects of one's adopted environment, which were initially a cause of sharp surprise—whether tinged with scepticism or pleasure—begin to seem perfectly ordinary. After a while, it becomes absurd to think that one is "in exile."

Where is one, instead? That question, of course, is much harder to answer. Is the counterpoint to exile defined as being "at home" or "belonging"? These too are terms awaiting fuller and deeper decoding. And "at home" where, in which frame of reference? Exile and emigration are usually thought of as political circumstances, in which one leaves a nation or is expelled by the state. And yet, one also leaves the particular place, village, or city; a web-work of non-ideological memories and affinities. On the other end of the journey, I find the notion of "place" a good antidote to the idea of nation. It is difficult to take on a new national identity completely if part of your life, and all your longer history, has taken place elsewhere—for national identities have to do precisely with history and its interpretations. But it is possible to develop palpable attachments to a place where you actually live, which you come to know through your own senses and motions, and with which you develop countless ordinary or extraordinary connections.

The enigma of arrival is more difficult to analyse than the drama of departure. It is much easier to define one's position in reference to something else than by a definite location. Indeed, physicists think that in the molecular realm, such a feat is impossible unless a particle is stationary, and particles—perhaps like humans—never are. The formative lessons of exile will never leave me, and my first language and cultural formation are inescapably part of my psychic storehouse. But by now, I have been formed by my subsequent cultures and experiences just as strongly. I have become inescapably hybrid, with new elements undoubtedly to be still added.

Such shifts may be difficult even to notice, but I think it's important to acknowledge them, if only to avoid the idealization of exile—its, so to speak, theoretical seductions. Historically, "exile" was thought of as a tragic or a pitiable condition, but recently it has been redefined as somehow interesting, morally heroic, even glamorous. The exilic position is isomorphic with exactly those qualities, which are privileged in a certain vein of post-modern theory: marginality, alterity, the decentered identity. On a more lived level, the situation of the outsider, while hardly easy, has its consolations and even its comforts. It provides not only a ready-made identity, but also an explanation for one's existential condition and its discontents. For a writer, there are the considerable advantages of the oblique vantage point, a perspective from which nothing can be taken for granted, and everything is strange and new. Indeed, the position of the writer—at least the modernist writer—maps easily onto the position of the outsider, and some writers have famously chosen exile, precisely for the bonus of that sharp angle of vision, the bracing coolness of distance and de-familiarization.

For a while, exile can be a wonderful stimulus to perception and imagination. It can also be an existential challenge and a moral task. But I have come to think that if the "exilic position" is maintained for too long, it can become not fertile, but arid; not a prod to creativity, but an instrument of fixity. The Israeli writer, A. B. Yehoshua, indicated some of the dangers in the essay title, "Exile as a Neurotic Solution." In that essay, he speaks of the collective temptations, for a group (in his example, the Jews in their long Diaspora) to remain displaced, and marginal to the society at large. Such a location allows you to look back, or forward, with longing, toward an ideal home, but it leaves you free to be un-implicated in the mundane problems and conflicts of the place where you actually live. On the individual level, too, the posture of detachment can turn into a kind of wilful separatism; the energy of critical distance into a mannerism. The habit of dividing the world into "before" and "after" can render one oblivious to the changing realities both in the country one has left behind and in the world of the present.

The very possibility of writing in exile and observing one culture from the perspective of another—indeed, the very processes of translation and self-translation—are enabled by the underlying elements of commonality among diverse cultures; a kind of common palette of human perception and experience. Cross-cultural contacts, or literary exchange, would be impossible without such underlying similarities or foundational universals, which enable us to attempt to understand each other, despite and across the tensions and the interest of cultural difference. Eventually, I think, every writer wants to—or needs to, if the imagination is to be kept alive—address such underlying existential or ethical questions or to confront the broader realities of the human world, no matter how much they are inflected by particular locations, or languages, or cultures. Indeed, one way to arrive at this stratum of character, or perception, or the human situation, has always been through a full and deep exploration of the particular. Witness, for example, the work of Czeslaw Milosz, which—through sending deep probes into particular landscapes and memories—converted his localities into a universal vocabulary.

The social realities of our world, in the meantime, and the conditions of cross-cultural movement, have been changing so radically as to transform the very meanings of exile and of home. Since my own, Cold War, emigration and the "strong" forms of exile generated by the geopolitics of that period, the Iron Curtain has lifted, the Berlin Wall has fallen, borders within Europe have opened up, and differences between East and West are blurring very fast. I think it can be safely said that (barring some unforeseen developments) the era of European exile is over. Not so in other parts of the world. There are countries that eject their citizens forcibly or make it impossible for them to stay. There are still refugees streaming from various parts of the world in the forlorn hope of finding safer or better places and people fleeing their countries of origin for fear of their lives. I do not mean for a moment to underestimate the hardships of such circumstances. But even in such extreme situations, the changing nature of our world is changing the character of cross-national movement. Even when people emigrate ostensibly for good, they usually know that they can eventually go back, that friends can visit, that they can avail themselves of all the means of contemporary travel and communication. At the same time, the sheer amount of cross-cultural movement has been increasing exponentially. Migration, dislocation and various kinds of nomadism are becoming the norm rather than an exception. It sometimes seems that lives rooted in one place and in a sort of narrative continuity are becoming the interesting aberration. But the extreme mobility that characterizes our world relativizes even the most stable identities. Even if we stay in one place, we know how easy it is to leave. Even if we live in countries with long histories and traditions, we are inescapably aware of the world's multiplicity and in most cases the heterogeneity of our own cultures. We know we are not the only centres of legitimacy. There are certain words that used to be a routine part of our vocabulary and no longer seem to apply. "Native country," "foreigner," "alien": None of these sit easily with our perceptions or slip naturally off the tongue. The strong contrasts between home and elsewhere, the native and the stranger, have given way to something less polarized and more fluid. In a sense, everyone's subjectivity is becoming hybrid. And, whatever I have become, I can no longer think of myself as the Other—the outsider to some putative outsider. But then, in the new fast-changing circumstances, these positions themselves are increasingly mobile. Yesterday's outsiders are today's insiders—and sometimes, vice versa.

We are living in a perpetually mobile, nomadic, and intermingled world. We also live in an increasingly globalized culture—the matrix of digital technologies, Facebook, Twitter, and 24/7 whole-world news. It seems quite possible that such a world will create a more mobile personality—less rooted in a particular place, history, or tradition but also more flexible and playful. It is possible that the shaping force of distinct national cultures itself will lessen, and that the very intensities of feeling experienced by the Cold War emigrants on being prized out of their original culture may come to seem quite strange. The younger generation of immigrants and voluntary nomads is likely to tell us to lighten up.

How do these changes affect the literary imagination? It certainly seems to me that the changing topography of the world profoundly alters our consciousness of the world. The task, for a certain kind of writer, is precisely to catch these deeper shifts—to imagine the present, so to speak, in all its flux and unfamiliar strangeness. How to grasp it, articulate it, narrate it? What forms are sufficient to the distinctly non-linear circumstances that increasingly define us? Certainly, the writing coming out of various diasporas, and cross-cultural lives, has moved from the literary margins to centre stage. What styles, or stories, or genres will be invented to describe a world that is no longer divided between peripheries and centres but in which movement is multi-directional and no centre privileged; in which the individual self is shaped less by history or culture than by other factors entirely; in which the very idea of the "cultivated," stable self may be losing its significance and hold. In short, what kind of literature we need to represent our fast-changing present and rapidly approaching future and interpret them for ourselves and others remains to be seen. But one thing that seems clear is that in our current, globalized conditions, a global—or a world—literature is not only possible; it is, surely, both necessary and inevitable.

Index